MODERN LIBRARY

Administration and Automation

MODERN LIBRARY
Administration and Automation

Savita Mittal

Ess Ess Publications

4837/24, Ansari Road
Darya Ganj
New Delhi-110 002
Phone: 51563444
Fax: 51563334
E-mail: info@essessreference.com
url: http://www.essessreference.com

First Published 2005

ISBN: 81-7000-438-1

Ess Ess
Rs.750/-

Published by:
Ess Ess Publications
4837/24, Ansari Road, Darya Ganj,
New Delhi-110 002.
Phone: 51563444
Fax: 51563334
E-mail: info@essessreference.com
url: http://www.essessreference.com

Printed in India at:
Printline, New Delhi

Preface

The rapid and exponential growth of information has made it necessary for librarians and information scientists to employ new techniques to cope with the massive proliferation of literature in all the subject fields. Research in sciences and social sciences has led to high productivity in document publication. To bring this vast amount of information under bibliographic control and to render it useful and accessible to potential users is a great task. The information is valuable and useful only if it is retrieved timely and cost effectively. The scientific application of knowledge has necessitated keeping abreast with the latest information and this means keeping in constant interaction with the advancements. So, in this age of information explosion/overload, keeping track of information resource and managing the same are the key to success.

Acquisition, organisation, storage and delivery of information have always been the main tasks of a library. Emerging new technologies offer new ways of handling these tasks. Today, libraries are adopting the new sophisticated information technology tools to provide accurate and instant information and to cope up with the demands of new knowledge, the enormous increase in the collection of documents, problems of their storage, retrieval and dissemination of information.

The term 'library automation' is used to refer to the extensive use of mechanical, electronic or micro-electronic equipments to perform the functions and activities associated with the functioning of a library, such as, acquisition, serial control, cataloguing, circulation and also to perform other functions like library and information services and networking.

The computers are of great significance with the advancement of telecommunication and reprography technologies in automating the library. Sharing information over the vast distances becomes possible in no time when these computers are interconnected by some of the modern communication vehicles. The computers are increasingly being used in library and information services for information processing and repackaging of information and on improving products and services of library and information centres. They offer a versatile tool for organisation and retrieval of information.

The administration and automation practices of modern libraries are elaborately discussed in the present volume. It is intended for library and information science students and teachers who are undertaking study on library automation and computer application to library and information services. Working librarians who are interested in automating their libraries will also find this work informative and useful.

Savita Mittal

Contents

1

Modern Library Administration

This chapter outlines some of the management considerations that should be recognised and planner for. Although phrased variously by different writers, the issues with which management should be concerned usually include: (a) determining objectives, (b) preparing plans for achieving the objectives, including developing cost and time schedules, (c) authorising and controlling the required work, (d) monitoring and evaluating progress towards the objectives, (e) identifying alternate corrective action as problems develop, and (f) informing staff of the effects of the program upon them. Among these issues, first, and perhaps most important, the library management has the responsibility of determining the objectives to be achieved by the mechanisation program, including the definition of priorities. In doing, so, the systems analysis staff may well provide a picture of present operations and future possibilities, but the ultimate decision among the alternatives must rest with management. Second, the costs involved in mechanisation are so great that budgetary allocations for each stage of development and implementation must be carefully planned. Development, no matter how carefully controlled, is very likely to be delayed at a number of points. On cause, having little to do with technical problems, arises from unforeseen delays in funding. This imposes a real and important constraint on the planning process, since the development plan itself must be designed to provide for intermediate systems whose operations can be continued even if later systems must be deferred for an indefinite time. Third, the time schedule for development must be defined by library management.

Again, the systems analysis staff can provide the technical support by defining likely series of events in time, but so many issues must be reconciled-many of them essentially nontechnical in character- that the library management must ultimately determine when things are to be done.Fourth, the management of the actual development and implementation itself rests with library management. Unfortunately, it is a kind of management relatively unfamiliar to the librarian.

The work is highly technical issues involved. Furthermore, usually it is a one-time project, rather than an on-going operation such as the library itself represents. As a result, the management problems are very different from those normally encountered in library administration.Fifth, the development of a system requires may compromises to be made among conflicting require-ments and capabilities. Great care is required to avoid an overcommitment to the demands of one or another specialised interest—to those who regard the aim as effective utilisation of equipment. To those whose concern is with cost/effectiveness, to those concerned with day-to-day operations, to those with some ideal of perfection.

Conflicts among these interests can be exemplified by the issues of filing rules—simple alphabetical sorting which makes for efficient machine utilisation, or cataloging code which better fits the requirements of the staff and users? Where the conflicts cannot be resolved on technical ground, library management must weight the issues involved and arrive at a judicial decision.Sixth, a mechanised system will introduce significant changes in the relationships among the library, its staff, and its readers. The library management must therefore plan a program of education for the staff and public relations with the readers to ensure an understanding of the effects of mechanisation and acceptance of them. This chapter introduces these issues of management planning—objectives, time schedules, and budgets; project management; training and public relations. Before doing so, however, it seems important to establish the context within which management decisions will probably be made.

Generally, it can be described in this way: Automation of library clerical processes is not a trivial problem even though, superficially, they seem to be little more than analogues of business data processed which have now been computer-based for years. There are vitally significant differences which must be recognised in management planning.Libraries are concerned with files of truly enormous magnitude. For example, whereas an inventory control file for a very large company might contain ten million characters, the catalog of a typical library will contain ten times as much- one hundred million characters. That of a large research library will contain over one billion characters, and the National Union Catalog has been estimated at one hundred billion characters!

The conversion of such immense files into machine language is almost prohibitively expensive, but the storage and maintenance of them on a continuing basis is even more expensive—particularly since ready access to the catalog is essential.Unfortunately, again in sharp contrast to business data processing, there is not a comparable degree of utilisation by which to justify incurring such expenditures. For example, whereas 10 per cent of a typical inventory control file will be active each day, less than 0.1 per cent of a library's catalog will be used each day. There is thus a relatively small base of activity over which to spread costs. The investment in conversion, storage, and maintenance must therefore be justified by increased benefits to a much greater extent than in business data processing. And such intangibles provide an especially difficult basis for library management planning, because of the limited discretionary resources usually available.In fact, libraries operate on a very marginal economic basis, with remarkably small budgets for the amount of work they do.

As a result, there is little of the organisational "fat' that developers of mechanised systems usually depended upon for demonstrating economies of operation.Perhaps even more significant in management planning is the fact the library data processing involves the very substance of the library's functions. In this respect, the library's catalog, serial records, and even its circulation control files are comparable to the manufacturing component of a company and not to the bookkeeping records. Changes in the basic records of the library, which are almost certain to occur with mechanisation, therefore affect the character of the library service themselves and not simply of peripheral accounting procedures. It may be for this reason that library data processing involves a degree of intellectual judgment far beyond that in normal business data processing. For example, catalog filing rules are with good reason much more complicated than simple alphanumerical sorting.

In fact, in this sense mechanising library data processing is comparable in difficulty and complexity to the development of a total management information system for a company. It is therefore especially important that management planning make adequate provision for the effects upon library service of the changes resulting from mechanisation.Finally, library operations and their costs are relatively ill-defined, at least in the form required for mechanisation. Only recently have libraries added systems and procedures personnel to their staffs, and few libraries, even now, have procedures manuals in the detail to be found in a business. There are still relatively few people available who combine knowledge of libraries with that of data processing. Management planning therefore must recognise the necessity for adequate systems work, including procedures analysis, and accommodate the difficulties in finding or training personnel capable of doing this work.

OBJECTIVES, TIME SCHEDULES, AND BUDGETS

The first and most important step in the management of a mechanisation program is the definition of objectives for it. Because program objectives must be compatible with library policies, the library administration must being by reviewing existing policies, both as documented and as generally understood. In doing so, it will probably find it necessary to develop some new policies and to document many previously undocumented ones. Then, the situation which led to the decision to undertake a modernisation program should be analysed. Typically, these might include demands for change coming from higher governing bodies; requirements for new services in response to changing conditions; increasing backlogs due to inadequate budgets, staff, or space. In any case, program objectives must be established which reflect both library policies and current or anticipated needs. The most ambitious general objective might be the orderly development of a total system which not only exploits as many of the new technologies as possible, but does so with optimum balance of cost and effectiveness and compatibility with other (state, local, or national) library systems.

A more limited one might be the documentation and analysis of existing library operations with the aim of limited improvement, through reorganisation or simplification and through limited use of proven equipment techniques and technologies. Very limited and specific objectives could include faster processing of new book orders, better control over technical processing routines, availability of more comprehensive statistic, better management information, reduction in routines performed by clerical staff, availability of better bibliographic descriptions of the collection, more effective utilisation of professional staff, improved reference services, better control over the physical collection, reduction of patron involvement in the charging transaction, and better circulation control. In defining objectives, the librarian is confronted not only with the uses of cost and effectiveness of services as required now. He should be even more concerned with the quality and quantity of services required in the future (in 5, 10 or 15 years). Will the library, with its present means, be capable of furnishing them? What must be done so that the expected service will be made available? As a result, the librarian must make predictions and projections about the future as well as clearly understand the present roles and purposes of his library.

Admittedly, the dynamic development of our educational and cultural system, together with the revolutionary developments experienced by library science in the past few years, all tend to decrease considerably one's confidence in any prediction. Nevertheless, even poor projections are better than none, and they can be revised often (perhaps once every six months) in order to maintain a reasonable, albeit minimal, degree of credibility. For this reason, it is particularly important to develop objectives in terms of a planned progression of systems starting from the present ways of doing things and leading to some ultimates system.

The importance of such an approach to library automation should not be underestimated. Libraries, as operational agencies, require that throughout development there be some level of system at all times in regular, full-scale operation in the library. Even more significant is the necessity that any interim system be capable of sustained, economic operation indefinitely. There is always uncertainty with respect to both the future and the actual progress in development of new systems. For example, related programs elsewhere and the actual availability of technology are completely outside the control of the individual library and yet essential to its planning. The progression of steps must be designed to articulate well with those programs as they actually develop, Because of these considerations, such a progression should be planned around a logical succession of systems which perform essentially the same functions but at increasing levels of sophistication. It may therefore frequently be desirable that less sophisticated objectives be met first, as the basis on which later systems are built. Only in this way can the library avoid the pitfalls of overcommitment to some ultimate concept, on the one hand, and of a refusal to proceed (because "new machinery will soon appear") on the other.

The management planning task, assisted by the library systems analysis staff, is to delineate those functions which are to be served at each stage in the progression. Some of them will simply be continuations of existing function, unchanged in any substantial way. Others will represent significant changes-such as a book catalog replacing a card catalog. Still others will represent totally new services-perhaps mechanised information retrieval or facsimile transmission. And some will represent the need to interface with other libraries.

The criteria used in this planning process include: (a) the economic value to be expected from including, changing, or even deleting functions, (b) the logical progression in conversion from an existing function to another, more sophisticated one (e.g. in transition from a card catalog to a computer produced book catalog to an on-line computer catalog), (c) the need to relate with others in other libraries, (d) the availability of budget and personnel, (e) the availability and reliability of the necessary hardware and software (f) the flexibility and ease of change, (g) the consistency with the ultimate objectives. We have already commented on the necessity to define a planned progression of stages. Each of them must satisfy a clearly delineated set of requirements, appropriate to the available technology and knowledge of how to do things; each of them must embody an equally well defined set of administrative and operational control; and each should be carefully planned so as to be consistent with the ultimate objectives. But each of them must also be based upon equally well-defined financial considerations. The basis of financial support therefore should as well planned as the technical implementation of hardware and software. In particular, cost/effectiveness measures of performance should be the primary basis for evaluation, and the decision about whether to automate in large part should be based on a comparison of cost of manual versus machine methods. While cost/effectiveness is especially difficult to evaluate when it is applied to systems development which progresses through a number of stages, spread over a period of years, this merely serves to emphasise the importance of a carefully planned progression of steps as an integral part of the development program.

The process of development and implementation of a mechanised library system is complicated and involves a large number of people. Therefore, the management of this effort must also be planned in advance, the tasks that are to be carried out assigned to development staff, and time estimates established for each task with target dates for their start and finish. The process of creating any mechanised processing system involves the performance of activities in a series of phases, commonly used in describing and planning computer work in both government and industry. They represent a natural sequence for development of mechanised library systems as well.

1. Feasibility analysis.
2. Requirements specification.
3. Detailed design.

4. Computer programming and check-out.
5. Computer program functional test.
6. Installation and implementation.
7. Maintenance.

Each of the seven phases encompasses a set of tasks, which culminate in milestones, or concluding events. The successive completion of them becomes an objective measure of progress achieve.

Phase 1—feasibility analysis. Based on a statement of the library's requirements, an estimate must be made of the resources required for the project. A summary project plan must be prepared, and a cost-versus-benefits comparison made. During this step, the level of analysis of the library's operating system is only that absolutely necessary for cost estimation and preliminary planning purposes.

Tasks: Assemble documentation on library policies and practices. Determine necessary development activities, including number and identify of any subsidiary efforts.

— Estimate development costs for each step or task.

— Check reasonableness of estimates.

— Perhaps summary budget plan for development.

— Estimate costs of both existing and proposed systems.

— Prepare cost-benefits evaluation of the proposed application.

Phase 2—requirements specification. This step consist of the detailed study of the existing library system, and the formulation of the operational requirements for the proposed system.

Tasks: Determine library's system requirements in detail.

Analyse library's environment including projects with which it must be compatible.

— Determine needed computer program characteristics.

— Compare with similar systems.

— Prepare performance specifications.

— Assure concurrence of library policy-makers with system performance specifications.

Phase 3—detailed design. Based on the requirements specification, this step proceeds to the definition of detailed design for both the computer system and the library personnel involved. It results in documents that detail the functions to be programmed as well as the operating procedures for personnel.

Tasks: Interpret requirements specification in terms of specific equipment, volume of activity, response times, and operating environment.

Phase 4—computer programming. Based upon the detailed design specifications this step proceeds with all work necessary to produce, document, and test computer programs. Included are such activities as flow charting, coding, integration of individual programs into a program system, preparation of test data bases, detecting and correcting errors, compiling or assembling operating programs, and listing of code. It results in a completed computer program end product, tested for conformity with detailed specification.

Tasks: Flow chart each component computer program.

— Specify all input and output forms.

— Write programs from detailed flow charts or other program design documentation.

— Compile and check program code, and make necessary error corrections.

— Test the performance of each individual program and of the total program system.

Phase 5—computer program functional test. This step covers demonstration tests of the computer program system, for the library management, usually in a simulated environment at the library. Included is conduct of the demonstration tests (based on test plans prepared as a part of Phase 3, above) and analysis of the rest results. All necessary work to remedy design deficiencies revealed by these tests should be charged to the appropriate previous steps. The results should be a computer program that is proven to be in conformance with the detailed design specifications and accepted by library management.

Tasks: Conduct test according to plan.

— Analyse test results.

— Initiate any modifications needed for computer programs.

— Document test results.

Phase 6—installation and implementation. This step covers all work necessary to install the system at the library. It includes training as well as activities for conversation from the existing manual operation.

Tasks: Prepare documentation for library staff.

— Supervise conversion of data required to make system operations.

— Develop training plan for library staff.

— Conduct training program.

Phase 7—maintenance. System maintenance is required for improving, changing, and correcting operational computer programs. Revisions are need because operations requirements are continually changing during the both the development and operation of the system. Although operational needs are projected during requirements analysis, in most cases they can be neither totally defined nor totally implemented in the imposed time schedules. Also, corrections must usually be made to the computer programs because errors and operational deficiencies not detected in the routine testing of the programs are usually discovered when the system becomes operational. Much of the work of program maintenance personnel must be devoted to the handling of emergencies; the remainder to modifications required to meet environmental changes.

Tasks: Develop maintenance plan and organisation.

— Provide continuing communication between library operating staff and computer programmers,

— Establish change procedures.

— Process system changes.

— Work breakdown structure

The formulation of such a comprehensive program is perhaps best accomplished by the definition of a work breakdown structure and an associated cost accounting structure. The work breakdown structure shows the component tasks of a library development project in detail and, as a basic for effective program planning, it insures that no major program activity is overlooked. It provides graphic representation of the relationship of the various components of a complex program to each other and the achievement of stated program objectives. Finally, it provides a convenient means for monitoring progress towards achieving the objectives of a program.

In this example, the total library system has been subdivided into three major subsystems, each of which has then been further divided in to more detailed modules, which represent work of a manageable size for program control. Each such module will then call for tasks within each of the seven phases in development, as have been outlines above in the description of those phases. In summary, the work breakdown structure produces a classification of work as follows: The library system is analysed into subsystems, each of which is analysed into modules; the work for each module is analysed into phases, with tasks specified for each phase.

Various analytical tools have been developed to control activities of this kind. One example is the PERT chart, essentially a flow chart tied to the work breakdown structure, in which the time dimension plays an especially important role. It has particular value in helping to determine the sequence of events which represent the longest delay in project schedule, called the *critical path* in the development.The mechanics of preparing a PERT diagram are relatively simple.

The next step is to determine the activities required for the completion of each of them and to specific milestone events by which to measure progress. Then dependencies among the individual tasks and corresponding milestone events must be identified. That is, the initiation of each activity will require the completion of one or more prior activities. These time dependencies can be visualised as a sequence, from lift to right, of the corresponding events, with arrows going to an event from all prior events necessary for its initiation. The real value of the PERT chart lies in the use of estimates of the time required for the completion of each activity. Usually, these estimates are expressed as both a range (from most optimistic to most pessimistic) and an expected, or most likely value.

When such estimates have been developed for each activity, an elapsed-time analysis can be produced by adding together all the estimated times for completion of the progression of activities and determining for each event the cumulated elapsed time to that point. Where several sequences of activities converge on a single event, the sequence (called the critical path) requiring the longest period of time determines when the corresponding activity can be initiated. In other words, all sequences of activities upon which an activity depends must be completed before that activity can be commenced. Those sequences leading up to an event which require less time than the critical path will have slack time (waiting time) built into them. This can be used for adjusting schedules so as to concentrate effort on other tasks or to minimise peak manpower, equipment, or facilities loading.

When the elapsed time analysis is complete it may be determined that the total elapsed time estimated for the program is incompatible with the required program completion date. If this happens, it will be necessary to reinspect the program logic in an effort to identify activities originally planned to occur in sequence which can, in fact, occur in parallel. Such a change in the plan, however, will almost always imply an increased risk of failure to perform as planned.

Sometimes it will be possible to compensate for the increased risk by adding additional backup efforts or by assigning the same activity to two different groups for simultaneous, parallel performance. Upon closer scrutiny it may be found that some of the activities originally thought essential are, in face, only desirable and can be eliminated from the plan entirely. Eventually, this strategy will force the planned program elapsed time to be compatible with the program completion date specified by the program manager. Next, it is necessary to analyse each week of activity in the planned program to determine what level of manpower or special facilities will be required. This may reveal, for example, that during the first weeks of the program there are heavy demands being made on various categories of manpower, and that later in the program there are periods when practically no demand is made for the same categories of manpower. It usually is possible to minimise the peaks by shifting some of the activities to later times when fewer demands are being made.

Cost Accounting and Control

An integral part of the planning function involves the budgeting and control of funds required for the various program activities. A convenient structure for doing so is the work breakdown structure itself. During later stages in the planning, all of the specific activities required to accomplish program objectives will be identified as tasks in the work breakdown structure. Each of the tasks (or portions of a task) may in turn be assigned a cost account number for which funds may be budgeted. The cost account structure is used in imple-menting cost accounting routines. Each increment of cost (man-hours or materials dollars) is posted periodically against each of the cost account numbers.

The individual elements are added together in such a way as to provide cumulative cost records at each of the summary levels in the cost account structure. At the highest level in the structure the total cumulative cost for the entire program is summarised. This number is plotted on a program status chart and monitored closely by program management. Any significant deviations of actual cost or performance from the planned cost/ performance curve is the signal to program management to initiate appropriate corrective action.

Education and Public Relations

Among the most important activities which should be included in project planning is the education of both staff and users in the operation, implications, and effects of the system. It is necessary for several reasons.

— Staff are rightly concerned about the effects which automation will have on them personally. Unless they have a sense of involvement, this concern can turn into outright fear and antagonism. A well-planned program of education, scheduled to proceed in parallel with the development project can help overcome this concern.

— The staff will need to change many of the ways in which they have carried out their assigned tasks. Some of those tasks themselves may even change. In principle, the procedures manuals and task descriptions generated as part of the programming work during development are sufficient to show each staff member how work should be performed. In fact, of course, intensive training is usually required, if only to show each person how his work relates top the system as a whole. In this respect, it must be recognised that while automation of clerical processes may not change the basic professional content of librarianship, it will change much of the detail. Even professionals, therefore, will need to see why these changes may be necessary and how they relate to the major objectives.

— Directly related to the second reason, is the fact that many times only the staff is really in position to recognise a serious flaw in an operating procedures. Unless they have been given the opportunity to see what the purposes are, they can hardly begin to bring out what would otherwise be only intuitive feelings that "something's not right".

— Any change of system (even from one manual method to another one) is bound to produce temporary traumas. Failures, changes from the familiar, bruises to esthetics- all are bruises to occur, if only because something is new. Since this is the case, particular care must be taken to prepare both staff and readers for these traumatic effects. This means that not only is a program of education needed, but public relations as well.

Orientation of Library Staff

It is therefore very important for the library administration to plan and carry out a careful program of orientation. It must make the staff knowledgeable about what the equipment coming into the library will do and what their own part will be in the new system. Only then will they be willing and able to participate with personal interest in successful operation. Fortunately, time is great factor which contributes to the ease adjustment to the encroachment of the machine.

Automation does not take place from Friday night to Monday morning. The library administrator can take advantage of the year or two or even three that the development will require to get his staff actively involved. And this should not be a voluntary involvement, left to the discretion of "interested" personnel, which ignores the very person who most needs to be drawn into the activity. It is especially important to inform staff from the time of their first awareness of the planning for a change in system.

The decision to introduce a new system is made only after extensive analysis of the impact which the new equipment and system will have on the library's interests. By the same token, the employee is just as anxious to learn what impact the new system is likely to have on his interests. Frank and open discussions by management are therefore necessary to reduce rumors that otherwise may give a distorted view of the situation. A well-planned information policy throughout the organisation has advantages even after a commitment is made to obtain equipment. If the introduction of a new system is tactfully presented, it can generate pride and satisfaction in the organisation, but the program should not be oversold or potential difficulties minimised. The important point is the realisation by management that all employees need complete and accurate facts.

It should be apparent therefore that an orientation program requires intensive and careful planning comparable to that carried on for the other aspects of the development and installation. The different requirements of various types of library staff and users for information about the system must be considered.

Appropriate techniques must be developed for the dissemination of necessary types of information. The procedures for conducting the orientation must avoid interfering with on-going operations.

The first step should be to get the staff acquainted with automated data processing in general. Such indoctrination could commence with a tour of an existing computer facility, preferably one associated with a library. A special course in data processing, with emphasis on applications within the library itself could be organised. Certain of the library staff could be sent to special training schools operated by the equipment suppliers. Once the library personnel are somewhat familiar with data processing, the professional staff should be involved in planning the introduction of automation to their respective departments. In this manner, they will see the project in terms of their own needs and will be motivated to plan and execute it well.

Furthermore, if the response of the personnel directly involved with the pilot operation has been favourable (and such attitudes are typical) these people can be counted on to sell the system to other people who will be working with it. In some cases it may even be possible to provide some on-the-job training in the pilot operation prior to the full implementation of the new system. Descriptions presented on the spot while touring through the library can help individuals visualise the characteristics of the new system. Other techniques can be used to maintain a high level of interest in the new system during the time just preceding the installation. Appropriate posters, demonstrations of new equipment or techniques, as well as lectures and directed reading can stimulate continued interest in the new system. The installation phase is critical since at that time the majority of the library staff are exposed for the first time to the system as an operational entity. This is a period in which the basic attitudes of personnel who must operate and depend upon the system are solidified.

2

Dynamic Library Functions

To analyse the various dimensions of the multifaceted concept, the study of organisations has drawn on a range of different perspectives. These can be presented in an historical and dialectic sequence of *thesis, antithesis* and *synthesis.* Theories of organisational behaviour grew, initially, out of the Industrial Revolution and the development of the factory system. The classic statement of this early approach was Frederick Taylor's *Principles of scientific management* which advocated the application of 'scientifically' deduced methods to the production process.

Taylor's recognition that manufacturing processes can be systematically analysed and divided into a sequence of single tasks led to time-and-motion studies and the 'assembly line' concept. 'Scientific' management viewed the organisation from an engineering perspective generally described as 'mechanistic'—the organisation as machine. This provides the initial thesis of organisational theory. However, this approach takes little account of the human dimension. People were seen as cogs in the machine, motivated by material rewards, and told what to do by management. An emphasis on 'human relations', emerging from the perspectives of social and behavioural sciences, provides the antithesis of this view. The classic starting-point for the 'human relations' school is the so-called 'Hawthorne effect'. A series of experiments were conducted in the Western Electric Company's factory at Hawthorne, near Chicago, between 1924 and 1932.

These were intended-in the manner of scientific management-to explore the relationship between working conditions (levels of lighting, structure of the working day, etc.) and productivity. What was discovered, however, was that production increased, not because of changed working conditions, but because the workers felt important and appreciated as the subject of scientific study. The 'Hawthorne effect' is the effect of making people feel special. It underpins the maxim already quoted that 'People who feel good about themselves produce good results'. This approach stresses the importance of individual psychology and social interaction. Motivation, the importance of peer-group relationships, the informal, 'hidden' networks of the organisation—the dynamics of the organisations are analysed in terms of interpersonal relations. Two examples have already been used, showing the insights that can result from the application of social/ behavioural sciences to management studies.

One is Mintzberg's research into the nature of a manager's work. The other is Pettigrew's research into the political dimension of organisational decision-making. A number of studies offer a contrast-an implicit comparison of thesis and antithesis-between a 'scientific management' approach and a 'human relations' approach.

Rensis Likert distinguished four types of management style. The first two are authoritarian, one autocratic and exploitative, the second more benevolent. With these styles, the organisational structure is tall and narrow with centralised decision-making and little delegation. Likert's third style is consultative. Staff are asked their opinions which may, or may not, be taken into account when decisions are made. The fourth style is genuinely participative with the work group sharing their views and making decisions collectively. The 'managerial grid' developed by Robert Blake and Jane Mouton provides a framework within which to compare the relative value given by a manger to 'concern for people' and 'concern for production'. At the end of the latter scale is an overriding concern for output and efficiency. At the end of the former scale is a 'country club' approach with comfortable personal relations, a relaxed pace of work, and low concern for output. The '1.9' position (the 'country club' approach) is excessively orientated towards human relations. The '9.1' position (concern for output above all) is excessively mechanistic. A midpoint on the grid shows a 'middle of the road' approach ensuring adequate output and satisfactory morale. A high score on both scales (the so-called '9.9' position) indicates an excellent performance in terms of both interpersonal relations and work output. Management style is often described in terms of a continuum of possibilities from autocratic to democratic-from authoritarian to participative. In reviewing work done in this area, Charles Handy uses the more useful distinction between structuring and supportive styles. This less emotive terminology gives a positive value to both types of approach. Structure, direction, clear mechanisms and a focus on the job to be done are needed; so too is support for the individual, and awareness of social processes, and recognition of the 'psychological contract' between individual and organisation.

There is, then, a need for synthesis between the 'mechanistic' perspective and the 'social/behavioural' perspective. This is currently provided by the 'systems' approach to organisations. The perspective here is partly biological or ecological-the organisation seen as an organism, evolving and adapting as a result of internal and external stimuli-and partly that of systems theory as developed in computing and cybernetics. The organisation is seen as a system consisting of two principal subsystems. The 'technical' subsystem incorporates the 'mechanistic' elements: plant and machinery, work-flow, routines and processes, etc. The 'social' subsystem includes the 'human relations' dimension. Both co-exist and management must give due regard to both.

The standard representation of an organisation as system includes inputs, processes, outputs and a 'control' loop providing feedback on outputs in order to regulate and adapt inputs and processes. However, organisations do not have built-in mechanisms of feedback and control, as do certain machines. Nor do they have automatic processes of adaptation and evolution, as do animals and other organisms. Organisations need to introduce sophisticated communications systems in order to simulate this feedback/control/adaptation process. A central point in Peter Drucker's Innovation and entrepreneurship is the importance of information flow into and within the organisation. Drucker notes that the model of technology has shifted from mechanical processes to biological processes organised around information. There is currently considerable interest in the nature of organisations as information systems, from the perspective of computing and cybernetics (that is, the science of systems of control and communications; in particular, study of the human control system of nervous system and brain, and experimentation with applications of computing technology to intelligent processes).

The systems approach implies two important points. The first is that an organisation is a dynamic, changing entity. It is never static. An organisation chart may appear to show a fixed structure, but a fixed framework still allows for considerable freedom and flexibility of organisational behaviour-and the structure itself will adapt over time. The second is that there is no one 'best' form of organisation. Rosemary Stewart sees the major contribution of social sciences to the understanding of organisations as being this awareness: 'that different types of behaviour need different forms of organisation and that the appropriate kinds of organisation can change with the company's situation'. This 'contingency' theory-that is, the theory that the nature of an organisation is contingent upon its situation-reinforces the importance of information.

The 'systems' approach and the concept of the 'adaptive' organisation (that is, the organisation as open system or organism, adapting to meet changing circumstances) is very relevant to libraries. As organisations, libraries clearly illustrate the coexistence of technical and social subsystems. In terms of service delivery these concepts are formalised in the traditional structural division, in academic libraries, between 'technical services' (relatively mechanical - and nowadays often automated- processes of acquisition, cataloguing, circulation control and so on) and 'reader services' (services involving the social process of interaction between staff and customers).

The library needs to be 'adaptive' given a context of discontinuous change. The customer community, the library's governing framework, and a range of external considerations all form 'contingent factors' to be taken into account. Finally, libraries, like other adaptive organi-sations, need good information systems. These are necessary partly because of the point mentioned by Lupton-in order to adapt to contingencies, an organisation needs a continuous flow of information about the contingent factors surroundings it. They are also necessary as feedback/control mechanisms. The pressure of accountability requires that management demonstrate efficient use of resources, effective service delivery, and value to the customer.

Changes in size, new patterns of service provision, and

the impact of information technology have all produced a considerable amount of restructuring of library organisations in recent years. Many public library departments in the UK have been restructured into larger directorates-of leisure, recreation, education, culture, etc. An emerging pattern in some British and American higher education institutions is the linking of library services with computer services to provide one integrated support network of information systems and services. In schools and colleges, libraries have, in many instances, become part of a wider structure of 'learning resources'. These changes in size reflect changes in the pattern of service provision: each is designed to provide a clearer direction and focus. So, in theory, the fundamental purpose of a UK public library within a 'leisure' ethos is distinct from that of a public library in 'education'—although, in practice, sharp distinctions in public library service, arising from their directorate contexts, are not yet evident. In educational establishments, however, there is a clearer link between this organisational restructuring and the nature and purpose of library service.

The concept of the library as a 'learning resource', for example, gives structural reinforcement to the view that a school or college library is the 'foundation of the curriculum'—a central part of the educational process, providing resources to enable students to develop learning skills. In public libraries, the link between structural change and the pattern of service provision is more at 'grass roots' level than directorate level, with the development of the 'community librarian' approach. Sheila Ritchie links the community-orientated approach to service with a consequent need to restructure the library organisation. Ritchie contrasts a passive, building-based approach to service with a more pro-active, developmental approach which gets much closer to the customer community and seeks to meet need as well as expressed demand. The latter, she suggests, requires a decentralised structure with participative decision-making, 'bottom up' communication, and delegated authority. Her implication is that the passive, building-based approach is delivered through a centralised structure with management mechanisms which are essentially 'top down'. An important point here is the distinction between geographic decentralisation and managerial decentralisation.

Public library structures have always been decentralised to a degree, provided through a geographic scatter of branch libraries. However, the management structure has often remained highly centralised with branch librarians having very little real delegated authority. Indeed, the term 'branch library' is a literal statement of the management structure-the library as the local branch of a centrally-determined service. In England, some local authorities-particularly some London boroughs-are developing a decentralised approach to services which are not, traditionally, delivered directly at local level: social services, for example, or housing repairs. Islington, for instance, is evolving a pattern of 'Neighbourhood Offices', each serving a local population of between 4,500 to 8,000 people. By bringing services to this 'neighbourhood' level, the local authority hopes to avoid the problems which are often attributed to centralised services-inefficiency, remoteness, inaccessibility, lack of responsiveness. In order to do this, the 'neighbourhood' concept does not just decentralise service delivery, it also decentralises management authority. Each Neighbourhood Office, and service department within that Office, has a considerable degree of autonomous authority for decision-making and resource allocation. Indeed some local authorities, including Islington, are developing mechanisms for involving local residents, directly, in decision-making at neighbourhood level.

As well as changes in size and in patterns of service

delivery, changes in technology are also having an impact on the structure of library organisations. In order to take full advantage of technological opportunities there is a need to build 'systems' skills into the management team. The automation of 'housekeeping' processes and technical services can mean a reduction in the number of staff employed in these areas. The possibilities for the development of new, IT-based, services can mean the emergence of new elements in the organisation chart-staff responsible for online searching, database creation (for example, the provision of community information using videotex), or the 'repackaging' of information into state-of-the-art reports, current awareness bulletins and SDI services. Technology may affect the process of communication between staff as well as the staffing structure. Networking and electronic mail offer opportunities for improved interactive communications across a geographically scattered organisation and this may have an impact on participation in the decision-making process.

Technology raises a further issue which has an impact on the structure of library organisations; the balance between what is provided from within the organisation and what is contracted out to external agencies. Much of the 'behind the scenes' work of processing and cataloguing, for example, is no longer carried out within libraries. It is handled externally by bibliographic cooperatives (cataloguing) and commercial suppliers of library stock (processing). Indeed, some commercial suppliers are now offering a full range of bibliographic services including facilities for stock editing and collection development. There is thus no longer any need for a large section of the organisational structure to be devoted to bibliographic services and stock processing. Similarly, electronic publishing and document delivery is changing the structure of reference/ information services.

Online information, interlending networks and facsimile transmission are-to a varying degree in different types of library-replacing or supplementing library holdings of printed books and other documents. Again, the balance changes between what is directly provided (in printed form) and services which enable the library to gain access (electronically) to information held elsewhere. Structural change in the balance between 'providing' and 'enabling' is becoming a highly significant issue for public libraries in the UK as the government extends the application of compulsory tender testing to local authority services. This discussion of current structural issues illustrates three key points. The first is that a 'structure' cannot be regarded as a fixed and unchanging framework. Changes in size, service provision, technology, the balance between providing' and 'enabling'—all are 'contingent factors' which impact on and influence the library's evolving structure.

The second is that an organisation's 'structure' serves a number of purposes. The organisation chart indicates the reporting structure-the lines of command (of authority and accountability) necessary in order to coordinate and control the work of the organisation. Another diagram might be needed to indicate lines of communication-for example, the horizontal lines of communication between staff on the same management level but in different parts of the organisation which will not be shown in hierarchical lines of command. As well as coordination/control and communication, the structure needs to incorporate a 'development' dimension, if service delivery is to be pro-active and customer orientated. A further diagram might be needed to indicate the ways in which people come together in order to plan service and think ahead.

The work need to be divided up in an appropriate manner-yet it also needs to be coordinated and integrated to a common purpose. In order to get 'close to the customer' there is a need to delegate authority so that staff dealing directly with customers have some autonomy-yet there is a need to provide mechanisms for overall control and accountability to senior management. A pro-active and 'adaptive' organisation will wish to support innovation and creativity-yet there has also to be a measure of stability and conformity to accepted procedures, agreed objectives and shared values. Essentially, this is a conflict between elements of centralisation and decentralisation. A major challenge for those library managers involved in any restructuring exercise is to keep these elements in balance. The lines of command and the characteristics expressed in the left-hand checklist operate through hierarchy and bureaucracy. The hierarchy enables everyone in the organisation to know to whom they are accountable and for whom they are responsible. The bureaucracy lays down rules and procedures.

The hierarchy expressed the levels of power and authority from Chief Executive to the bottom rung on the corporate 'ladder'. The following illustrates how this reporting structure might look for a library assistant in a public and an academic library:

Library Assistant	Library Assistant
↓	↓
Branch Librarian	Assistant Librarian
↓	↓
Area Librarian	Sub-Librarian (i.e. Section Head)
↓	↓
Deputy Librarian	Deputy Librarian
↓	↓
Chief Librarian	Chief Librarian

In both (rather simplified) cases, the hierarchy has five levels; the Chief and Deputy as senior management; the Area Librarian or 'Sub-Librarian' (a curious term used in UK universities) as middle management; and the Branch Librarian or Assistant Librarian as junior, line management. One of the challenges of organisational structure is to keep the line of command as short and tight as possible by reducing to a minimum the number of levels in the hierarchy. This is a challenge because of the need to keep each individual manager's 'span of control'—the number of people for whom that manager is responsible-within manageable proportions.

In the example above it might be possible to remove from the public library hierarchy the middle-management level of Area Librarian, but all the Branch Librarians would then report directly to senior management. This is fine in a relatively small public library organisation. But if the organisation is large-say, of four areas each containing six branches-then the Deputy and Chief would have 24 Branch Librarians reporting directly to them. In terms of the span of control it would probably be more effective to retain the Area Librarians.

There is, then, a need to consider three points when examining the hierarchy of an organisation

— overall size of the organisation
— levels in the hierarchy
— spans of control for individual managers.

A fourth point which has a crucial impact on organisational structure-and which relates to the right-hand checklist (division, delegation, etc.)—is the need to divide the work to be done into a number of departments. Traditionally, there are four ways in which this can be done.

— by function
— by product
— by territory
— by customer group.

The classic division of public library work is by function-reference, lending, bibliographic services, etc.-and by territory, though a structure of branch libraries. In academic libraries there will be an element of functional division (bibliographic services, interlibrary loan, circulation desk, etc.) and also some division by customer group with the establishment of subject-based departments within the library. Public libraries also divide work on the basis of customer groups; traditionally with the division between adult and children's services and, more recently, with the targetting of services to particular customer groups-elderly people, unemployed people, people from particular minority ethnic groups, etc.

Finally, there is also some division by product-for example, music libraries, community information services, current awareness bulletins, etc. The fact that libraries use all four ways of dividing work into departments illustrates the complexity of library organisations and the difficulty of finding a structure which integrates all elements to meet service objectives. Departmental separatism-by which the organisation fragments into several departments which rarely communicate with each other-can be a characteristic of large library systems. There is no real communication between 'central' and 'the branches', between sites or subject libraries, between technical and reader services, etc.

Equally, it can be experienced by the library itself in its relations with the other parts of the parent organisation. In some large corporations, the library can appear by passed and marginalised as the web of corporate communications and decision-making processes seems not to include the library staff.

There are a number of ways by which departmental separatism can be avoided. One is through a formal system of meetings and committees where staff from different departments come together. Similarly, interdepartmental project teams and 'task forces' can be set up to tackle particular initiatives and programmes. A third, less formal, strategy is that of individual managers 'networking' across the organisation; building up personal contacts in a number of departments. A further way of providing integration-and also an important element of professional development for the individual job-holder-is by creating a 'matrix' structure. This gives individuals a 'line' management function-for example responsibility for a particular service point-and also membership of a 'team': for example, the team of librarians charged with providing service within a particular geographic area.

The job description will give an indication of the relative proportion of time to be spent in each role (say, 60% line management, 40% team membership). A more sophisticated matrix may link the individual librarian to a particular territory (area team), a specific service (for example, children's services of reference work), and a section of stock (such as adult fiction). In this structure, the day-to-day administration of service points is likely to be delegated to Senior Library Assistants, thus creating an element of career progression for non-professional staff.

One value of 'team librarianship' as developed in public libraries is that it can help to break down barriers of department separatism; as well as offering a cost-efficient means of deploying professional staff. A number of other 'teams' will exist within the organisation to contribute to the process of integration/coordination and to the process of planning and forward development. There will be a Management Team of senior staff. There will also be various 'expert' teams bringing together staff with a particular area of expertise; for example, a team responsible for developing staff training programmes or for a particular area of service delivery-children's services, online searching, etc. In addition to these permanent or long-term teams, there will be teams brought together for a relatively short time to plan a particular project or deal with a specific task; for example, the implementation of an automated circulation control system. As well as breaking down departmental separatism by bringing together staff from different sections in order to tackle a common objective, these teams also bring an element of flexibility and innovation into the organisation's bureaucratic framework.

The concept of bureaucracy tends to get a bad press because of an association with complex regulations and procedures which tends to stifle initiative and promote inertia. But bureaucracy has positive values, in that it instills rationality and continuity into an organisation. Bureaucracy is expressed through:

— specification; structure shaped by job functions, not by particular individuals.

— stratification; hierarchy providing defined levels of authority.

— systems; of rules and procedures.

As well as an element of stability and consistency, the bureaucratic approach also leads to impersonality-and thus to fairness and equality of treatment. Bureaucracy can be a safeguard against arbitrary and over-personalised dealing and decision-making. However, bureaucracy can lead to an overemphasis on rules, procedures and conformity. There are two strategies which can help to inject a capacity for innovation and adaptation into the necessary bureaucratic framework. One is the use of short-term teams. The other is described by E.F. Schumacher as the fundamental task of achieving 'smallness' within an organisation.

'Smallness' is designed to avoid the problems normally associated with large organisations:

— remoteness and lack of commitment; an individual's feelings of personal responsibility for the success of the organisation diminish as the organisation grows.
— disaffection arising from the feeling of being 'just a cog in the machine'.
— 'red tape', inflexibility, delay, inertia (i.e. bureaucracy).

In terms of organisational structure, 'smallness' is achieved by decentralising the organisation into a number of small, relatively autonomous units. Library organisations are usually decentralised in structure-into a number of relatively small departments or branches-although management tends to remain centralised so that these small units have little real autonomy. A particular value of 'smallness and the use of teams is the sense of 'team spirit' than can be generated. Group dynamics and the generation of team spirit emphasise the important of seeing an organisation's structure as a social system as well as a technical system. Bureaucracy and the organisation chart may be impersonal, but the success of an organisation-the quality of library service-depends on people. There is a link between changing patterns of service provision and changing organisational structure. But structure alone does not determine the nature and quality of service. In order to bring in the 'people' dimension, considerations of structure need to be supplemented by the concept of organisational 'culture'.

Organisation and the Concept of Culture

The concept of organisational 'culture' is difficult to describe with precision because, unlike structure, it cannot be codified into a series of organisation charts, a cycle of meetings, or a manual of procedures-although part of it can sometimes be captured in an organisation's mission statement or set of core values.

— the impact on management thinking of the 'enterprise culture' vigorously promoted in the UK by the present government.

— the development of an organisational 'culture' which puts the customer first.

— the need, in an adaptive organisation, for a 'culture' which stimulates innovation, supports individual initiative, and accepts risk-taking; and which gives a 'bottom up' as well as a 'top down' dynamic to communications and decision-making.

— the 'loose-tight' concept of individual autonomy and selfcontrol within the framework of a strong corporate 'culture' which constantly reinforces a few key values.

These examples suggest that culture is, at bottom, attitudinal. It is a set of attitudes-feelings, beliefs, values-which shape, and are reinforced by, actions. It is thus at the heart of the organisation's social system. In all organisations the formal structure co-exists with an informal, 'hidden' set of dynamics. One example has already been seen: the informal but influential 'politicking' based on the 'King's Parade', which co-exists with the formal decision-making structure.

One aspect of the 'hidden' organisation, then, is the informal power structure of influence which co-exists with the formal power structure of authority. Traditionally, this 'hidden' organisation has been developed and reinforced through the social relationships which evolve within peer groups; and through the history and heritage-the corporate memory-of an organisation. It finds expression in the emergence of 'cliques' (tight knots of people who commune closely together, often to the exclusion of colleagues), the existence of an informal communications 'grapevine', and the establishment of 'unwritten rules'. These are an important guide to the workings and attitudes of the 'hidden' organisation and cover issues such as

— who to approach for information or advice on a particular issue.
— how to communicate with colleagues; when to write, or phone, or go to see someone.
— how to address colleagues; first names, or a more formal approach.
— dress codes; shirt sleeves? ties (properly tied, or loosened?)? jeans? skirts or trousers? etc.
— at work early or late; a sign of diligence-or inefficiency?

These 'hidden' dynamics are a powerful force in socialising individuals into the 'norms'-the accepted attitudes and behaviour-of the organisation. This 'hidden' organisation has considerable value. It provides peer group support, extends communication networks, and so can assist with the smooth operation of the organisation. Rosemary Stewart suggests that it can even be responsible for the continued existence of organisations which would otherwise have collapsed; people develop informal methods of coping when organisations fail to adapt, formally, to changed circumstances. The 'hidden' organisation, because it is based on social relationships, is naturally organic and adaptive. What is important, from the management perspective, is that these 'hidden' dynamics do not get out of line with the formal structure and objectives of the organisation.

A successful-and happy-organisation is a single community where formal mechanisms and informal, 'hidden' dynamics work in harmony, mutually reinforcing each other. When this happens the organisation can be said to have evolved a healthy and coherent 'culture'. Charles Handy's Understanding organisations, which focusses on the 'psychology' of organisations and the people who work in them, offers a useful typology of organisational cultures. The power culture is entrepreneurial and competitive. There is little bureaucracy and much individual autonomy. Communication is verbal, decision-making is a highly 'political' process based on the power of individual personalities. People are judged on results. This is thrusting and dynamic culture which can work well in small organisations and at a time of rapid change. However, size can be a problem. Handy uses the image of a web to portray this culture-and the web can break if it gets too big or tries to link together too many activities.

The role culture suits large organisations operating in a stable environment. Power is based on position in the formal hierarchy. There is a clear structure of departmental responsibilities and bureaucratic procedures. It is important that individuals follow the correct process. This culture offers security and predictability, but change in the external environment can be a problem. Handy's image is of a Greek temple-and the foundations become insecure when the ground shakes. Task culture is focussed on getting the job done. People and resources are brought together into project groups or task forces to 'get on with it'. Within the group power is based on expertise. Handy's image is of a net or network. This culture is good where flexibility, adaptability and responsiveness are needed. However it does not lend itself to control/coordination or to building strength in depth. It also needs an appropriately bountiful resource environment. When resources become limited, senior management has to control methods as well as results, and teams begin to compete, using political influence, for available resources. The task culture changes to a role or power culture.This analysis of the resources environment's impact on organisational culture is particularly relevant to library service where, currently, there are often severe resource constraints. The task culture can provide the adaptability and innovation needed at a time of discontinuous change-hence the use of matrix structures and temporary teams within library organisations. But the need to allocate resources in a context of competing priorities shifts the emphasis to a role power culture. Decisions have to be taken which will be unpopular with some people. A current difficulty within library management is to reconcile these conflicting cultures.

Considerations of organisational culture have to take into account the 'psychological contract' between the individual and the organisation. This is the 'hidden' contract, based on expectations and motivation, which co-exists with the formal contract of employment.

> This psychological contract is essentially a set of expectations. The individual has a set of results that he expects from his organisation, results that will satisfy certain of his needs and in return for which he will expend some of his energies and talents. Similarly the organisation has its set of expectations of the individual and its list of payments or outcomes that it will give to him.

An important element in this 'contract' is affinity between the culture of the organisation and an individual's expectations and aspirations. An individual with a need for security will feel comfortable within a role culture. This might feel stifling to an individual with a need for recognition and 'self actualisation' (that is, 'stretching' oneself to realise one's full potential); that person might have the strength, confidence and ruthlessness to operate successfully in a power culture. On the other hand, and individual with a need for group affiliation or the expression of expertise might find the most suitable niche in a task culture.

When managing change and dealing with the restructuring of organisations, it is important to remember the interaction between organisational culture and individual psychology. A change in culture can have a profound effect on the 'psychological contract' which conditions the attitudes and behaviours of individuals within the organisation. The person culture in which the structure or organisation only exists to serve the cluster of individuals within it. 'Barristers' chambers, architects partnerships, hippy communes, small consultancy practices, families and similar organisations can have this person orientation. In this culture, influence is shared and when power is exercised it is on the basis of expertise.

Although there are few organisations where this culture predominates, there are many individuals whose personal preference is for this type of approach. 'Specialists in organisations-computer people in business organisations, consultants in hospitals, architects in city government-often feel little allegiance to the organisation but regard it rather as a place to do their thing with some accruing benefit to the main employer'. This cast of mind is relevant to library service for two reasons. First, because of the increasing number of non-librarian specialists being employed within library organisations-people with expertise in systems, marketing, personnel, finance, administration, etc.-whose 'psychological contract' with the library may be shaped by this viewpoint. Second, because librarians themselves can think in this way. As specialists with a particular expertise their expectations and aspirations may well be framed in terms of 'the profession' rather than the organisation in which they find themselves currently working. This is one possible reason for the barriers which can build up, in some libraries, between professional and non-professional staff. The latter think of their work in relation to the organisation and, ideally, the customer community; and they sometimes perceive professional staff as being more interested in furthering their professional careers than in serving the needs of that library and its customers.

There are a number of factors which can determine the culture of an organisation:

— the size of the organisation;
— the age and history of the organisation;
— the organisation's purpose, objectives and activities;
— the resource environment within the organisation;
— external environments which form 'contingent factors' for the organisation;
— the people in the organisation; their expectations, aspirations and motivation.

From this list it is clear that there can often be a mix of different cultures within the same organisation. For example, the activities of a cataloguing department lend themselves to a culture-thoughtful and precise application of rules suggesting a role culture-different from that of a team of community librarians, where a strong focus on the team and the job suggests a task culture. The list also suggests that organisational cultures changes over time and through changing circumstances. Cultural change, however can be a slow and sometimes painful process, bound up as it is with the need for attitudes and behaviours to change. To operate successfully within an organisation, a manager needs to understand the dynamics of how that organisation works.

Those dynamics are based not just on the formal structure but also on the 'hidden' organisation which co-exists with it. Structures are made up of people, and the manager needs to be aware of the psycho-dynamics of individuals, interpersonal relations, and groups. It is this psychological dimensions which drives the attitudes and values underpinning the concept of organisational culture.

— The manager as coach, not just devising plans, but motivating people by careful and detailed attention to them as individuals.

— The manager as value-shaper, reiterating and reinforcing the core values of the organisation by speech and action.

— The need for managers to 'walk the talk'; to show integrity and consistency-practise what they preach-in order to shape values and motivate individuals.

— The need for managers to get around the workplace, visibly and approachably. The Excellent books all stress the value of MBWA (Managing By Wandering Around). In addition this 'wandering around'—in the customer community as well as within the organisation itself-keeps a manager in close touch with current situations and information to which the organisation may have to respond or adapt.

— The importance of 'small stuff-the succession of brief encounters that characterise the manager's day of, in Mintzberg's phrase, 'brevity, variety and fragmentation'.

Making the best use of these brief encounters is the fundamental message of The one minute manager by Blanchard and Johnson which stresses the importance of brief ('one minute') but effective sessions of goal-setting, praising, and reprimand. Books like the Excellence sequence and The one minute manager are sometimes dismissed as 'pop' management. In fact, they present-in clear and often vibrant language-fundamental insights into the dynamics of organisations and the psychology of individuals at work. The three issues on which The one minute manager focusses (goal-setting, praising, reprimand) are, for example, core elements in the process of 'developing people' which Peter Drucker sees as an essential part of a manager's job.

In search of excellence and the winning streak both offer a checklist of the key attributes of 'excellent' organisations.

Although these attributes appear in different sequences, are expressed in different terminologies, and refer to different nations, there is considerable consensus regarding the characteristics of successful organisations. What follows is a synthesis of those attributes, arranged under four main headings

- *Purpose*
  - clear sense of the fundamentals of the business
  - clear objectives
  - no dilution by diversification
- *Market orientation*
  - continuous market research
  - feedback from customers
  - care for quality control and customer service
  - integrity in dealing with customers
  - care to develop a good public image
- *Organisation*
  - structure
    - kept simple
    - few staff at headquarters: most out 'in the field'
    - decentralised, with delegated authority and considerable autonomy
  - control
    - concern for the planning process
    - clear objectives, with feedback on results
    - constant reinforcement of core values
  - culture
    - 'hands on' involvement by mangers: to transmit

core values, and to generate commitment, enthusiasm and pride

— attitude supportive of innovation and entrepreneurship: a positive attitude to risk-taking (with tolerance of mistakes as part of the learning process); a bias for action and experimentation-try it out, get it done.

— *People*

— productivity through people

— respect for the individual

— care for the motivation and morale of individuals

— recognition that 'rank and file' staff are the root source of efficiency and quality of service

— leadership

— visible management (e.g. MBWA)

— creation of an environment which encourage the exercise of leadership at all levels of management.

This checklist provides a useful summary of the key issues raised in this book so far. It also illustrates how much organisational dynamics are intertwined with the psychology of people. Implicit throughout the checklist, for example, is the connection between excellent organisational performance and good interpersonal communications.

Importance of Communication

The Excellence literature illustrates the link between communications and organisational performance. The one minute manager shows the link between communications and effective management. In these books, the focus tends to be on management communication which is *ad hoc* and verbal. Every organisation will also contain two other types of communication: the formal communications structure, usually of meetings and memoranda; and the informal 'grapevine'. It is important for managers to realise that, however much an organisation becomes a single community, there will always be a network of communication and social relationships from which management is excluded. Ken Jones suggests that these informal communications networks play a vital role in easing the 'psycho-social strain' which individuals can experience in a bureaucratic organisation. They do this in three ways:

— as a socialising force, giving people a sense of 'belonging', of being a member of the group with whom they communicate.

— as a part of the 'politicking' process, enabling people to attempt to influence the decision-making process.

— as an information network, transmitting news more rapidly than the 'official channels'.

The informal 'grapevine' is also, of course, one of the key ways in which an organisation's culture is developed and reinforced. Stories circulate through the grapevine and then become part of the 'oral history' of the organisation to be reiterated from time to time. These will inevitably focus on an individual or an event in a way which promoted certain values and attitudes. Formal communications usually exist on paper. The written document provides a record and tends to be worded more precisely than a verbal interchange. Of course, simply writing and sending a message is no indication that the message has been received or understood or acted on. There is no (immediate) feedback. However, much communication in organisations tends to be of this one-way, paper-based type-memos, reports, bulletins of 'routine instructions' to all staff.

Meetings form the other major element of formal communication-regular committees, or specially convened meetings. There may well be considerable verbal interaction at these meetings, but the official record of discussions and decisions will be the 'minutes', a document written up afterwards and formally approved at the next meetings. Discussion will also have been largely limited to those items included on a preset 'agenda' of issues for consideration. This formal, bureaucratic process is important-it provides a stable, impersonal and regular means by which issues can be raised and decisions made. But it is likely to be somewhat slow and ponderous. The vast majority of useful communications will take place around these meetings, rather than in them.

Communications within an organisation can be described in terms of four directions:

— downward, following the hierarchical chain of command.

— upward, through a variety of mechanisms; reporting systems designed to monitor performance; participative planning and decision-making structures; the machinery of consultation and negotiation with trade union representatives.

— horizontally across, between peers in the same work groups, or departments and individuals on the same level of the hierarchy.

— diagonally across, for example, when a department in one part of the organisation needs the assistance of a senior specialist from another section.

In each direction there can be barriers to good communication. Within the hierarchy the quality of communication can diminish as it filters down-or up-through the chain of command. The desire to spread only good news gets in the way of full and accurate upward communication; information is 'laundered' as it passes higher up the hierarchy. A sense of status and of 'only telling people what they need to know' can obstruct the flow of information downward. This can lead to what has been described as the 'mushroom management' syndrome-people are kept in the dark and occasionally get a pile of fertiliser (or something similar) dumped on them. In libraries, the split between professional and non-professional staff can lead to breakdowns in communication based on hierarchy.

Non-professional staff are rarely included in the organisation's cycle of formal meetings and are heavily dependent on their line manager-often a relatively recently qualified professional i a junior management position-in order to feel included in the communications network. Barriers to communication across the organisation can include geographic dispersal and the compartmentalism of different departments and specialisms. Library organisations can have particular difficulties here. Library organisations are often geographically dispersed with a lack of communication between 'central' and the branches in public library systems; or between the 'main library' and the site libraries in some academic institutions. There is also sometimes a lack of communication between functional departments (lending, reference, bibliographic services, etc.) Technology may well be able to help in breaking down some of these cross-organisational barriers.

Electronic mail is a valuable hybrid which can have (like verbal communication) an interactive element and which can be (like written communication) precisely worded and formally recorded. Email networks enable staff to communicate frequently irrespective of geographic dispersal. A number of the 'integrated systems' (automating cataloguing, circulation control, acquisitions, serials control, etc.) in use in large UK libraries have the capability to support an Email network. It may be that Email will become a useful tool by which management can widen communication flow and increase participation in discussions and decisions within library organisations. Good communications are essential to a healthy organisation and a contented workforce. As Anne Mathews emphasises 'high morale and motivation stem from open communications'. There are a number of things which can be done-aside from exploring the potential of new technology-if managers wish to increase the effectiveness of organisational communications. One is simply for management to be aware of the need to review communications.

The concept of the 'open door' (as in 'if you want to come and see me, my door is always open') illustrates the discrepancy which often exists between a manager's self perception and the way in which that manager's style is perceived by other members of staff. The manager may think the door is open-but in practice the manager is often out of the office, or busy, and staff may feel inhibited about just 'popping in for a chat'.A second strategy is to create an environment which encourages communication. This involves managers taking pains to listen more effectively-too often, meetings become a series of monologues rather than a dialogue or true discussion. It also involves creating a climate of trust. Staff will not offer their observations, opinions or information if that material is then used to exploit a situation, condemn an action, or gossip about an individual.

The third strategy is to create 'communication opportunities' within the organisation. The use of temporary teams and matrix structures is valuable in this regard, as is a culture which supports the concept of 'management by wandering about'. Coffee (or tea) breaks and lunchtimes are also excellent opportunities for informal communications, as is the time-honoured tradition of 'a quick drink after work'. Some managers also see social events-Christmas parties, summer barbeques, charity sports events, etc.-as an important part of this process and act as a catalyst for such events.

Social events bring people together and can build a feeling of collective identity and 'team spirit'. They can help to break down barriers of status and formality and so can contribute to better interpersonal relations. They bring people out of their departments and into the organisation as a whole thus encouraging integration and a sense of overall purpose. Above all, they can take people out of their job-roles and enable them to 'be themselves' as human beings. Of course, this can be dangerous. The stereotype is of the 'office party', fuelled by alcohol and spiced with romance, which leads to embarrassment or calamity. When people are taken out of their usual roles the results are unpredictable. There may be people- particularly those who subscribe to a 'role' culture- who feel uncomfortable or out-of-place at such events, or who chose not to attend and then feel 'left out' of the group. But the potential for positive outcomes, in terms of team-building and networking, can outweigh the possibilities for discomfort or disaster.

An organisation is a community, a mix of the mechanistic and the human, of technical and social systems. formal structures co-exist with the 'hidden' organisation of unwritten rules and alliances. Explicit contracts of employment co-exist with the implicit 'psychological contract' between each individual and the organisation. Feelings, beliefs and shared values form the 'culture' which shapes attitudes and behaviour. This 'soft stuff of people and their motivations is a key factor in determining the 'hard facts' of organisational performance. All are linked by formal and informal networks of communication. Charles Handy writes of management style in terms of 'structuring' and 'supporting'. Clearly, managers need to give attention to both functions-and good communications are central to both. It is important to review organisational structures, bureaucratic processes, and formal channels of communication. It is equally important to be alive to the 'hidden' dimensions of individual psychology, organisational culture, and social networks. To promote a sense of community and nurture the social systems within the organisation, it makes sense to provide opportunities for informal socialising outside the roles and restrictions of the organisation itself.

Each organisation performs certain office functions for implementing various decisions taken by the management from time to time. A library also performs similar functions, though in a modified forms due to its special functions and jobs. These office functions fall under the following categories:

1. Committee work.
2. Personnel administration and coordination.
3. Finance and Accounts.
4. Publicity.
5. Binding.
6. Building and equipment.
7. Correspondence work.
8. Stores, stationery and Printing.
9. Maintenance of Library Records.
10. Preparation and Publication of Annual Reports.
11. Maintenance of Library Statistics.
12. Conducting Library Surveys.

Correspondence Work

The correspondence work consists of the following distinct jobs:

1. Inward correspondence/Receipt of Mail.
2. Replying the letters/Fresh Correspondence.

3. Outward correspondence/despatch of Mail.
4. Filing work.

A library gets the following types of letters etc. through either mail, chief mail or urgent mail, and by hand from various sources:

1. Readers' letters containing suggestions for book selection, applications for admission to the library, remittance of fines, refund of cash deposits etc., requests and suggestions for improvement of library services, reservation of reading materials etc.
2. Book lists and catalogues from publishers.
3. Indents from members of the Book Selection Committee/ Heads of Departments.
4. Bills and Receipts from book suppliers.
5. Correspondence dealing with other sections of the library.
6. Misdelivered mail.

The following routines are involved in dealing with the inward correspondence:

1. Receipt of the whole correspondence by the Librarian.
2. Sorting and classification of correspondence.
3. Registering in the Inward Correspondence Register and stamping and noting the Receipt No. and date.
4. Posting of the number and date of receipt of reply against appropriate items in the concerned Outwards Correspondence Register.
5. Transmitting the correspondence to various sections of the library after entering it in an appropriate diary and obtaining and verifying the signatures of the concerned person of the section.

6. Preparing the list of inward correspondence in arrears.
7. Disposing of the misdelivered correspondence by transmitting to proper quarters.

Replaying correspondence/Fresh correspondence

Each section takes steps for disposing of the correspondence. The following jobs are involved:

1. Drafting the reply.
2. Getting it approved from the Section Incharge/Librarian.
3. Getting fair copies typed/written in hand and comparing these with the original letters.
4. Drafting, stencil cutting and duplicating circular draft letters.
5. Filing the stencils and cleaning the Duplicator.
6. Preparing copies of lists of books and other items.
7. Sending the correspondence to the Librarian for his signatures and transmitting it to Outward Correspondence Section.

Outward correspondence/despatch of mail

In the outward correspondence section, the following routines are involved:

1. Storing, classifying, arranging and signature verifying of the outward correspondence received from various sections of the library.
2. Entering the particulars of each letter etc. in the appropriate Outward Correspondence Register and assigning concerned despatch number and date on the copies of each letter despatched.
3. Preparing an envelope for each letter and writing full address of the addressee on it.

4. Closing each envelope, weighing it and affixing postage stamps of appropriate value on each of the despatched letters and posting them against each item.
   (The letters which are to be delivered by hand through a messenger to the local offices or persons are not stamped.)
5. Sending the mail to the post office and other offices through messengers asking them to deliver the letters and obtain necessary acknowledgments.
6. Verifying the acknowledgements.
7. Posting the number and date of each letter despatched against the concerned item in the Inward Correspondence Register.
8. Preparing the stamp account and posting it in the Postage Stamps Register.
9. If the stamps are likely to be exhausted, an order for the supply of stamps is prepared and sent through the office accountant.
10. Receiving the supply of stamps and accounting it in the Stamps Register and storing the stamps in the Stamps Chest.
11. Sending the office copies of the despatched letters to the concerned sections for filing in the respective files.

Filing work

1. Each section receives back the copies of the despatched letter.
2. Each such copy is filed in the concerned file.

Stores, stationery and printing

Stores Section is concerned with the acquiring, storing and distributing of all store and stationery articles required in a library. Besides the store and stock articles required in a modern office, the following articles should specially be kept in store:-

1. Forms and Registers as required by various sections of the library.
2. Catalogue Blank Cards.
3. Binding Materials.

Acquisition of stores

Except some stray articles, which may be acquired occasionally from the pretty cash account, the supplies of stores should be acquired annually on sanctioned and competitive rates from approved firms either by the parent body or by the library itself by calling quotations for the supply of requisite store articles, forms and registers. The quantum of supplies should be based on the following:

1. The Maximum to which stock should be bought up periodically-say, once in a year.
2. The minimum below which the stock should not go i.e. when the stock reaches that figures, steps should be taken for replenishment.
3. The annual consumption.
4. The quantum of issue.

This work involves the following distinct jobs:

1. Asking various sections of the library to send their store requirements for the coming years.
2. Preparing the rough indents after taking into account the consumption of articles in the previous year for each section.
3. Preparing a final indent after consulting the Librarian. Care is to be taken that the cost of the indented articles is not more than the budgeted amount for the purpose.

4. Sending indent to the parent body/central executive for acquisition of store articles.

5. Receiving the bills from the suppliers; passing them after necessary verification; certification; transmitting the bill to the Accounts section for payments; and noting down Voucher Numbers in the Stock and Store Register.

After the supplies are received from the suppliers or the parent body/central executives, these are to be stored in a classified order according to the numbers allotted to each of the articles. These are to be kept in appropriate cartons, tins or other containers so that these are not spoiled by rain, dust, dirt or vermin. The Store Room should be kept scrupulously clean and tidy.

3

Management Approach

The distinction is especially apparent if one compares management theory as derived from the work of Weber with the work of the 'human relations school' of Mayo and, later, Likert. Weber, working at the beginning of the twentieth century, developed a model of bureaucracy which emphasised division of tasks for greater efficiency, standardisation of the methods of performing tasks and a centralised, unified, role of making decisions inherent in a principle of legitimated authority. Control is exercised through a chain of command which is hierarchical and compliance is sought through a system of rewards for technical proficiency.

The individual characteristics and personalities of those working within the bureaucracy are largely suppressed. Mayo, working in the 1920s, focused attention on the characteristics of the small, often informal, group which employees quickly formed in the workplace. The operation of strict standards of behaviour exercised a powerful means of control over group members which was independent of legitimate authority. Likert, writing in the 1960s, developed this idea and integrated it with the concept of formal organisational structures to create the notion of 'organisational families' where work groups are formed, often with overlapping membership, with leaders in each group acting as a link with the next higher level in the hierarchy.

The group, acting with the leader take decisions concerning the tasks to which they have been assigned. The progression apparent in these theories is from a unitary concept of leadership towards a pluralistic concept based more on negotiation than coercion. The trend is especially marked in organisations, such as libraries and formation services, where groups of professionals are responsible for serving a user group more or less directly.

The close professional contact between information worker and user and between information workers should foster cooperation and a sharing of information about how best the user can be served. There should be a recognition that every participant has something to contribute and that progress and change are group activities in which all share. Power is an important consideration when thinking about the activities of such groups.

A basic definition of power might be 'the ability to achieve change'. It implies that others may share in the process of change but that they, individually or as a group, allow their own interests and concerns to be subsumed under those of a leader, for some period. It does not imply that tenancy of the position of leader is permanent or even long lasting. The function of leadership should be carefully distinguished from the concept of titular authority: though some are labelled 'Senior Assistant' or 'Librarian-in-charge' this does not mean that they will necessarily assume, or be recognised in, the role of leader in all circumstances.

The concept of 'power bases' May be helpful here. There is much discussion in the management literature about what constitutes leadership, whether leadership skills can be taught and in what circumstances leaders may best function. Steers lists several 'bases' of power which can be used to achieve compliance. The first is 'coercion': the use, or threat, of physical sanctions. This is rarely possible, and perhaps not desirable, in the working circumstances of libraries and information services. The ability to reward through the allocation of tangible benefits such as salaries, wages and fringe benefits is another power base. Such rewards may also extend to less obvious area such as allocation to places where working conditions are more attractive or where there may be greater possibility of engaging in activities which the recipient especially values. 'Social' or 'normative' power connotes the ability to award marks of esteem or prestige. Within a group, this is an important means of control. To those who accept the norms of behaviour of the group, membership of the group is granted, the individual is recognised, accepted and receives response and feedback from other group members.

The individual who does not accept such norms, or departs from them, risks alienation. As social animals, most people depend upon group membership and shared identification with a group or groups to foster their own sense of identity. Being cut off from this source of social gratification is very threatening to the individual and, in most cases, the aberrant behaviour quickly ceases. It can also be quite subtle in its operation: refusing to respond or laugh at another's jokes, for example, can cause considerable discomfiture. This pattern of behaviour can occur in all kinds of social group, be it work group, a group of friends sharing a meal, members of a sport club and so on. Three other power bases are commonly recognised. The first is legitimate or authority-based power. Formally, an organisation confers on someone a title; that person is ordained, or set apart, from the rest of the group and has responsibilities to the organisation. The successful use of legitimate power depends on the willingness of others to recognise and respect such authority and is not, except in cultures which emphasise hierarchy and deference, a strong position from which to promote change. 'Control of resources; is another base. Most changes require the ready cooperation of workers and the use of physical resources, materials and equipment. Use can be denied or hindered, often in subtle ways.

Non-cooperation through direct refusal may be inappropriate or considered rude; instead, the required resources will be deemed to be in use for other purposes, inappropriate, or otherwise not available. Charismatic power represents the final base. Some individuals are strongly imbued with personal qualities which make them attractive to others and capable of inspiring loyalty. It is the opposite, perhaps, of the qualities of the unfortunate individual whose assessment for promotion included the memorable phrase: 'His subordinates would follow him only out of a sense of curiosity'. Charismatic power is a quality which has been displayed by some, such as leaders of religious groups, statesmen, military leaders and businessmen. It is, perhaps, not a quality which is very evident within professional circles.

Since this kind of power is tenuous and so strongly dependent upon the continuing success of the individual, it is probably no bad thing that the information profession tends to rely upon qualities other than messianic zeal to achieve its ends. Power is an intangible concept; insubstantial difficult to define and very difficult to control. The effects of its exercise are sometimes subtle. The publicly acknowledged power structure, usually based on authority, is one small aspect of the place the concept of power occupies in managing organisations. All managers should be aware of the overlapping, intersecting bases of power present in the culture of their organisations and should regard them not as a threat but as a natural expression of human behaviour. The must be taken into consideration when planning change but they are also one of the tools which can be used to facilitate change if the power-holders can be identified and persuaded to cooperate. It might be thought that organisational change in any organisation is simply a matter of senior management determining what is best and then arranging to implement it. Except in the most authoritarian cultures, such a view is naive.

The culture of society, modern management thinking and our professional approach dictate the need for consultation before major changes are decided upon. A group of professional librarians and information workers is a structure quite unlike the arrangements one might find in many factories or large commercial organisations. In the latter surroundings, work is divided into stages, departments are formed and many workers have little contact with the eventual recipient of the product; there are exceptions, notably the work group method of car assembly which was developed by Saab-Scania and Volvo in the 1970s, but these are far outweighed by organisations using functional divisions.

The group of librarian and information workers is more like a collective where some have 'backroom' jobs, somewhat remote from the public, whilst others have jobs which bring them into contact with users in client relationship. Many professional librarians and information workers have a strong identification with their users and will measure any proposed change against the likely effect on those users. In such circumstances, consultation should become a natural process, drawing on the health of information help by the group. A hierarchy may still be quite evident: some on in a senior position will have to sanction expenditure and lead the group to implement the change but the direction of change should emerge from a process of discussion and sharing of views, information and beliefs. Increasingly, the emphasis in library and information work is towards a team or group approach, a development which is also reflected in other 'caring' professions, such as health care and social work, and in the organisation of parish clergy into team ministries. The ideal of unanimous view of change emerging from a group whose members are aware of the likely impact on users is difficult to achieve. Any change is bound to have its proponents and opponents; senior management are likely to be affected and drawn in to the debate even if they are not, themselves, on one of the sides. It is helpful to view changes as a forum in which various stakeholder groups argue and debate, from alliance, threaten and seek to conciliate with each other.

The notion, of a new system design emerging after an episode of dialectic is unrealistic in most circumstances: instead, the issue of change should be looked on as a vehicle for arguments about the power relationships within the organisation and between the stakeholder groups. In addition, few libraries or information services represent either a purely hierarchic or a purely democratic structure.

Most represent a mixture, often of a type where the formal structure appears hierarchic, with departments and fonnal lines of communication, but the informal structure for the professional staff emphasises something of a collegiate approach, where ideas are shared and power is defined more in terms of the power base of information than in terms of authority or resource control. Progress is achieved rather through seeking an accommodation with others than through appeal to higher authority. Katz and Kahn suggest that hierarchy is associated with the division or responsibility to minimise the risk of failure. An authority structure implies the existence of a supervisory function by which supervisors guide, instruct and communicate requirements to those under their control. The supervisory function is explicit at each level of the hierarchy: thus a set of supervisors at one level will themselves come under the influence of another set at the next higher level, and so on until the top of the hierarchy is reached. The authority structure encourages a degree of specialisation, so departments are formed, committed to carrying out a set of defined tasks. A supervisor thus has a power relationship with a group or groups and is subject to a power relationship defined by contact with a superior.

The extent of the power relationship is defined by what it is relevant for a supervisor to seek to control. Thus, aspects of a person's social life which influence job performance may be recognised as being subject to a degree of control whereas behaviour outside of working hours may not be so considered. Both supervisor and supervised groups gain their sense of identity in this kind of structure from their positions as defined by the power relationship. A consultative approach to organisational change may threaten, or appear to threaten, the authority structure of an organisation. Consultation implies that those consulted will be given all necessary information for them to be able to make an informed judgment about the most beneficial path for the development of new system designs to suit their perception of the organisation and its role; it also suggests that those in a senior position who are responsible for arranging the consultation will accept and evaluate such judgments. This implies a change in the relationships between a supervisor and the supervised group.

The relationship now becomes one in which communication is two-way and in which the supervisor has to recognise, and respect, the distinctive competence of the supervised group to comment upon the area of work for which they are responsible. For the best kind of supervisor, one who does not rely overmuch on authority as a power base, this presents few problems. But, in circumstances where the working relationship is not quite so good, where a condition of trust does not appertain between the supervisor and the group, this recognition would be perceived as a loss of power by the supervisor.

The result may be a refusal by the supervisor to set up the necessary consultative meeting and to rely, instead, on personal experience and opinion to answer question from senior management about the desirability of features of a new design, or the establishment of meetings at which the input of information from both sides is partial and the manner guarded. Clearly, both outcomes are undesirable. One approach to overcoming this difficulty might be to use the systems analyst to conduct such meetings.

The systems analyst, being outside the authority structure, should not upset the working relationships. However, this is too simplistic a view. In some circumstances, the analyst may be perceived as an extension of management. In addition the analyst's expertise may hinder communication because participants may feel inhibited. If workers represent stakeholder groups then the analyst is also a stakeholder and thus cannot be viewed as being disinterested. Without care, the interests of stakeholders other than the analyst and senior management may be ignored or not even recognised. It is also possible for a stakeholder groups so to dominate proceedings that the ideas of the group gain ascendancy even though they may not be as good or effective as those of another group. Rational debate may be replaced by strategies such as bargaining, covert threats and the release or concealment of important information.

Stakeholders may also take the view that they are the subjects of manipulation by senior management. This view takes as its premise the existence of a solution which senior management have already accepted and to which they are committed but the existence of which they have not revealed. The purpose of consultation is then seen to be to provide a forum for selling the solution rather than informing participants of the options and seeking reasoned response. Any volunteered information which seems to strengthen the management case will be welcomed but information critical of the case will be rejected or explained away.

The stakeholder group will feel that it is responding to a hidden agenda and is being manipulated in order to give justification to the management plan. Bearing such beliefs, the group may become increasingly uncooperative or may simply decide to put up only a token show of resistance to being led in the direction indicated by management. It is important to recognise that there need not, in any objective sense, be a management plan already in existence. It is enough for the stakeholder group to believe that it is being manipulated for the responses to become dishonest or, at best, for there to be a cynical acceptance of the management plan by the group. Consultation also implies that management will be willing to modify its views. This may be far from easy especially if the project has already gained their interest and support. When considering the response to a long-cherished plan it is tempting to rationalise criticism and become convinced that critics do not understand the plans.

So far, it has been assumed that consultation is desirable whatever the circumstances. This assumption needs consideration. In examining, the range of work which might be undertaken by a manager, it is clear that a distinction can be drawn between making decisions about matters which are urgent and those which are not. The day-to-day administration of a library or information service will require many urgent decisions and it would be unrealistic to suppose that full consultation could ever be contemplated before making such decisions. Provided the manager is aware of any relevant information, has experience of similar situations and is confident in that experience, there is no reason to suppose that the outcome will not be a feasible solution arrived at in a comparatively short time.

There may be an advantage in making some decisions in this way: one persons, considering all the evidence may be able to discern and concentrate on the salient points and set aside other matters. A better decision may emerge because of this ability to focus on the problem. The individuals in a group considering the same problem will bring a range of information and opinion which will need to be shared and then evaluated so that some judgment about the importance of each item can be made. Members may need to be convinced because their own beliefs and experience may be contradicted by others.

Various strategies may be used by the group to resolve difference but, in most circumstances, the group will adopt a satisficing approach: that is, a group view will emerge which minimises the differences between members. The need to establish truth may give way to the need to keep the group intact. This strategy is rarely acknowledged openly; instead, a selective view of the evidence will be constructed by the group in an effort to rationalise its decision. The decision which eventually emerges from group discussion will be one with which most, if not all, of the members can agrees but it may not be the best, when compared with a dispassionate review of the evidence, and it may take a long time to appear. 'Group think' is a term which has been applied disparagingly to the outcome of such meetings. It is unfair, though, to reject group approaches to some issues simply on the grounds that the solutions cause the minimum of upset to participants. What a manager must consider at every point where a decision is needed is whether the impact of the decision is likely to be confined to one person or one part of a process, or whether it is likely to have a wider impact. In the latter case, a group decision many be more persuasive and may help commitment to change to be built more quickly than if the decision is solely the product of one mind. Balance theory, first propounded by Heider, is a useful means of considering and explaining how a group tends to operate. Kotler and Andreasen explain that a fundamental assumption to balance theory is that individuals like to have an equilibrium in their system of values, beliefs and understanding. When confronted with some piece of information which does not seem to fit or contradicts notions already present in their minds, their response is to try to restore balance. How had and sustained that attempt is depends on the degree of imbalance and the perceived importance of the information.

For an indication of how the balance theory might explain group behaviour. Here a source is represented as giving some information to a group about some object of common interest. The source might be another group or an individual; the object of interest might be a fact, an aspect of behaviour, a plan, an individual, or whatever. The attitude of the group towards the source is represented by an algebraic operator, either a plus or minus sign, to represent a positive or negative attitude. Similarly, the group attitude towards the object of interest is either positive or negative, as is the attitude which the group perceives the source to have towards the object. Balance theory suggests that the system is in the balance whenever the combination of algebraic signs, through multiplication, becomes positive. Thus, three plus signs represent balance, as to do minus signs and a plus.

The remaining possible combinations of three minus sign or two plus signs and a minus indicate system which is out of balance. If the system is out of balance, the group will adjust its perceptions in an attempt to restore equilibrium. Consider an example, Suppose an individual is presenting a scheme for the introduction of fees for conducting online searches. If the starting position of the group is broadly in favour of the scheme, but it is perceived that the source is not, the group response will depend on its attitude towards the source. If the attitude is positive then the system will be out of balance. There are four possible responses.

The first possibility is that the group may change its attitude towards the scheme: in other words the personality of, or respect for, the source may be strong enough to induce the group to change its view of the desirability of the scheme. In the second case, the group may change its attitude towards the source. This implies that the group is very firmly convinced of the correctness of its view of the object and this is sufficient for its positive view of the source to be replaced by negative, critical, view. A third possibility is that the group distorts its perception of what the source has said. This means that the group imputes additional, undisclosed, motives to the source for representing arguments against the scheme and conclude that the source is really in favour of it. The final possibility is that the group decides to reduce the perceived importance of the issue to a point where it can live with the residual tension and created by the imbalance. Clearly, the first possibility is desirable if the intent of management is to persuade a group of the need for change. The choice of source will be crucial.

The Role of the Systems Analyst

The team approach to management has been widely adopted in libraries and information services; even in small-scale services the sharing of managerial decision-making is recognised as desirable because it enables expertise to be shared and encourages commitment. In conducting the analysis of a system, team work is vital if the necessary information is to be collected quickly and without disruption and if full understanding of the findings is to be fostered. Someone has to take on the role of analyst, a key position, and one of considerable power. It is especially important, therefore, that the person selected has the right qualities for the job. The ideal is to have someone from outside the organisation: a consultant who has no obvious axe to grind, no departmental sensibilities to protect. Such a person will be able to give an objective view of the system, its good and bad points, and the opportunities for development and change.

Good analysts will be able to call upon a body of experience, both their own and the corpus of professional knowledge to which they have access; they will be able to import new ideas into the service. Sometimes, however, this may be a focus for trouble. It all too easy to dismiss such imports as unlikely to be suitable: 'it wasn't invented here' is often the underlying theme of objections to new ideas. The need for a sensitive and confident approach by the analyst is vital. An outside consultant is rarely able to enforce change: the consultant is only able to influence the direction and progress of change.

In other words, the power base of the outside consultant is information and change will only come about if this power is allied to the power of people in key positions within the organisation. Such individuals or groups have to be convinced that the direction and pace of change proposed *is* consonant with the objectives of the organisation and will meet the needs of users. Only then can they begin to lead the rest of the staff to accept change. It is rarely possible to justify employing an outside consultant for anything other than very large or sensitive projects. Usually, someone already on the staff must be selected to take the role for the duration of the project. It is possible to divide the role up and allocate parts of it to a number of people but coordination of the work may then become very difficult, especially if the system being investigated is complex. Another approach is to appoint a small group: the appointment of a team leader with responsibilities and authority for management of the team and coordination of the investigation is important.

Having the analysis conducted by an in-house person or team has an additional value: if the systems approach to planning is to be used again there will be always be a need for someone with analytic skills to hand, responsible for monitoring, testing, and investigating. This may not necessarily be a full-time role, but the cumulation of experience, the cast of mind and the development of the approach will be valuable attributes which can also enhance other roles.

The trend in many areas of management, notably of libraries and information services, has been to develop permanent, or semi-permanent, project team often based on a 'matrix' view of the organisation and managerial responsibilities. As well as functional, 'line', responsibilities, each manager has an overview of some area of development and is responsible for alerting the group to interesting ideas or emerging possibilities. The placing of an analyst in a team is helpful if ideas are to be developed from the conceptual stage to reality. In choosing a person for the job of analyst it should be borne in mind that the person conducting the analysis is not just using a set of techniques, but is involved in the process of change.

The analyst is often viewed as an agent of change and may thus be resisted or welcomed depending on how those being investigated view the desirability of change. Although change represents a normal and healthy state for a system it also presents many problems, most of them related to human behaviour. The analyst needs to be sensitive to such problems, but not overawed by them. Similarly, it is necessary for managers to be aware that the focus of interest of the analyst should include some consideration of human and social factors, as well as a study of technical factors. What qualities should be look for in a system analyst? The following list of personal qualifies is an ideal: it is unlikely that some on with all will be found, but it isolates those areas of character which should be fairly strongly represented. Perception is a key quality: in analysing any task it will be necessary to link the information given to that given by other people. Imagination may be needed to perceive the relationship between the piece of information supplied by one person and that given by another.

Odd scraps information may be collected during the course of the investigation. It may be some time before they can be fitted into the general picture but the analyst must remember them and be able to see, at the appropriate time, how they may be used to complete the picture. It is a rare that all the information can be gathered in an orderly fashion and the information may be incomplete: the analyst may persist in questioning and observing until the loose ends have been discovered and tied into the general picture. This calls for stamina! Strength of character may seem to be an odd trait to expect. It is included because the analyst is expected to be objective and not to take sides. Those being analysed may think otherwise and try to press the analyst into acting as their channel of communication to the management.

Being in the middle in such circumstances is uncomfortable and should certainly be avoided if the clear analytic view is to be preserved. This is one point on which the internally appointed analyst may be at some organisation may be difficult to surmount and a proper sense of objectivity may be difficult to sustain. Conversely, a person placed in this position may respond to behaving in an aloof manner and not, seemingly, be willing to respond to the legitimate concerns of fellow-workers. Either response is unhelpful and will result in distortions. It will be difficult for the internally appointed person to avoid either extreme: for management, this consideration reinforces the need to select the person with care, to pay careful attention to the need for training and to recognise the mental stain under which an analyst may be forced to work. Breadth of outlook is concerned with the ability to remain interested in whatever level of work the analyst is observing. It may be very exciting to analyse the work of senior management but the work of others lower down the hierarchy should not then be looked upon as tedious and not worth the effort of full analysis.

Work, at all level, contributes to the overall success of any enterprise; it is especially the case in library and information services that the public image depends largely on the work of library assistants and those close to the users. Orderliness and discipline are key qualities: analysis creates a lot of information, which will need to be organised. This is not a rewarding task, but the analyst has to be a paragon in this respect. Spotting loose ends is only possible if the recording system in use draws them to the attention of the analyst. This means creating orderly files and using a standard method of documentation for recording the results of interviews, questionnaires and observation. It also relies upon the earlier mentioned quality of perception to link all this material together.

Discipline is necessary if the result of a hard day's interviewing or observation is to be documented. Leaving it until tomorrow may result in the loss of a fleeting impression or small clue which can lead the alert analyst to a significant, but hitherto unrecorded, fact. The analyst's day needs to be carefully organised to allow adequate time for recording, administration and thought. During the task of investigation, the analyst will encounter people of very different character, levels of education, degrees of responsibility and so on. These people must be persuaded to cooperate, whatever their state of mind or position in the organisation. Some may be very defensive: 'we've done this job for years.

Some may need encouragement since they may not believe that their jobs are important or that anyone could be interested in the details. Some may need encouragement to talk: the analyst may have to steer the conversation discreetly back to the matter in hand. The analyst must not only be interested in what is being said but must also convince the other person that the conversation is interesting.

Momentary inattention or faint signs of boredom are enough to reduce people to silence and to foster non-cooperation. Equally, it is easy to create distrust and dislike by appearing to talk down to people or by making assumptions about their work. The problem may be exacerbated for the internally appointed analyst by the power structure of the organisation. If the analyst occupies a higher or lower position in the organisation, relative to the person being interviewed, trust may be an important issue. This may be especially true in an organisation where the power structure emphasise hierarchy, status and position but less so where a collegiate atmosphere prevails.

The function of the analyst is to create conditions in which people feel comfortable and able to talk about their work. High social skill is one of the most important characteristics of the good analyst. When appointing an analyst from outside the organisation it is normal to prepare terms of reference for the project. These provide an agreed statement about the duties, responsibilities and behaviour of the analyst. It is much less common for terms of reference to be prepared for internally appointed analysis: somehow custom and practice, good sense and an awareness of responsibility are expected to take the place of formal statements. This is unfortunate because if there are questions about the conduct of the analysis, behaviour of the analyst, duties and responsibilities, there is nothing tangible to which reference may be made. It is also unfair to the analyst who will be occupying a demanding role within the organisation. A formal statement may offer guidance on moments of uncertainty and may provide some authorities backing in the event of disputes. Such statements can have additional roles if they are made known within the organisation. First, they will act as an introduction to the idea of systems analysis and help to define the role of the analyst.

Secondly, they will outline the scope of the work to be undertaken. It is especially important that staff are aware of survey arrangements: does the analyst have permission to approach them directly and arrange appointments for interviews or must the analyst first seek permission from a departmental head? Some of the information which may be elicited could be confidential or critical of those in authority and staff may need reassurance about how the information is to be used.

It is best to prepare written, agreed, statements outlining:

— scope of the investigation;
— objectives
— constraints
— resource available
— conduct

For an investigation employing outside appointment of consultants these details will need careful and extensive consideration. For the small-scale, in-house job there is a temptation not to define matters too closely, relying on good sense and day-to-day contact to clarify any misunderstandings: this can work quite well, but *some* terms of reference need to be agreed otherwise the analyst may find it difficult to decide when to finish the investigation and move on to producing the feasibility report. In dealing with any organisation the analyst must recognise that most are complex structures which have evolved over a considerable period of time and continue to evolve.

They are also complex mixtures of people, structures and expectations loosely bound together by some common purpose. The background of the organisation and its human aspects constitute two major areas which the analyst must consider. In discussing the background of an organisation the analyst must remember that the system which have evolved represent its structure and purpose. Such systems do not necessarily reflect stated objectives: the objective of most organisations, once set up, is to survive but few would openly lay claim to this as their purpose. Instead, a statement of mission will represent the function of the organisation to the public.

The analyst may discover many curiosities of arrangement and administration, some of which may be difficult to link with the mission statement. This is often the case in organisations with long histories or those which have evolved quickly: structures and processes may be retained long after their usefulness is exhausted, simply because no one has questioned their continuance. The analyst should not worry at this: it is something to be noted for further discussion. Systems are devised and are then influenced by the people who have to work with them. It is a common finding that a system designed now will, in six months time, have been changed subtly by workers.

The most stringent rules and procedures can be established, intensive training can be given and yet, in some small respect, each of us will adapt any task which we are given. It is an expression of individualism, an opportunity to exercise a little autonomy, a chance to remind ourselves that we matter. Once again, the analyst should not be surprised if procedures laid down in staff manuals are not followed completely or accurately. What is important is for the analyst to discover what *is* being done and to asses how efficiently and effectively it is being done. Organisations are a mixture of formal and informal systems. The analyst may first discover the formal system enshrined in an organisation chart, procedures manual or summary description of objectives.

These present a picture of the divisions, departments and hierarchies. They will lay down the routes for reports and outline the authority structure but will not show the way in which the organisation, considered as a set of social groups really operates. The 'grapevine' is a familiar example of the informal communication structure which operates in all organisations: everyone who has been accepted as part of a group is plugged in to the grapevine and sends and receives information, rumour and misinformation.

The network of relationships represented by the grapevine is not reflected in the formal organisational chart. A senior manager may find that a colleague at a lower managerial level or in another department is the point of contact. The jest that 'if something's going on the janitors are the first to know' has a ring of truth about it and certainly reflects the power of the grapevine. The 'gatekeeper' concept, often exploited in setting up current awareness services, is another manifestation of the notion that certain people in an organisation are key collection and distribution points for information. Inform them, and quite quickly, almost every one will know. The grapevine is one example of an informal system.

Others can be seen if the pattern of working relationships is observed. The most important, from the point of view of the analyst, are work groups. These are formed of employees, often in the same department or carrying out similar tasks. Norms concerning rate of work, starting and finishing times, problem-solving and general behaviour are quickly established and a group leader often emerges. Some behaviour may stretch or defy the formal rules of the organisation, though often in fairly trivial ways: taking 20 minutes instead of 15 for a coffee-break, for example.

On the other hand, such groups can support members experiencing difficulties of having 'off days. They can also discipline members whose rate of work is, for no good reason, less than the group norm. Group thus provide a form of control which members are willing to accept in return for the social benefits and closeness which such structures afford. Most people, with the possible exception of sociopaths, prefer the company of others and will seek to be accepted by a group. Group membership extends throughout the hierarchy of the organisation: there will be work groups at senior management level as well as amongst clerical assistants and middle-management.

Some work groups may have a life outside the internal environment, reflected, perhaps, in common membership of a club or the pursuance of a leisure activity. This sharing of work and other activities encourages the formation of strong bonds of loyalty which individuals will be unwilling to transgress for fear of the disapproval of the group. Leadership may be shared, the particular skill or knowledge needed at the time being the deciding factor in the choice of leader at a particular moment. In many cases someone emerges as leader, perhaps the person who normally initiates activities. Groups commonly allocate roles to members. 'Leader' is one such role; others are 'facilitator', the person who tries to organise resources so that things are done; 'conciliator', who tries to bring about agreement where there is conflict; 'shaper', who tries to mould ideas from the group: 'jester', the person who can be relied upon to break an awkward moment with a joke and so on. Why should a consideration of such matters be important to the systems analyst? Consider the problem of implementing a new system.

It is quite likely that working relationships will be altered by its introduction. Some groups will be split up, and some individuals will find themselves working with members of other group. There will be an alteration in the power relationships between individuals and between groups.

A large group, perceived as powerful by other groups, may be split. Its power will be seen as diminished whilst another group may be seen as having gained power through increased membership or the accession to membership of particular individuals. This will disturb groups and individuals who perceive themselves as losing power. The change to group membership and the change to the power structure will be resisted and a period of conflict will ensue. The acute analyst will recognise the likelihood of this occurrence and plan for its management, if it cannot be avoided.

Sensitive design of process and the internal environment can reduce the incidence of outbreaks of conflict but complete avoidance is too much to expect. The best that can be done is to alleviate the effects and to facilitate the development of new groupings and new norms of behaviour as soon as possible. During the process of investigation of the system the analyst must be alert to the need to discern what groups exist and how they are organised. In particular, a knowledge of which workers are regarded as group leaders can be very useful when trying to promote change. Discussion with leaders can often prove helpful in spotting problems in existing processes and new designs and for reducing the potential for conflict. It is also helpful at the start of an analysis to spend some time in gathering information about the history, present and past objectives and anticipated future of the organisation.

A consideration of these statements will reveal what the members of the organisation *think* it is doing and how they like to think the organisation is perceived by users and society in general. It is rare to find that these expectations are borne out by the analysis. The Hillingdon study for example, revealed many apparent misapprehensions by members of the public about the library service, its facilities and ambience. But, were these mistaken views or evidence of a mismatch between the perception of the library service as held by the staff and that held by those outside? Only a careful investigation of the services offered and how well these met the needs of users and potential users could reveal which is true. In any case, the fact that some people perceive the library service in unfavourable terms is important.

Analysis may also reveal that a belief that the organisation is carrying out some function cannot be supported by evidence. For example, a company information service manager may believe that some of the needs of the marketing department are being met by circulating details of products made by competitors. If no one in the marketing department follows up such information, or if it is obtained more quickly from elsewhere, the information service manager would be foolish to continue to assume that this aspect of the service was successful. It is often the painful task of the analyst to draw attention to the differences between belief, expectation and actual performance.

Systems theory suggests that all organisations exist within an environment consisting of the rules and conventions of society, laws, stakeholder groups, and physical, economic and other factors. The 'general' environment can be distinguished from the 'operating' environment which may be thought of as being constituted of rules, stakeholder groups, such as suppliers and users, and physical, economic and other factors. An organisation also has an 'internal' environment—the procedures and groups, such as staff, which constitute the system. The general and operating environments may provide opportunities for growth, development and change but the characteristics of both may curtail or circumscribe what it is possible to do. For example, a company information service may be permitted by the managing director to reorganise its facilities to provide a more effective service subject to the constraint that the running costs remain the same: the operating environment sanctions change in one direction but subjects it to control through an economic factor. The internal environment might, in the same example, put a brake on change because of some limitation in the availability of resources. If the proposed changes require staff to be trained in skills such as word processing the change cannot take place until this is achieved. The constraints on, and opportunities for, growth presented by the general environment are long term and reflect changes in the social and cultural life of a society or country.

The gradual shift from rate-supported, supposedly 'free' services to direct charging is a response by the operating environment to economic and legislative changes within the general environment. It is usually very difficult to recognise, record and assess such changes early in their development because their evolution depends so much on public and political debate followed by government action. For service organisations, the best approach is for the management to be aware of the political process and to be prepared to consider the implications of the arguments presented in such debates as may be evident: when the operating environment is subject to change, it will not come as a complete surprise. The essence of success is the ability to anticipate the need to respond strategically rather than reacting to a stimulus.

This is not to suggest that managers should neglect opportunities to influence the general environment but it is a suggestion that bringing about social and political changes are long-term activities, involving professional attitudes and beliefs, rather than the short-to medium-term activities which comprise resource management.

The tasks of the systems analyst are to seek out the factors in the operating and internal environments which control or circumscribe change and to consider what effect such control might have on any proposals. The aim is to identify the difference between what facilities are needed for a successful change and those which are available.

Once identified, the management of the organisation can consider whether the environments can be influenced in some way to make the acquisition of the necessary facilities feasible. Sometimes a complete solution can be realised, sometimes only partial achievement is rendered possible: it is for the analyst to guide management into thinking about the problem. The discussion has centered on the characteristics of the organisation. People, too, will exhibit certain characteristics which the analyst must consider when undertaking any kind of study. A new recruit to an organisation comes with a set of beliefs and attitudes formed by experience, contact with family and friends, and the surrounding culture.

The first days within the organisation are a process of socialisation, during which the new recruit is exposed to the values, attitudes and beliefs of those already in the organisation and to statements about its role and functions. In turn, those in contact with the new recruit are affected by the 'mind set' of the recruit. This process of accommodation and acclimatisation can best be considered as 'establishing a psychological contract'. Such mental contracts complement formal, written, contracts of employment in that they summarise a set of beliefs and expectations about the organisation and work within it. If, for example, the recruit observes that up to five minutes late arrival is not remarked upon then the belief that such behaviour is ignored will form part of the contract.

The stated organisational objectives of a public library might indicate that its purpose is to serve the information needs of all members of the surrounding community but the actual experience of the recruit might be that certain sections of that community are favoured. Thus, a set of attitudes and beliefs about work and the organisation are formed. A major problem arises when different sets of attitudes and beliefs are held by various groups. This is almost inevitable because the daily experiences of a library assistant, for example, are different from those of the manager of the library service.

Each encounters a distinct range of people, problems and opportunities and each has a range of ways of responding. It is unlikely that the range of experience, and the beliefs, of the two will concur. Each will have different expectations about work.

A senior manager may see this as offering a more effective control of resources, better service to users and more amenable jobs for assistants. Surely, no one would object? The assistant working on the issue desk may see it as an imposition which will break up satisfying working relationships and replace a variety of manual routines with one invariant routine in which all skill has been replaced by the boring activity of scanning bar-coded labels with a light-pen.

The senior manager may have a unitary view of the library, in which everyone is 'just part of one big, happy, ship'; the assistant may see it, instead, as being a set of rowing boats all facing in different directions. If automation is to be introduced without too much disturbance and dispute some accommodation between the views has to be reached and the starting point for this is the recognition, at the outset, that different opinions are held. The analyst is in the best position to be aware of such differences. Resistance to change is a fact of organisational life. It will impinge upon the work of the analyst in several ways. The initial stages of the study of an organisation are based on discussion, interviews and observation. The success of each depends on cooperation: willingness to engage in the study and not to mislead or to withhold information. Sabotage need not be an over act: a strongly defensive attitude may be enough to prevent a free flow of ideas and thus prejudice the outcome of the investigation. Later stages may depend on willingness to learn new, or modified, techniques.

Successful learning depends on the self-motivation of the trainee. Resistance to change will hinder the development of this self-motivation. The success of the design of a modified process may depend on the response of users to a model or prototype: resistance to change may lead users to withhold or suppress critical comment or to engage in destructive criticism. In each case, true responses are coloured by resistance to change. The task of the analyst is to anticipate such resistance and to be prepared to allow the feelings engendered by it to be expressed as openly as possible. Only when they have had a good airing, been formally acknowledged, and any misconceptions recognised and corrected, can the development of more positive attitudes be assisted. Almost as serious is an uncritical enthusiasm for change. This usually results from unrealistic expectations about the transformation of working life by, for example, the use of new technology.

A justification for introducing computer-assisted systems is their ability to replace the so-called drudgery of work with a manual system. A rosy picture of a future free from tedious tasks is painted for the benefit of library staff. It is true that the nature of the process is changed but many assistants would question whether the quality of their working life is materially improved. This is not to suggest that those responsible for the design and implementation of the new systems are mendacious: rather, it is a case of inexperience and an unwillingness to assess critically the experience of others engaged in similar projects. The analyst has an important role in keeping management and users in touch with reality, which often means explaining that the new system *will* have problems though they may be different from those experienced with the previous system. It is also important for managers to realise that improvements to one part of a system may simply move a problem to another part.

Solving the acquisitions department bottleneck may increase the cataloguing department backlog unless some attention is given to balancing the work flow in both departments, for example, An over-enthusiasm for change can lead to concentration on one part of system to the detriment of other parts and, ultimately, the whole system. Being perceived as an agent of change can make the analyst vulnerable to the attentions of those having some wish to alter the power relationships within the organisation.

Such people may seek to use the analyst as a tool, or channel of communication, to spread ideas and discontent and to seek to consolidate their own position within the organisation. The analyst has the difficult task of gaining their cooperation without becoming party to a conspiracy. There may be problems originating from the senior management level as well. This may arise from commitment to an idea or proposed new system. A strong identification with a project may lead senior management to assume that their enthusiasm and commitment is shared by others. It may frequently be necessary for the analyst to remind the senior management that the implementation of new ideas should be viewed as a process which involves many stakeholders all of whom will need to be informed and involved. It is also important that the sense of a project being someone's 'baby' or personal idea is abandoned early on. Neglecting to facilitate this 'letting go' will result in the 'owner' of the project becoming defensive in the face of legitimate criticism and this will stifle improvement and development. The process of consultation is of critical importance to the sound development of a project. The responsibility for establishing circumstances which facilitate the process is shared between management and the analyst. If the analyst is already in a senior position within the management structure then it may be supposed that this task will be easy because groups can be summoned and discussions initiated almost at will but a consideration of power relationships and the process of consultation should warn against any such supposition. It is certainly possible to summon groups, explain the circumstances and reasons for the meeting and then invite comment. It is most unlikely that much will be elicited and what is given will probably reflect the group's perception of what it is the manager wants to hear.

The analyst lower down the management structure of the organisation has an easier task when dealing with those at the same level but may have to cope with defensive behaviour when dealing with those above or below in the hierarchy. The analyst from outside the organisation is often best able to facilitate consultation, for several reasons. Such a person has novelty value: a new face, and an evident willingness to listen, will often encourage groups and individuals to be open and ready to discuss.

The outsider may be perceived as having no 'axe to grind', no link with the established power structure. Because the outsider lacks the detailed historical knowledge of the organisation which can only come from having worked for it for some time, each point or suggestion which is made will need to be explained and its context outlined. Essentially, the advantage is one of encouraging flow of conversation: the difficulty is in starting the flow. The need to explain will provides a conversational 'ball' which can be exchanged between the analyst and the group.

Whatever the managerial position and status of the analyst, the major problem in facilitating a free exchange of ideas and opinions is in being perceived as a tool of management. The first steps that management can take to reduce this appearance is in the establishment and promulgation of the terms of reference of the analyst. A clear statement of purpose intent and methods of procedure will encourage the view that project development is to be conducted openly. The ideal is to have already the kind of organisational culture which assumes consultation will take place and that the views of all are welcome and important.

Many libraries and information services tend not to have strongly hierarchic management structures: the conditions are good, therefore, for the encouragement of consultative processes. How should this be fostered? The first step is essential: senior management must accept that group relationships and the processes of discussion are important areas for the development of the organisation. Secondly, the process of learning should be structured around a problem though it need not, initially, be clearly defined.

Thirdly, the process should involve all levels in the organisation: in this way, the new culture is seen to affect everyone and will not be perceived as a sop to those lower down the structure. Assume that it has been agreed to call a consultative meeting of senior staff to discuss an apparent problem with training. Ideally, participants will have been selected who are stakeholders and thus have some particular interest in the problem. Since the problem is, at present, ill-defined this may include many people.

The purpose of a first, or exploratory, meeting is to determine more precisely what the problem is perceived to be: that is, how does each member of the group see the problem and in what respects do these views differ? It is important that the analyst should not dominate the meeting or seek to lead discussion. Instead, the analyst should invite the principal stakeholder, who is usually the person who first identified the problem to state briefly what the problem appears to be. Thereafter, the analyst should ask questions which seek to sharpen the problem statement and should invite other participants to make similar statements of the problem as seen by them.

A helpful technique is to ask each participant in turn to present a brief statement and to suppress, for the moment, reactions to the statements of others. This facilitates a flow of comment and encourages involvement. Another important condition at this point in the process is to discourage evaluation: in this respect, the technique has something in common with 'brainstorming'. Evaluation of idea is essential before action is taken but at this stage it is rarely helpful and will certainly discourage others. It is important to realise that approving of something is as evaluative a comment as disapproving of it. Both positive and negative comments should be discouraged. The second stage of the consultative process is concerned with testing how open the participants are prepared to be.

The analyst should be aware of attempts at concealing motives, of confusion over the role of the analyst and an unwillingness to proceed with discussions. Nothing fruitful will be achieved until the existence of these feelings has been acknowledged. The analyst is being perceived as the 'expert': the analyst may be seduced into discussing the problem in some depth and will thus begin to 'own' it and think about its solution. This kind of identification is to be avoided: whatever solutions are to emerge should come from the group and the role of the analyst is to facilitate its development.

The analyst must avoid the appearance of aloofness: trust is a vital component in the relationship and will only be built up if the analyst is willing to engaged in the discussion. Response from the analyst is important but that response does not need to be evaluative. Rather, it should aim to encourage discussion. Reflective questioning is often helpful, especially if the analyst senses that an important fact, opinion or feeling has been hinted at but not openly stated.

The technique is simple: the analyst reflects the comments of a participant, thus passing the 'ball' back. Another useful approach is for the analyst to summarise the points which have emerged but using the analyst's words. Quite often, this will elicit the comment: 'That's not quite what I meant...' Once again, flow of conversation has been encouraged, a misapprehension may be corrected, and some additional information may emerge. The analyst is also in a good position to observe the process of group discussion: who talks to whom, whose comments tend to be ignored and who introduces new ideas. In this way, some appreciation of the power structure within the group can be formed.

Non-verbal behaviour may also provide a valuable clue to the level of involvement of each participant. Signs of boredom, avoiding eye contact with the group, extensive doodling, may indicate someone who has yet to build up sufficient trust to be committed to the process of consultation. The analyst may have to guide conversation so that the person is more directly involved or, if this is not successful, may better discuss matters in private with the individual. It is important to ensure that apparent indifference is not ignored because it can be used to cloak a much deeper-seated unease about the consequences of whatever project the organisation has in mind. Part of the process of communication is the giving the receiving of feedback. In the first stages of the consultative process, much of the analyst's work will be concerned with facilitating the flow of conversation and ideas but the time will come when the participants will ask the analyst to respond to them: in essence, the question is 'How do we seem to you?' What is not required at this point is a discussion of the ideas which have been presented but, instead, feedback on how the group behaviour is perceived by the analyst.

The request will only come when an atmosphere of trust has been engendered but if people are not yet ready to hear something the result may be that the accuracy of the feedback is challenged or the views presented by the analyst may be distorted and rejected. What the analyst chooses to comment on will depend upon experience and how well the participants and analyst know each other. In the initial stages of consultation, it is best to confine feedback to areas concerned with the way in which the group is working rather than comment on individuals.

Staff organisation in the large academic library, though an intriguing area for speculation, has received relatively little notice in the professional press. Even in the United States it is only in quite recent times that it has assumed the appearance of a major preoccupation. Indeed the study of management generally as applied to university libraries was quite late to appear in journals of librarianship. It seems reasonable to suggest that this delay reflected the slowness of academic librarians in grappling with management problems. 1939 was the earliest data that could be set as the starting point for informed interest in management problem, that being the year in which the Library Institute of the University of Chicago was centered on that theme. It was also, he noted, the year in which the first formal survey of a university library by a committee of experts was undertaken.

For both this seeming neglect and this concentration on one continent there are understandable if no necessarily universally acceptable reasons. 'As to the latter point, in a matter of simple geographic dispersion, large academic libraries, however one defined the term, are thicker on the ground in the United States than anywhere else in the English-speaking world. As to the former, their appearance there in significant numbers has been a phenomenon only of the present century. At the same time those few large British libraries which predated that transatlantic phenomenon have not been characterised by published contributions to the theory or practice of large-scale management. Indeed as recently, the librarian of one of them was able to speak of 'the recent growth of interest in management problems on the part of British university librarians', and to date the beginning of this interest to no further back. But one can at least postulate two further factors contributing to the late appearance of a substantial literature on staff organisation in large academic libraries. The first is the long tradition of non-professionalism among the directors of such institutions.

The predilection for the appointment of scholars rather than professional librarians in the United Kingdom, and indeed the enormous and long-standing difficulty that university libraries had in relating to the profession generally there up to very recent times, is sufficiently well-documented to require no further discussion. These tendencies have been less prevalent in the United States but the appointment of non-librarians to direct the large academic libraries there is still by no means unknown. One has only to instance Harvard, Yale and Princeton in recent years to establish the point.

The second factor surely is the considerable inertia of the large, well established organisation. Inertia does not necessarily cannot apathy. Resistance to change in a large academic library can well be rooted in a persistent appreciation of the mismatch between the demand for services and the resources to supply them. A harassed chief librarian or director may be quite prepared to accept the possibility, perhaps the probability, that improvements in performance might follow an organisational 'shake-up' and yet be unable to envisage or to risk the inevitable slipping back of services during the shake-up period. Like Alice, he may find it impossible to stop running long enough to find out how to run faster. Finally, one must not forget the relatively recent appearance of management theory as a whole as a widely discussed, or even acceptably academic subject.

One most repeat, however, that university librarians were not early ventures onto this sea, even after it had been charted. In this it must be admitted that, as in other ways, academic librarianship lagged well behind the more professional approach of public librarians. Johnson points out by the end of the 1930s public librarians had been experimenting for nearly four decades with various forms of organisation'. Even if, as he makes clear, the public librarians interest was largely in facilitating ease of use of collections, rather than in improvements in management per se, their experiments exposed them to the problems of staff organisation long before their colleagues in the academic world. If there are reasons then why interest in staff organisation problems has been late in developing, what is the explanation for what can only be described as a major recent upsurge, not only in North America but in Britain as well? It is surely that the administrative problems of the large academic library have become too substantial to be ignored. Inertia has been overcome by the concentrated energies of cumulated internal stresses. In addition, an added stimulus has been given by mounting external criticism.

In this context the Atkinson Report can be seen to be no more than a local irritant compared with a much more widespread impression of concern about the future of the large research library. What are these internal pressures? Most flow directly and inevitably from size itself. The big academic library exists in large measure because of the palpable economies of scale that it achieves. Yet paradoxically, these very economies are countered by the operating disadvantages which size eventually brings in its train.

From the strictly productive point of view, it is clear that beyond a certain point there begins to operate a law of diminishing return, by virtue of which the addition of further staff does not achieve a proportionate increase in output. This situation has brought about a considerable acceleration in the automation of library operations and has contributed to the growing awareness of a need for more effective resource-sharing among libraries. Each of these endeavours to counter the disadvantages of size, however, has brought additional administrative complexities in its train. Size has other effects which also bear, even if indirectly, on output.

The systematic approach to management emphasise a high degree of specialisation but this in turn restricts the nobility of employees within the organisation, with consequent effects on morale and recruitment. Size leads to communication failures, which increases the possibility of a mismatch of talent and job requirement and is further destructive of morale. A particular problem of job satisfaction is posed by the increasingly administrative preoccupation of the professional staff as the organisation expands. All these reasons have provoked recently a spate of suggestion for modification of the staff structure of the academic library.

As is so often the case, the literature tends to record proposals and accounts of success and to omit mention of non-implementation and failure, but five general areas of discussion have emerged and we propose to consider each of these in succession, as the ideas have been ventilated in the United States and Canada in the United Kingdom and in Australia. The five areas, which of course merge considerably into one another, are: basic patterns of organisation; job satisfaction for the professional the impact of new technologies; communication; and participation in management.

Basic Patterns of Organisation

There can be observed an oscillatory, or perhaps cyclical, phenomenon in the development of basic patterns of organisation in academic libraries. As an inheritance from their days of more modest size it was common for even large libraries to have highly-centralised patterns of staff organisation up to thirty years or so ago in America, and in Britain until much later. McAnally stated in 1952 that 'as recently as 1940 the average college or university library was organised along departmental lines'. This was still the situation in virtually all Australian university libraries up to 1965 and it remains today a fairly standard pattern in Great Britain for the majority of university libraries. Typically, such libraries are organised as a series of discrete departments or section, with the head of each reporting directly to the chief librarian. Such a pattern, with its assumption of universal competence on the part of the chief librarian has been found in the experience of many libraries to be two cumbersome, and indeed too disruptive.

Each of the rigidly compartmentalised departments defend its territory against the others and the far from omniscient director must suffer the advice of a wide range of subordinates who are all-too-often mutually suspicious, if not mutually anatonistic. An interesting paradox is frequently posed by the regular existence of a deputy chief librarian to whom, in such circumstances of fragmentation, it seems difficult to assign line responsibility and whose energies are thus all too often dissipated on trivia at the very time when the director's span of control is unduly extended. This pattern of a highly centralised grouping of functionally based departments remained fairly standard in American academic libraries until after the Second World War when, as a conscious effort towards integration and towards the certain of a reasonable span of control for the senior executive, three emerged the two -divisional pattern, a structure based on a major division into reader services on the one hand and technical service on the other. McAnally notes a reference as early as 1938 to the emergent trend towards a divisional head for technical processes but states that it was the early and middle 1940's that saw the real development of the two-divisional pattern and that in the seven years since 1945, divisional organisation has proved so satisfactory that most of the major libraries now have a small group of capable administrators at a level immediately below that of the librarian.

He claims that by 1952, indeed, the bifurcated organisation was widely accepted in the United States. This pattern came to Australia in 1966 with its adoption at the University of Sydney and is still the commonest from of organisation here. It has hardly impinged, however, on the British academic scene. But the two divisional structure has brought stresses of its own, of which the major ones are the polarisation of staff attitudes and loyalties, and the difficulty of accommodating functions that either include elements of both reader services and technical services or do not fall satisfactorily into either area. Problems of this kind have provoked a further phase of the cycle. On the one hand several libraries have increased the number of divisions.

On the other hand, the number of miscellaneous extra-divisional activities, commonly reporting directly to the librarian, has increased alarmingly, once again threatening to over-extend his span of control. The present generation of proposals and experimentation with organisational structures aims to preserve integration while avoiding rigid canalisation, to improve career opportunities and to widen the range of participation in management. Before considering these developments, however, it is necessary to note a variant to the division pattern as so far described. An organisation-by-subject division enjoyed a vogue in the United States in the 1940s and 1950s and has reappeared, in one form or another, in Britain in recent years. Once again, this development originated in the public library field. Maizell credits William F Poole with the concept, as early as 1881, of organising a large public library as a series of broad subject collections, each having its specialist staff, with the prime project of facilitating reader use.

This idea was transferred much later to the university library field, beginning with Brown University in 1939 and from then until the 1960s a total of twenty-fix academic libraries in the United states espoused its according to Johnson though as be points out, due to the speed with which some libraries thereafter abandoned the concept, there were never more than twenty-two exponents at any one time. The first to drop the idea was Duke 1972, and by 1977 there were only fourteen substantial academic libraries in the United States still committed to it. Johnson speculates on his brief flourishing and sees it as having been basically a response to greatly increased and considerably changed demands on the American academic library in the immediate post-war period.

The development of interdisciplinary studies, continuous pressure for specialised subject assistance and the general education movement in the United Stated were accompanied by the sudden expansion in the student numbers and a growing awareness of the specific needs of undergraduate readers. A possible answer to those problems was seen in the double example of the public libraries organisational patter and the subject divisional academic structure of the universities themselves. In many cases too, the subject divisional pattern offered an attractive theory to sustain the re-integration of a decentralised library system. This last was an ironic twist to an organisational modification which in public libraries represented, to some extent at least, a measure of disintegration. Why did this form of organisation not survive in American academic libraries? Johnson sums it up succinctly by stating that when the subject divisional plan did not coincide or harmonise with constitutional goals and problems, no amount of effort, regardless of the strength of administrative will, could "squeeze" it in where it did not fit'. Basically as with the public libraries, the subject divisional plan was adopted as a device to facilitate the use of collections and not really as a means of forwarding organisational efficiency, but it was not long before such enthusiasts as Frank Lundy of Nebraska had build a whole organisational theory about it and indeed, in Lundy's case, a whole philosophy librarianship. Lundy's credo rested on the development of the subject specialist, the coining of the term 'dual assignment' and the promotion of the idea of the practice of librarianship clear across the board. The subject divisional organisations created in some British university libraries in recent years, in most cases, are no more than super-structures resting on the idea of the subject specialist and discussion of them has been left largely to a later section of this paper, but it is very interesting to note that the subject divisional concept should have emerged with such vigour in Britain at the very time it was sinking rapidly into eclipse on the other side of the Atlantic.

One must except from this generalisation the system of subject libraries established at University College, London, some years before any American university library was moved to consider the subject divisional pattern. Remarkably enough, there was a similar late start in Britain in relation to the subject organisation of public libraries. Thus, as Overington has pointed out, while Savage had tried to establish subject departmentalisation at the Edinburgh Public Library between 1932 and 1935, it was not really until Chandler reorganised the

Liverpool City Library in 1961 that it could be claimed that any major British Public Library had espoused the system completely. This is despite Gardner's optimistic statement as early as 1955 that subject departmentalisation... for large libraries is here to stay and McClellan's experience of Tottenham Public Library. McClellan attributes this slow emerges in the public libraries in part to developments since 1920 which had lead to the general readers adviser as the openly specialist in British Public libraries outside the technical services area. It was almost as if public libraries had been moving towards the bifurcated pattern favored by American academic libraries. He also hints at the extra cost involved in the subject organised library, a point confirmed by Overington who is constrained to say that 'the only categorical absolute costs for subject departments will be higher support is that absolute costs for subject departments will be higher than for a conventional organisation in the same library.

In Australia there have been only two significant instances of subject divisionalisation in major public libraries. One, to no-one's great surprise, is the National Library of Australia, reorganised by Dr Chandler after his appointment as Director General in 1973 after his years at Liverpool. The other is the State Library of Western Australia, similarly restructured by F A Sharr as early as 1956, thus preceding by some years Chandler's metamorphosis of Liverpool.

The first Australian university library with any appearance of a subject division pattern was Monash University Library, which elected to counter any centrifugal tendencies by establishing, on its foundation in 1958, three physically separate units on a subject divisional patter in addition to a central library. This arrangement, however does not dominate the staff organisation pattern. The same can be said of the University of New South Wales which decided in 1974, to establish subject divisional libraries, but these sit administratively within its division of reader services. For organisation, WOPSO proposed a broader base than the existing two divisions, in order to involve a wider range of experienced staff in the process of decision making.

This aim it translated into recommending five divisions in place of two, together with four central offices reporting directly to the librarian. The question of working environment was taken up in recommendations relating to an elaborated supporting committee structure, as well as to staff development and the process of intra-library communication. It also appeared, however, in recommendations about one of the new divisions, a resource division in which was developed a degree of subject specialisation and dual assignment. In the event of we approved an increase from two divisions to four, adding to the existing reader services and technical services divisions a separate division for branch and department libraries and a division of support services, which brought together the separately reporting offices suggested by WOPSO.

A second Australian example is the University of Melbourne Library. In 1973 a newly appointed librarian added to a very conventional centralised pattern a corporate planning group of four senior officers with no line responsibilities but with 'portfolios' for administration, resources, services and systems respectively. As an organisation, this has much in common with the structure for Columbia proposed in the Booz, Allen and Hamilton study. Interestingly enough, if only to prove the point that three matters do pursue a cyclical progression, more than twenty-five years earlier McAnally was reporting at Yale, harvard and Texas experiments with a floating research and planning staff responsible to the director. A feature of many recent proposals has been an increasing reliance on standing and *ad hoc* committees. While this development can be regarded as designed to improve communication and enhance participation, from the point of view of structure it can be seen as a positive attempt to smooth off the corners, to handle the problem of interdivisional topics and to provide a device for the easing in of new developments. Guelph University Library provides an example of heavy reliance on the committee device.

Here a two divisional structure was replaced by the creation of fourteen departments held together by eight coordinating committees. The conception of committee is, of course, a heady exercise and it carries with it the occupational hazard of 'overkill'. It is worth bearing in mind the multiplicity of committees established at the University of California and their subsequent reduction in numbers.

Job Satisfaction for the Professional

This aspect of the problem has been aired increasingly in the professional literature, particularly but not exclusively the American literature over the last ten years. There are two subsets to what is described variously as frustration for professionals and waste of professional talent. The first is the increasing absorption of professional staff in administrative tasks as libraries increase in size and capacity.

The second is the desire for a collegial rather than a bureaucratic relationship within the institution on the part of workers who consider themselves to be as well-qualified professionally as their superiors in the hierarchy, and this second facet of the problem is treated more fully below under 'Participation in management'. The various proponents of professionalism have identified different areas of library work where it is claimed not only that the professional is required about where alone he will gain satisfaction. It is instructive to note the range of these areas and to speculate on the reasons, geographical and chronological, that have led to their successive promotion. Except in British Isles, jealous retention of the complete cataloguing process as a professional preserve appears how to be no longer acceptable. And even in British academic libraries it is clear that, except in institutions where age or size or both convince the administrators that it would be too difficult to adopt standard practices, cataloging is no longer the professional mystery it once was.

Of course, some sections of cataloguing remain, justifiably, in the professional sphere. Particularly for large-intake institutions with wide-ranging subject and language interests, cataloguing copy from outside sources is not available for current material. In the case of older books there remain specialist areas, for example the description of incunabula, which must remain the domain of the professional. Even in those even the practice of copy cataloguing, there are many in Britain which do not accept the classification and subject cataloguing provided with 'outside' copy. Thus the subject analysis of material to the library has to retained as a professional areas. After cataloguing, perhaps collection-building is the most frequently identified area to need professional attention.

The development of the position of bibliographer in several large American libraries illustrates the point that book selection is a main activity for the professional elite in several British libraries. In at least two Australian university libraries selection and collection building are identified in major separate administrative unit with a high professional staff content, instead of being absorbed within an acquisition department or division. The most recent area to have been marked out as a professional domain is that of reader services. Again there has been a chronological development. Reference services, long established in American academic libraries have been much slower to develop in the United Kingdom. However, they are early candidates for reservations by the professionals, and in Britain these services have been given a considerable boost, in the guise of information services, by grants from the former Office of Scientific and Technical Information and the translation to universities of former colleges of advanced technology.The development of direct services to readers in Australian academic libraries has been fully described recently by Whyte. It is notable that here again Australian libraries moved more quickly then their British counterparts and, like American university libraries, with what seems to have been a much more definite awareness of public library practice. A later service to be identified within the reader services are, has been the concern with reader education.

Again the American experience dates much further back than the British, but especially in the newer UK universities, a concern with reader education has appeared in some strength in the last decade. It has been important in Australia since the early 1960s. In marking out areas of professional mystery the academic librarian operates at a considerable disadvantage compared with his public library colleague, in that he must be prepared to encounter a fairly substantial cynicism among the most influential section of the reader population, the academic staff.

The in built and explicable arrogance of the academic, employed because of pre-eminence in certain areas of scholarship, may well persuade him that the operations of a library carry no particularly heavy intellectual demands. Moreover, academics frequently see their own success as having been achieved despite the confusions and inefficiencies of the libraries they used, and may feel contemptuous of any suggestion of the need for professional expertise in the assistance to readers. For these reasons, the librarians's abandonment of the bibliographic mystery of cataloguing, which academics did conceive of as an occupation for professionals, has made it even more difficult for academic libraries to preserve and increase the number of professionals posts on their establishments. In all this the American experience has differed significantly, in part because the very size of American academic libraries and the relatively recent and rapid attainment of that size have created protected positions for them in their institutions. If the British have been on weaker ground in establishing acceptance of a professional content for librarianship in academic libraries, paradoxically they have had more success in securing academic acceptance for those positions on the library staff already accepted as professional.

The question of faculty status, which has so preoccupied American writers on academic libraries, has become quietly and almost universally accepted in the United Kingdom. This has come about in part from the careful preservation of the tradition of the scholar-librarian, in part from the firmer retention of the cataloguing mystery and in part from the attempt to bring together in one person responsibility for a combination of the professional areas, accepted and non-accepted. Thus, to take the case of the most recently established British universities, though their size does not warrant their serious consideration as large academic libraries, it is almost the norm to have a high percentage of senior positions at academic equation filled by officers with respectable able academic, though not always professional, qualifications. These officers, frequently designed subject specialists, undertake some combination of subject analysis, collection-building and reader service, including reader education. The development is not limited to the newer institutions. We found that only a dozen or so of the sixty-one British university libraries we visited in 1975 were not consciously practicing some form of subject specialisation. As noted earlier in this account, subject specialisation appeared too as an element in the passing enthusiasm for the subject divisional plan in American academic libraries. It is remarkable again that, with one notable exception, the British interest developed at the very point that the American was waning. The first substantial reports of British subject specialism appeared in the mid-1960s with the articles of Humphreyss, writing from a large library, and Guttsman writing from a new one. They were echoed with some caution in the Report of the Parry Committee in 1967. By contrast, Lundy, the most vocal American advocate of subject specialism has expressed the opinion that the practice of librarianship clear across the board was finally abandoned in 1971. A much earlier British prefiguration, it must be admitted was to be found at University College London where Chambers built a staff organisation in the 1930s deliberately used on the continental system.

It is important to note that Lundy's 'across the board' concept is by no means an accurate description of the practice of many libraries which purport to employ subject specialists. Indeed subject specialism seems to be more of a spectrum than a clear concept and subject division of tasks is to be found in even the most functionally organised of libraries. Perhaps the determining criterion should be the practice of dual assignment whereby one staff member includes both technical service and reader service operation within his normal day-to-day occupation. By this standard the number of British university libraries committed to the practice of subject specialism reduces perhaps to less than twenty.

As far as Australian academic libraries are concerned, the subject specialist in the Lundy sense is still virtually non-existent, though the University of Adelaide has announced a wholesale staff reorganisation based on this scheme. Several problems have arisen with subject specialists which apply, mutatis mutandis, to the whole concept of a professional cadre.

— the attempt to give professional satisfaction can be clearly seen in many cases to have produced considerable dissatisfaction among support staff. Elites are seldom popular.

- The mechanics of dual assignment introduce considerable complexities. The question of the most appropriate physical location of an officer working at both technical service and reader service activities is difficult to resolve, even on the basis of compromise. Once settled, the problem remains of dividing one's attention effectively between records demanding 'heads down' concentration and readers requiring 'head up' invitation.
- Having avoided frustrating the professional by locating them outside the main administrative structure, it seems we have condemned them to the much greater frustration of never acquiring the appropriate experience promotion to executive positions.
- The experience of some British university libraries recently and of some American libraries earlier suggests that 'subject specialism with this degree of range of influence over library operations brings the real danger of a new form of disintegration.
- There is some evidence that the distribution of elements of the technical service operation so slows up the total operation as to render impossible coping with major throughput requirements.
- There seems to be no doubt that administrative costs are increased by the system. The Parry Committee recognised this fact and it has never seriously been disputed.

All these reasons suggest some caution at least in adopting this method of increasing professional job satisfaction. It is notable that the Columbia University library proposal for a resources group was finally quietly abandoned and that, at the other end of the size scale, a similar fate befell subject specialisation at Leicester. Nevertheless the logic of putting professional talent to best use is irrefutable and the accompanying assertions of improved job satisfaction are attractive. As Guttsman puts it, 'if logic were the only guide and human sensitivities and psychological satisfactions did not count we would have a chain of command operating in military fashion'. However the same author had also come to the view, eight years after his earlier article, that the system was not universally applicable but 'probably fits best institutions with student populations of 3000 to 8000 and a fairly unified library system' and that 'problems of geographical disparity and complexity of communication which would follow from the decline in face to face relationships resulting from increased size would inevitably impose other solutions'. For the University of Sydney Library in 1975, as noted earlier, WOPSO recommended very strongly the creation of a resources division in which subject specialists would combine collection building, reader education and liaison with the academic staff.

The committee noted that Columbia, even after the Booz, Allen and Hamilton report, could not see its way clear in its own particular situation to bring together the development and use of resources', but considered that 'this interesting concept is possible in the University of Sydney library system'. WOPSO also emphasised that 'before implementation of the scheme there needs to be an investigation into whether there are sufficient staff available to put into practice the aims of the division without any diminution of service or activities presently performed'. In the event the librarian was unable to satisfy himself that there was or would be sufficient staff available.

The Impact of New Technologies

A problem for the director or chief librarian with a vested interest in a simple structure has been the emergence of new technologies which either do not fit into the organisational expression of library routine or have not yet been absorbed into the discipline of librarianship as developed and demonstrated by the formal organs of education for librarianship. Two areas spring immediately to mind: special materials, and systems work automation. The first is surely no more than temporary difficulty. Media specialisation has been a way of life in non-academic libraries for nearly a generation. It is now an accepted involvement of many academic libraries.

Again, if one may take the English example, the former colleges of advanced technology brought with their translation to university status a determination not to be book-bound. For the time being, however, audio-visual material, their selection, processing and exploitation provide another area which tends top cut across any neat conventional compartmentation into technical and reader services. Systems work poses a problem of a different order. To the extent that it depends on computerisation it connotes training and experience in a discipline outside—and all too often alien to—librarianship. Again, it may be said that the problem is but one of transition.

The field of library education is providing rapidly and increasingly for specialism in this area. In the meantime at least, however, the library administrator is faced with two sets of problems. The first is organisational. How can an operation which impinges on all area of the library's work be fitted into a functionally structured organisation? For a variety of reasons, mostly associated with an affinity of personal interests, libraries have often found themselves with their systems expert located, for example, in the technical services division. However logical this placement might be in terms of current activity, it can be observed that, sooner or later, it contributes to the polarisation which comes increasingly to characterise the two-divisional structure or to the inter-departmental strains that most centralised organisations demonstrate. Another answer, to keep the system office out of the basic structure and on direct report to the chief executive or his deputy, brings its own dangers of over-extension or span of control for the senior executive on the one hand and delusions of grandeur on the other. The second problem in relation to systems work is in the personnel area. Irrespective of their location in the organisation, what qualifications should be sought or preferred in a systems head, at least during a period when formal library education does not provide an appropriate dual qualification? Does one seek a library-enlightened computer expert or a computer-exposed librarian?

The treatment of these problems in particular libraries, or even in the three countries concerned, has not been pursued in this account since, as with most problems of relatively recent emergence, the attempted solutions which have been recorded are manifold and also manifestly unsatisfactory. In a sense too, one must repeat that they maybe no more than transitory, as both experience and professional education absorb the technologies into the library profession. Difficulties of an organisational nature will remain but they will be decreasingly differences in kind. It would be a truism to say that problems of communication increase out of all proportion to increases in the size of an institution. What is more, a hierarchical organisation is much better equipped, technically and in terms of personal expectation, for communication downward than upwards. A pressing problem then with the large academic library is communication.

The need is threefold; first, accurate communication downward to ensure that policy decisions are properly implemented; second, adequate information flow downward—and sideways—to keep members of the organisation aware of developments in policy and of the environment in which policy and executive decisions are made; and third, a clear channel of communication upwards. This last is quite vital. Two good selfish reasons should encourage the chief executive to have forwarded upwards all comments, suggestions, criticisms and complaints. The first reason is that members of staff will work better if it is known that what they have to say will be listened to and if there is a real alternative offered to the discontent engendered by the repressed complaint. The second is that constructive suggestions in detail on work flow and improved services are much more likely to be conceived at the work face than through armchair ratiocination by executives. Significantly, the WOPSO investigation at the University of Sydney Library unearthed much more discontent about communication failures than about staff structure or job satisfaction. The same evidence appears in other investigations. Two developments are open to the administrator in this area and both have been aired in the literature.

The first is to tidy up existing channels of communication and constantly to monitor their efficiency. The second is to open further channels by judicious modification or expansion of the committee structure within the library. Again, the latter possibility impinges on the question of staff participation in management and will be considered under that heading. Reverting to the former suggestion, it is surprising what results can flow from quite minor modifications to administrative routines. Even the determination to publish more widely the minutes of reports of various meetings can, at least on the negative side, remove the argument of ignorance, and on the positive side can provide an opportunity for dissemination of ideas and the provocation of debate. The publication of a house organ is a useful device but again often one that loses its effectiveness as institution grows in size, since its editing and appearance tends to remain the concern of an over-occupied senior executive instead of being delegated.

The real time involved in developing and maintaining these various possibilities needs to be weighed as carefully and as realistically as possible, of course, against the likely return. It is as easy to be over-obsessed as under-interested. Once again these comments are not accompanies by any particular reference to actual practice. The literature includes as sufficiency of reports of how it is 'done good' in one place or another. Merely on the grounds that the Australian scene may be less well known to readers, one could refer to the contributions by Fielding in this are of Australian academic library administration.

Participation in Management

The other problems so far discussed involve proposals for readjustment and modification of existing structure and philosophies, some of which are by no means minor but most of which are scarcely fundamental. On the face of it the question of staff participation in management is of a different order. Careful analysis of those proposals and actual modifications which have been reported, however, suggest that they may not be quite as revolutionary as might be either feared or hoped, depending one one's point of view.

Very few have attempted seriously to overturn the prime requirement that the chief executive of the library is accountable for all decisions made within the province of the library's independence of action. He may, depending on his management style, delegate the responsibility for making day-to-day decisions in particular areas, but only in the most extreme propositions of committee 'government' has the suggestion been advanced that his decision-making powers be over-ridden or supplanted by those of any intra-library officer or body.

Interestingly enough, one of the earliest articles on participation in management was also one of the very few to grasp this nettle of ultimate accountability. Kaser suggested, in

1970, retaining a pyramid of organisation, but only in association with a parallel structure of peer authority. Thus, in conscious imitation of the academic model, the chief librarian would assume at appropriate times a dean-like function in order to enable the group of peers to arrive at decisions and then revert to the role of director to implement those decisions. This duality of operation is seen as continuing down a line of delegation throughout the staff structure. Even if decision-making is left with the director, the possibility still remains that his office would not be permanently vested with the one incumbent. Proposals have been advanced for a rotating or elective headship shared among a group of peers, by close analogy with an academic department. We are not aware of any implemented practice of this kind in the United Kingdom, and in America it must be very rare. It certainly does not exist in Australasia. One would essay the suggestion that the analogy of the academic department breaks down on this point.

A multi-chair department is possible since each professor is appointed on his own scholarly merits and without reference necessarily to specific teaching or administrative responsibilities. A multi-chair library seems the less tenable if chief librarians are appointed for professional rather than scholarly qualifications, and given that a library is essentially an administrative organisation with a finite area of activity. Nonetheless one is aware of proposals to have more than one appointee on professorial equation in at least one British academic library. Semantically the possibility of what is basically a paradox is enhanced by the British use of the simple term librarian to describe the chief executive, as opposed to the transatlantic title of 'director', or even the not-uncommon Australian versions of 'chief librarian' or 'university librarian'. Leaving aside the question of whether the incumbency of the chief executive's position could change, what possibilities are open to him in relation to increased participation in management? It is enough first to repeat that delegation is of high significance in this consideration. It is not always appreciated that it must connote complete trust of subordinates and that it does not reduce the chief executive's area of accountability. It could also be said, of course, that it reinforces hierarchy and so tends to undermine the collegial basis to which reference has been made earlier. A further possibility is to widen the area of advice to the director and so provide increased possibility both for influencing decisions and for participating positively in decision-making. Care must be taken to avoid the charge of tokenism, however, and the director must be honestly prepared to be influenced by the advice offered.

The first opportunity to widen the advisory circle, as noted earlier, is to broaden the upper region of the structural pyramid by multiplying, within reason, the number of heads of divisions with direct access to the chief director. Regular meetings of this senior group can fairly easily establish a situation in which decision, though still in the hands of one person, are arrived at in most cases by consensus. The same pattern can be reproduced downward through the structure, with heads of divisions consulting the group of heads of their departments in regularly scheduled meetings. This hierarchically representative committee structure can be supplemented by other committees which either comprise more broadly representative groupings, or concentrate expertise for particular specialist areas, or to deal ad hoc with specific questions.

Prior to the WOPSO report on the University of Sydney Library, hierarchical committees were well-established, there was a broader advisory group and both specialist and ad hoc committees were in existence. On the strong advice of WOPSO this structure was further buttressed and it is worth, perhaps, listing in summary the various committees functioning in early 1978. This listing is included as an example of modest proliferation. Other libraries have suggested and perhaps even implemented much more elaborate schemes. UCLA's library administrative network envisaged twenty committees and, indeed, began life with that number, but it seems to have regressed to perhaps no more than ten. Equally, as with the more strictly communication-oriented devices, over-enthusiasm can push plans beyond the break-even point, where the return in increased efficiency and improved morale is countered by time lost from the job.

Participation in management is not a new topic. Twenty-five years ago McAnally pointed out that 'administrative councils' had been established 'since 1945' in many American university libraries, such as Chicago and Illinois and as long ago as 1956 a conference of eastern college librarians at Columbia University was devoted to staff participation in library management. There does not seem to be a voluminous literature on the topic in relation to British university libraries, but inevitably the question of participation arises with the status afforded to subject specialists and Guttsman and other writers have demonstrated their awareness of an area of difficulty in relation to ultimate accountability.

In Australia there has been discussion of the topic but perhaps rather little experimentation with the practice. The Sydney examples might be regarded as reasonably advanced for the Antipodes. It is intriguing to detect in American writing a concern that provision for participation may be the only alternative to unionisation, perhaps indeed the only defence against it. This theme appears as early as Kaser and has been echoed more recently by De Gennaro. The latter sees the two tends indeed as basically incompatible. It might be noted that the members of staff of the University of Sydney Library have been organised as a trade union for forty years. This fact seems to have had no significant bearing on that library's groupings toward staff participation in management.

One factor in staff participation in management which tends not to be aired frequently is staff's actual competence to participate. Kaser admits, for example, that one inhibiting factor to the successful operation of his proposed peer group is the possible lack of dedication of the would-be participants. The widespread 'democratisation' of university management itself in Australia by the inclusion of student representatives at virtually every level has been greatly affected by a lack of interest and willingness to apply themselves on the part of many of the new appointees. In the same way, meetings of consultative committees of library staff can degenerate all too easily into time-wasting if all members are not prepared to apply themselves in advance as well as during the meeting itself, to keep up with the professional literature and, in every respect, to equip themselves in the same way as the would expect the director to be equipped if he were to retain full powers of decision making.

4

Organisation and Motivation

The library is a social institution, it organisation is carried with laying down the theoretical principles and policies to be applied on a pre-planed structure while its administration puts those principles into practice on scientific manners. Thus library organisation is the bedrock of library administration and good administration is possible only when a library is well planned. L.M. Harrod had defined library organisation as the act or process of organisation, i.e. creating a systematic union of individuals in a body which officials, agents and members work together for a common end. Therefore, the basis of library organisation is to formulate the methods and guide lines for running a library and getting these methods into working order. Libraries are of different types according to the nature of their purpose and functions. They may be independent institutions like public libraries and the subscription libraries or part of other institutions like academic, commercial, industrial and other special libraries. The organisation of any library depends upon the nature of services it is supposed to render to its readers. The most basic function of any library is to make use of its resources for its readers.

ORGANISATIONAL STRUCTURE

Library is a social institution. It needs a simple and systematic organisational structure to achieve its goals and objectives. The Librarian should adopt various suitable criteria to structure necessary programmes and activities of a Library. He has to describe and to apply principles, useful for creating an organisational structure, and also to draw organisation charts explaining the inter-connections, inter-relations and inter-dependence among various sections/units of a Library. For organising the functions of a Library, its activities relating to each function have to be divided into works and jobs and grouped and arranged to form a structure. So it is a practice to divide and group the activities of a Library into desirable sections/units for getting best management results. Some suitable characteristics should be determined for division which would be relevant to fulfil the purpose. The following characteristics are now being used for creating sections/units in a Library.

a) Numbers,
b) Functions,
c) Territory (geographical contiguity),
d) Product,
e) Customers (users),
f) Process or Equipment,
g) Subjects,
h) Materials (books, periodicals, microfilms/forms, maps, etc.)

The most common form of organisational design is the functional structure. This divides a Library into functional departments/sections/units such as—Acquisition, Technical, Processing, circulation, Reference, Documentation, Extension, Maintenance, etc. The public and academic Libraries use the criteria 'subjects' which provides for more-in-depth reference and information services, requiring a higher degree of subject specialisation on the part of the staff. In academic libraries, subject departments are usually broad in scope to include all related subjects. Some libraries also get organised on the basis of materials they do serve such as books, periodicals, micro forms, manuscripts, maps etc.

The publication department/section of a library can be organised considering its information products such as Current Awareness, Bulletin, Indexing Journals, Abstracting Journals, etc. Special Libraries and Documentation Centres use the method 'process' or 'equipment' for organising their printing and photographic/micrographic units. In a national library system regional libraries are organised on the basis of their geographical character.

In the process of designing the organisational structure of a library, the dividing and grouping various library activities produce a number of horizontal and vertical units at different levels. So these units need to be structured relating them approximately, to produce a desirable organisational structure for effective administration and efficient management. This structure is essentially an establishment of appropriate relationship between various groups of persons working at vertical and horizontal positions of a Library. Therefore, it is necessary to adopt some useful principles for creating organisational structure such as:

(1) *Span of Management* which refers to the number of activities a manager can effectively manage. This emphasises on the limit to which a Librarian/Information Officer would be able to supervise, control and manager a number of activities efficiently.

(2) *Scalar Principle and the Vertical Hierarchy* which needs that there should be final utilise authority and the Lines of

authority should clearly extended downward to every subordinate position in a library.

(3) *Unit of command* which emphasises that each employee is supervised by only one supervisor who should make assignments and assess the employee's performance.

(4) *Delegation of authority and responsibility* which states that responsibility can not be delegated without accompanying authority. The process of delegation should consider certain facts such as:

(a) Assignment of tasks,

(b) the determination of the results expected,

(c) degree of delegation of authority for performing the tasks,

(d) exact fixation of responsibility for failure or success in performing the tasks of an employee in a Library.

(5) *Line and staff positions*: Line positions or managers are responsible and accountable for the tasks assigned to them in the achievement of organisations aims and objectives. Staff positions are those that provide advice, support and service to the line positions/managers in carrying out their tasks. Usually staff positions are created in big libraries to streamline operations on the basis of advice given to make right choice from different alternatives.

(6) *Functional authority*: It relates to supervisory power exercised on a section/unit by a position/manager/specialist outside the organisational section/unit by a position/manager/specialist outside the organisational section/unit. In libraries, often functional authority is given to specialists who complete a particular project work within specific time also sometimes they are known as co-ordinators because they have to work with employees involved in their type of speciality.

(7) *Co-ordination and integration*: The employees of a Library work in different positions to accomplish the desired result but these positions are not to be operated in isolation. So they have to operate in close cooperation and coordination with various units of a Library. Thus the final integration of different functions alone will ensure success.

(8) *Centralisation and decentralization*: In a library certain activities need to be centralised and certain others decentralised. But a judicious combination would ensure best results in most economical way. Therefore, in big Libraries house-keeping operations may be centralised and specific services may be decentralised.

Organisational Chart

An organisation chart is a useful visual aid for including the horizontal and vertical structure of an organisation. It is a graphic presentation of organisational structure showing different positions, span of control, relationships between line and staff positions, flow of authority and responsibility, relationship with Advisory Committees and such others. The process of organisation and also its administration must work upto this end. This S.R. Ranganathan has formulated his famous five laws of library science just to exemplify this basic approach of library organisation at different stages of its operation. The successive stages in library organisation are as follows:

(a) Planning and construction of Library Building.

(b) Equipping the Library Building with necessary furniture.

(c) Selection, appointment and duties of the staff.

(d) Co-ordination of the work of various departments and sections.

Library Building

The process of organisation of a library starts with the planning of its building. In irrespective of big or small, luxurious or plain, broad or tall, the library building must be primarily functional and it must suit the purpose for which it is planned and created. It must be built in keeping with the cultural need and taste of the local community but not merely as an architectural show piece for visitors. Hence J.P. Boyd has rightly stated, since a library is the cultural centre of a community, it has to render some specific services to the community. A library building has to be designed keeping in view its functions. The cardinal principles of library building planning, therefore, should be based on simplicity, efficiency, economy, flexibility, functional, usefulness and the avoidance of monumentality. The planning of a new library building must begin with the site. The location of the library must be in a central place easily accessible to all users.

The site of the library building must provide easily maximum natural light on all sides, adequate air space, free from danger of fire through adjacent buildings, a reasonable measure of calmness and adequate space around it for future extension. After selection of a good site construction of the library building should be well planned. The planning of a library building becomes an important function of modern librarianship. As the efficiency in the work of a library is assessed by the nature of its resources and the service it renders to its readers.

The building which house the materials also plays a vital role in extending efficient library service. So an ideal modern library must combine both function and design and it should be functionally efficient and economical. Therefore, the planning of the library building is very essential. Before finalisation of the library building is very essential. Before finalisation of the plan by the architect, the librarian must be consulted as a specialist in the field or a statement of the requirements of library prepared by the librarian known as programming, must be taken into account. The three important steps in planning a library building, i.e. programming, preliminary planning and working drawings can be possible through collaboration between the architect and the librarian.

In designing a modern library the following factors must be taken into consideration:

(1) It should be planned to accommodate some essential section such as—Acquisition, Technical, Circulation, Reference, Periodicals, Documentation, General Reading Room, Research Rooms, Special Reading Rooms, Browsing Room, Children's Wing, Auditorium or Lecture Hall, Exhibition or Display Hall, Binding Room, Record Room, Committee Hall, Librarian's Room, Staff work rooms, stack rooms, Toilets etc.

(2) It should be planned to observe economy of operation and maintenance.

(3) It should be planned especially for the kind of work to be done and the community to be served.

(4) The plan should be suited to probabilities and possibilities of growth and development, in future.

(5) It should be planned for any easy access to the building and comfortable use of books and other reading materials. Therefore, it should be located as centrally as possible and should be at ground floor level.

(6) Its interior decoration and arrangement should be colourful and attractive. Its exterior should have a glass front facing the road just to enable the public to see the interior of library building.

(7) Its reading room and stock room should have the benefit of natural ventilation and light.

The Library building is a vital ingredient in extending library services and attracting many readers. It resources and requirements will determine its size and the arrangement of different sections. In a small library all these sections will be close together on one floor. But in a big library these sections will remain far apart from each other in proper places spread out in two or three floors. However, small may be the building, the space allotment must be in keeping with the strength of the staff, readers and the size of the book collections according to the present needs and the possible future development. Therefore, the provision of space requirements is vital in the planning of a library building. Mainly the following four broad areas alongwith their allied and subarea are identified as common service areas in a library:

(a) Circulation Area which includes:

(i) Stock rooms or halls.

(ii) Charging/Discharging counter.

(iii) Public Catalogue (s).

(b) Reader Activity Area which covers:

(i) Reading room (s)

(ii) Charging/Discharging counter.

(iii) Public Catalogue (s).

(b) Readers Activity Area which covers:

(i) Reading room (s)

(ii) Microform reading room.

(iii) Research cubicles/study carrels.

(c) Study Activity Area which includes:

(i) Acquisition Section

(ii) Technical Section

(iii) Reference Section

(d) Other Areas which includes:

(i) Librarians/Senior professionals rooms.

(ii) Space for library staff

(iii) Seminar room

(iv) Binding section

(v) Reprography section

The interior planning of a library should be functional and it should be equipped with necessary furniture. The equipment for different sections of a library must be appropriate and held their smooth functioning.

The .furniture and equipment should be convenient, comfortable and durable. These should conform to certain standard specifications. The Indian Bureau Standard and University Grants Commission have made certain standard specifications for library and fittings. According to some experts in library planning in preparing a budget for anew library building at least eight per cent should be allocated for furniture and equipment in addition to the building. The different sections of a library should be equipped with the essential furniture:

(a) The acquisition section has to be equipped with tables, chairs, steel almirahs, accessioner's table, order file or trays.

(b) The technical section has to consist of classifier's table, cataloguers' table, chairs and card catalogue cabinet with trays. The catalogue cabinet manufactured from wood or steel are necessary for the storage of cards. These are available in varying sizes from four to seventy-two trays. Each tray is made of either wood or steel for cards measuring 7.5 x 12.5 Cms. The card cabinets should be placed in stands, and the overall height of the cabinet should not be more than 1.5 metre. This will accommodate six vertical rows of drawers of 12.8 x 7.8 x 40 Cm. dimension.

The standard size tray of a card cabinet can accommodate 1,000 cards. A metal rod which passes through the punched holes in cards is provided to keep the cards in order. The steel card cabinet usually manufactured in units of two or four trays. The catalogues' table consists of a number of drawers. The selflist cards are arranged in systematic order in these drawers.

(c) The circulation section must be equipped with charging desk, charging trays, sorting shelves, counter chairs etc. A circulation or charging desk consists of counter space to hold the trays of the charging system. The size of the counter space depends upon the use and it should have surface s at least 18" wide and its height from floor should be 32". In a big library charging and discharging counters may be separate. The charging trays are generally 2.5" wide and 18" long. In the circulation counter shelves are required for the sorting of returned books and reserved books. The library assistants who work at the charging desk need counter high chairs to seat. Normally the counter is designed for two persons to work at a time. Adequate knee space is provided at places where the library staff sit and work. The length and design vary considerably to suit the specific need of the library. Some of the common designs are rectangular L-shaped, U-shaped, etc. The counter is invariably made of wood, and usually have hard wearing top made of decolum or similar material.

(d) The periodicals section should be well equipped with reading tables, chairs, periodicals racks, periodicals display board etc. Wooden or metal tables and chairs can be used. The height of the table should be 30" from the floor and a table of 36 x 60 inches should have comfortable sitting accommodation for four readers.

LIBRARY EQUIPMENT

The equipment required for different sectional office rooms includes suitable chairs, tables, filing cabinet for pamphlets, maps, and other office-records, which can be prepared in standard specifications according to need of the Library. Also the library having a binding section, micro film unit should procure necessary machinery and equipments. Other essential equipments and fixtures like fans, lights, wear coolers, wall clocks are required to e fitted in proper places throughout the building according to the needs and conditions of a library. The standard institution of different countries have made their code to provide guidance to architects and librarians or library authorities in designing the library building, fittings and furniture. Various types of equipment that are generally found in a library can be categorised as follows:

(a) *Filing equipment such as*: Card catalogue, Roll dex, Kardveyer, vertical filing cabinets, Pamphlet boxes, Microforms drawers/cabinets, Microfiche steel cabinets, Slide boxes, Technical drawing cylinders or steel cabinets.

(b) *Record keeping equipment such as*: Kardex supplied by Remington Rand of India for Journal control system, Linedex for periodicals section.

(c) *Microform Reading equipment such as*: Microfilm reader, Microfiche reader, Slide projector.

(d) *Copying equipment*: Photocopying machine or Xerox machine, Microfilming Machine.

(e) *Non-Conventional Indexing and Filing equipment*: Termatrex, Filmsort, Rapid Selector or Filmorex.

(f) *Miscellaneous Supplies and Equipment such as*:- Electric Stylus, Revolving stands, Bulletin boards, stool or Ladder.

LIBRARY PERSONNEL

The staff, the books and the readers make up the fundamental trinity of a library. The success of a library largely depends upon the persons who are responsible for the effective use of a good collection of books in the hands of the readers. A library having good collections can not render best services to its readers without efficient and trained personnel. Thus for the fulfillment of desired objectives of any library sincere and organised human effort is essential. The basic aim of the library staff should be to place the right book in the hands of the right readers at the right time. They should ensure that no reader who requires help either in the choice of books, or in getting information from documents should go without it. According to Clara W. Herbort, "The organisation of a library is, therefore, of fundamental importance in the consideration of personnel administration. It is the house in which the members of a like profession live and should partake of the characteristics of a happy home. It should be well regulated, smooth running, cooperative, comfortable in which each member of the staff may find his rightful place". The personnel programme of a library aims at the securing of adequate and efficient staff in order to carry out the overall objectives of library organisation.

The staff management policy of different types of libraries will be influenced by their nature of services but their basic guiding principles will be the same. There is an absolutely essential need for a set of guiding principles which will assist the librarian or the personnel executive of a library in the formation of personnel policies, procedures and programmes as well as in the solution of personnel problems. The personnel policy of a library includes the ranking and grading, job analysis and job description, condition of service, recruitment, selection and training and strength of the staff.

The entire staff structure of library usually consists of certain ranks of employees of different grades. The "ranking" of employees is determined according to the type of works they perform, in other words, in relates to the number of posts at each level. The "grading" of the staff is made according to different classes of personnels blazing on their salaries and wages. The first requirement in getting the best out of a library staff is to make a clear-cut a separation as possible between professional and semi-professional work, as it will not economical to burden professional employees with non-professional duties or vice-verse. So all the employees in a library are divided into three categories—professional, semi-professional and non-professionals. The professional staff are engaged in performing professional duties whose minimum qualifications should be graduation with at least one year training in library and information science leading to post graduate degree or diploma.

The semi-professional staff of a library consists of employees who perform library routine and techniques under the guidance of professional staff and have received alternatively training in library science. Also some none professional (clerical) and unskilled workers are appointed to perform certain library works.

Job Analysis

As modern library is complex affair it becomes very necessary to define the duties and responsibilities of the library staff working in different sections. Therefore, an analysis shall be made embodying a general description of level of work and the responsibility of each grade or level of work. A detailed job analysis of each section of a library also needs to be attempted so that each member of the staff knows what he is supposed to do and what is expected of him. In deciding on the grade of the post, the general level of work and responsibility for a particular post should be laid down. Thus it can easily be determined what specific duties appropriate to each post, and what qualifications, knowledge, skill and aptitudes are necessary to perform the job.

Service condition is an essential ingredient of staff management. It includes such matters as hours of work, service regulations, pension, retirement and resignation policies and procedures, policy relating to educational and welfare facilities. Conditions of service in state and central government managed libraries both public and academic are laid down on a state or national basis. In order to relate the salaries of the staff to their work performed and responsibility attached the chief librarian or the Director of Libraries must use his professional knowledge to assess these. Also through joint consultation or negotiation between staff and management, the gradation, working conditions and scales of pay of the library personnel should be determined.

Recruitment, Selection and Training

The recruitment policy of a library is planned considering the nature of its services. Thus the recruitment policy of a public library differs from a school or college or University library or from any special and research library. Hence the recruitment of the library staff should be made by certain tests like aptitude test, personality test, interest test, intelligence test, etc. The tests are necessary and helpful in assigning the right job to the right person so that he can be able to develop his interest as a scholar, cultivate a real intellectual awareness and assist the research scholars, teaching staff and students to save their time in bibliographic search and information retrieval.

The recruitment of library staff should be proceeded by job analysis and job description. An analysis should be made to decide the number of posts required, types of jobs to be done, to specify the responsibilities implied in each job and to determine the qualifications required by a staff member to enable him to do the job satisfactorily. The minimum basic and professional qualification should be laid down for each job. As per the Report of the Library Committee of the University Grants Commission, India, the academic qualifications of the Library staff should be at par with those of the Professors, the Readers, the Lecturers and the Tutors. Apart from general academic qualifications of a high order, the librarian and his professional staff should also have professional qualifications of an equally high order. The selection and appointment of library staff should be done very carefully because much of the success of the library staff member on the job in a library depends upon skillful personnel administration. The staff of the library should be well organised so that each member can contribute his highest abilities and skills to the cooperative effort..

The usual method of selections either by open advertisement or through the Employment Directorate for the posts and prescribing the qualifications, experience and scales of pay. The head of the library or the principal librarian should be selected through a higher power selection committee consisting of Library experts. The librarian should be the person chiefly responsible for personnel administration and he should be called for an interview and the selection committee should prepare a panel of names in order of merit of performance so that, if the candidate placed at the top does not accept the job, an offer is sent to the next one. Thus the appointments to the different posts are made on the recommendation of the selection committee which should be very fair and honest.

After appointment, the library needs to ensure that new staffs are trained in their duties and that other staff improve their activities, so that they becomes more efficient and may quality for promotion. The existing staff should be trained in the use of new appliances and machines like computer photocopier, microfilm reader, electronic stencil cutter etc. Training may be imparted through (a) apprentice system, which equips the trainee with a practical knowledge of actual library work; (b) in-service training for those who are selected for promotion may also be required to take additional courses in library and Information Sciences or it they are in non-professional positions, so attend the library science courses over a particular period of time; (c) Under study method which enables an employee to work under another trained experienced employee; (d) study tour which provides scope for an educational visit to big modern libraries; (e) extension lectures, workshops, refresher course, seminars, conferences and meetings. For the purpose of training in librarianship or library and information science education, schools colleges and departments are established either by Government or by the library associations. The training for the semi-professionals is a undergraduate course where as the training for the professionals should be of the university standard and a postgraduate course, leading to B.Lib.I.Sc and M.Lib.I.Sc. degree.

Staff Strength

The strength of staff of a given library depends on the size of its collections of books, periodicals, manuscripts and other documents, scope of its service to the readers at different points, hours of opening, processing systems, the financial support, the number of types of readers served, etc. According to L.R. Wilson and M.F. Tauber in a University library the size of staff apparently bears a definite relation to the number of volumes added annually, the number of students and faculty members served, the teaching and research programmes of the university, the number of departmental libraries operated, the teaching and research programme of the University, the number of departmental libraries operated, the number of services desks maintained and the nature of the internal organisation of the library. The University Grants Commission of India appointed a Committee under the Chairmanship of Dr. S.R. Ranganathan to advice the U.G.C. about the development of libraries and their organisation. The Committee has laid down a staff formula to determine the size of the staff for different sections of a University or College Library on the following basis:-

1. *Book Section*:
   One person for every 600 volumes added in a year,
2. *Periodical Publications Section*:
   One person for every 500 current periodicals taken.
3. *Documentation Section*:
   One person for every 1000 entries prepared in a year.
4. *Technical Section*:
   One person for every 2,000 volumes added in a year.
5. *Reference Section*:
   One person for every 50 readers, other than the users of the text book collection in a day.
6. *Circulation Section*:
   One person for every 1500 hours for which one wicket gate of the library has to kept open in a year.
7. *Maintenance Section*:
   One person for every 6,000 volumes added in a year, one person for every 500 volumes to be replaced in a day and one person for every 1,00,000 volumes in the library.
8. *Administrative Section*:
   Minimum one library accountant, one steno-typist and one correspondence clerk.

9. *Supervisory Section*:
   One librarian and one Asst. or Dy. Librarian for two shifts for supervision, organisation, and solving the different problems cropping up in the work of different sections.

10. *Unskilled Staff*:
    One cleaner for every 30,00 volumes in the library, one attendant for every 6,000 volumes added in a year, for every 500 current periodicals taken, and for each of the shifts in the circulation section, besides unskilled and the semi-skilled workers normal to any institution.

Also the committee recommends for the provision of staff for leave substitute. Normally a person works only for about 250 days in a year and avails weekly holidays, notified holidays, monthly holidays, casual leave, medical leave and earned leave. But a University library should be kept open on all the days of the year except a few national days. Therefore, provision should be made to appoint staff on leave vacancy at the rate of one month in a year for each member in certain essential sections like the circulation, the Reference and the Supervisory.

Duties of the Staff

In the academic libraries, the librarian and his staff should make themselves familiar with the wave front of knowledge in which research is in progress. They should serve the staff with the nascent thought expeditious, exhaustively and pinpointedly. They should keep close touch with the progress of class room teaching programme and in collaboration with the teaching staff of different subjects should plan for the students to pursue, preparatory, parallel and follow up study by mobilising the resource of the library.

Also they should specialised in the bibliography of different subjects for book selection just to build a balanced book-collection in close-correlation with the current and future of research workers and students. Thus the Library staff should render their services to the research workers, teachers and students. Generally the staff of a modern library has many duties to perform but the most important one being they way in which information is channelised to the staff members. This is done through staff manuals containing standing instructions, occasional memoranda dealing with day to day changes and regular staff meetings to pass on information to all the employees of the library. The staff of Library should perform their duties in order to achieve its objectives. The main aim of a library is to utilise its resources to the best advantage of its readers. So the staff should investigate the reading interests and needs of the readers. They should attend sincerely to the technical and processing work such as classification, cataloguing, documentation, circulation, preservation and maintenance of the reading materials. They should extend their special services to the children and youths. The other important duties of the library staff are- Ordering and Accessioning of Books and other documents, processing payment of bills, salaries and sanction of leaves of the staff members, initiation and filing of correspondence, maintenance of staff records, the preparation of budget, annual reports, committee reports and proceedings, assembling statistical data, checking and certification of accounts.

Coordination of Library Work

Librarian as the chief personnel manager of a library should exercise his leadership within the Library. He must inspire confidence among his staff and should guide them properly to improve efficiency and attain best library service. He must delegate the authority of personnel function to the Deputy Librarian, Asst. Librarian, Sectional heads and other supervisors. Also he should discuss the problems of different sections with its heads to ensure smooth functioning, and proper co-ordination. Thus delegation of duties amongst the staff members is most essential for running a library smoothly and efficiently. Basing on the principles of scientific management the "line and staff" method of organisation is a suitable approach for co-ordination of library work with some modifications and adjustments according to the needs and requirements of particular library. The line staff officers are jointly responsible for the achievements of a library. A line officer discharges his responsibility by taking direct action but a staff officer discharges his responsibilities by furnishing information and advice to the line officer. C.W. Herbert in his book entitled "Personnel Administration in Public Libraries" has suggested the following guiding principles to ensure co-ordination and efficiency of library work.

1. The organisation should be as simple as possible; it should not be over organised with unnecessary overheads or under organised so that too many conflicting duties are placed on too few officers.
2. Authority must always go with responsibility, and these lines should be so clear as to be reading and generally understood.
3. Executives are of two types those who like responsibility for the execution of work and those who like planning. While the two qualities have to be combined to a certain extent in each executive, a large library needs to provide for both types with corresponding separation of duties.
4. The organisation should be built upon the basis of community needs and be sufficiently flexible to adopt itself to changing demands and conditions.
5 Personnel should be appointed to fit the requirements of the organisation than the other way round. This is one of the difficulties of reorganisation, since libraries must

naturally make the most of the capacities of the present members of the staff. Yet too great a consideration of these personal factors makes for an unbalanced development of the service as a whole.

6. The best organisation is the one gives the larger number of its members individual responsibility and opportunity for creative work and professional growth.

Thus library is a service organisation and its existence is justified by the degree of service it renders, to the clients and the Librarian at the helm of its affairs should have ability to command and guide this organisation safely. He should act as an able organiser, co-ordinator guide and controller of the Library staff should play an important role in the set of sound library organisation through co-ordination of their technical efforts.

Library Authority

In the first sense the word "Authority" means legal power or right and secondly it refers to a person or body exercising this power. The Library authority may be defined as the body responsible for library matters in its own areas. In case of different types of libraries it may refer to the Governing Body, Board of Trustees, Board of Management, Library Committee, Executive Committee, Local Body, etc. In England the people elect or nominate their library authorities and the library Committee or sub-committees work under them in order to reduce the amount of detailed work of the main Council of Authority. In U.S.A. and Australia, there are Library Boards and in India we have mostly library committees. Generally authority is of two kinds such as:

(i) Statutory which belongs to a given position, and

(ii) Personal which is a result of possessing qualities of leadership.

Authority may be delegated by the head of the organisation to his first sub-ordinate officer. Possession of authority must also involve responsibility for actions. In this manner the Chief Librarian possess statutory authority and he is responsible for all that goes in a library.

Library Committee

The librarian cannot bear the whole burden of management and policy making of a big modern library. So the library committee is appointed by the authority of a public or academic or special library to serve both as a co-ordinating and policy making body. In England the Public Libraries Act, 1892 lays down that urban authorities may appoint library committees and they may delegate powers to them.

The average size of library Act, 1919 also clearly states that library powers must be referred to the Education Committee which may appoint a Library Sub-Committee. This Sub-Committee is known as executive authority and library functions are delegated to it. So it is empowered to make decisions and to implement them. In U.S.A. each of the bigger and smaller local areas has got its own set of library laws to suit the local population and they select library authorities accordingly. In India, the State the Tamilnadu, Karnatak, Andhra Pradesh, Maharasthra, West Bengal, Manipur, Haryana and Kerala have library laws governing the establishment and organisation of public library system in the states. According to these laws library committees are constituted and they are responsible to the local authorities on one hand and the community on the other through the librarian.

A library may have a number of committees depending upon its size and number of activities and operations. However committees are usually constituted according to statutory requirements. The entire library committees can be broadly classification in to following five types:-

1. *The Executive Committee:* It is a committee with delegated powers by the authority. The local authority can not interfere in its work and it need not report its decisions to the library authority. It is autocratic in character.
2. *The Reporting Committee:* It has got powers to decide the policies within certain limits. Its decisions and actions are simple reported to the authority for its information. It is co-operating and helpful to the Librarian.
3. *The Recommending Committee:* It has no definite powers but it can recommend certain proposals for governing the library which are subject to the approval of the library authority. It is very slow in character. It is found in England.
4. *The Self-Perpetuating Committee:* It is created and exists in case of libraries operating under special character of statutes. It is practically independent having sole authority as regards the control and management of the library.
5. *The Adhoc Committee:* It is a special committee for the supervision and control of libraries. It is speedy in its decisions and it can accommodate co-opted members of performing a specific job. The Madras Public Libraries Act, 1948 has made a provision for the appointment of such a Committee.

In addition to above types of Committees there are also sub-committees which a library committee appoints in order to look after the functions like maintenance of accounts, purchase of books, appointment of library staff etc. The appointment of such committees depend on the size of the library system.

The Function of library committees

1. To formulate library policies and objectives.
2. To make proper selection of books and periodicals.
3. To compile and revise rules and regulations for the best use of library resources including the hours of opening admission to the libraries, condition of borrowing books and fines.
4. To check statistical and annual reports submitted by the librarian.
5. To keep a watch over the implementation of library policy by the library staff.
6. To check library accounts and expenditure, prepare estimates of anticipated expenditure and apportion of the library budget.
7. To approve the recommendation of librarian regarding selection of library staff and making the formal appointment.
8. To plan overall-library development programmes and activities.
9. To appoint Sub-Committees on book purchase, staff recruitment, staff welfare and financial provision, etc. for carrying on committee's business more expendiously.
10. To receive gifts, donations for the library.
11. To act as a liaison between the library and the public.
12. To evaluate progress and performance.

The Librarian usually acts as the ex-officio secretary of the library committee. He should have cordial relations with the members of the Committee and should carry out the policies as laid down by the committee from time to time. The librarian should advise the committee as to the provision of further library facilities in the state, district or local areas. He should also report to the committee regarding any repairs, alternations and additions required for improvement of the library buildings. He should have the full charge, direction and control over his staff so that he can appoint, suspend and dismiss personnel subject to the approval of the committee. He should also recommend to the committee from time to time the condition of service of the staff.

The Librarian as the ex-officio secretary should convene the meeting of the committee with the approval of its Chairman and should prepare the agenda for the meetings. On any library matter he should be answerable to the members of the committee. Generally Library committees meet once a month on depending upon the volume of business to be transacted. The minute of the previous meetings should be placed before committee for approval. In the meetings of the committee the Chairman usually presides and in his absence a senior member of the committee should preside. In most of the Indian Universities, the Library Committee is a Standing Committee of the Academic Council and as such the proceedings of the Committee are placed before the Council for approval.

The Committee is concerned with library policy and does not interfere in library administration. So the University or College Library Committee are intended to serve in an advisory capacity. In co-operation with the librarian, it formulates policies for the development of higher learning and research, allocations of book fund to the Library and different departments, and programme of library extension services. Thus the library committee can ensure better understanding between the readers and the library policies adopted. Moreover it can extend support for maintaining and enhancing the status of the librarians and the library profession.

Library Publicity

The public library is the only institution of the modern age which helps in raising the cultural level of the common man and no such other organisation, no school, no college or University does this service. so the public library is regarded as the "People's University". In a developing country the public library occupies unique position in all the problems of community life irrespective of age, sex, class and creed. but the public library service having great intrinsic value to the community does not attract the people of its own accord. Because it can not offer any immediate rewards of pleasure or of money unlike a film hall, and hence it is likely to be over-looked and neglected. Thus our modern scholars establishes the following reasons of non-use of libraries by the public:- ignorance of service, prejudice or misconceptions and the absence of desire to use books. The remedy for the cause of ignorance is a good publicity which is as necessary for the library as salesmanship for a commercial firm, in order that the ignorant may come to know of its service, resources and potentialities and derive benefits.

Thus library publicity means wide spread dissemination of information about the library, its location, when it is open, condition of loan of what it provides. Library publicity has its definite objectives based on a sound library policy. An effective publicity can be undertaken by determining its aims clearly, understanding its nature and the needs of the readers and realising the present and future capacities of the library itself in meeting the demands created by such publicity. It should not be presumed that once a library is established it will automatically attract the readers. Even in the western countries many people do not use the library either due to their ignorance of its existence and its services because they do not think it worthwhile to read.

Therefore, the facilities a library can offer are continually published through different popular media. Thus library publicity aims at the interpretation of library services, through annual reports, handbooks, bulletins and booklets, local newspapers, notice-boards, posters, exhibitions, book fair, advertisement, extension programmes and popular audio-visual media like radio, television and films. The annual report of a library contains the summary of whole work of the library and a brief statistics regarding book stock, periodicals, newspapers, research service, etc. It is attractively printed with illustrations, graphs and pictures, as a direct piece of publicity for the library and the most common medium through which the members can know its activities.

The periodically published bulletins of a library give interesting articles, information of local activities, list on monthly additions of books, reviews of popular books and periodicals and above all readers' opinions and suggestions. so that bulletins enable the participation of readers and also create special interest in them for books and for the library. Sometimes local newspapers spare a column or so in their weekly edition to include the activities of a library and publish the list of additions of books, forthcoming programme acknowledgments of gifts and other information on reader's services. Different types of displays, have contribution to the library publicity programme. The display board at the entrance of a library attracts the common reader as soon as he enters to the library and looks at the attractive book jackets along with book reviews.

Recent scientific advances, current political happening, biographical round ups of local or national interest and pictorial courage of library's activities all these and many more can draw the interested people to visit the library. Regular displays of recent books arranged simultaneously with extension programmes provide opportunities to the people to utilise the library properly. Also the anniversaries of great people, national or religious celebrations and important local functions on education and culture compells the people to consult books and other reading materials inside the library.

Talks, discussions, seminars on current topics can be arranged in the library hall or auditorium on such occasions which could be fruitfully supplemented by display of books bringing to the light many unknown books of the library. Besides these internal means of publicity the external audiovisual media, like occasional talks or radio and cinema slides, documentary films and television have widen the sphere of library publicity. The library primarily exists for helping the people in their individual and community interests and thus encourage all possible organised groups and associations to make wide library publicity by adopting it as a means of promoting their own particular interest. Also prejudice and misconceptions about books and reading can be removed by library publicity programme. The Librarian and his staff should participate in publicity work and try to make the library an entertainment centre.

Library Extension Service

The modern librarianship is not confined to the normal work of the library such as the provision of reading materials, reference service etc., but it has developed certain extension work to other related and associated fields such as the provision of lectures, exhibitions, film displays, musical and dramatic activities. The extension of normal work is regarded as Library Extension Service. The very purpose, of this service is to make the people library minded and thus to turn non-readers into readers, to create and sustain interest in good reading and to promote intimacy between the documents and the readers.

According to Dr. S.R. Ranganathan, extension service is an attempt to bring the library into a social centre whose function is the encouragement of reading. The success of a library service depends upon the best utilisation of its resources. The value of a library can be gauged basing on how much and how well it is used by the members of a community. Thus the library has to increase its utility and also to carry its message to the doors of many people in the inner sanctums of society who .for some reason or other, do not use it at all. This is chiefly due to ignorance about service, misconceptions and lack of desire to use books. Therefore, the extension work must adopt a few methods that have proved beneficial to display this apathy and to stimulate reading interest among the people.

The first step in this direction is to tackle the problem of non-readers. In the underdeveloped or developing countries having low literacy, like India most of our population suffers from the ignorance and illiteracy. The library can help to overcome these by joining hands with the local literacy drives, Story-telling, simple informative talks, reading programmes, heroic song recitals and similar attractive entertainment programmes can be arranged at suitable hours for local illiterates and neoliterate adults. These could be supplemented by providing simple and special books which the beginners and newly interested adults can easily read and follow. This can be achieved by the joint effort of local public library and adult education centre. Hence emphasis is given on the rural library as the main basic of rural reconstruction and our late Prime Minister, Pandit Jawaharlal Nehru cherished to have atleast one library in each village. According the sayings of Manu, "To carry knowledge from the doors of ignorant to educate them in righteous path; nothing can be equal to that form of charity; even to give always the whole world can ever come to its level."

Secondly the ways in which library extension service has been made and can be carried out in order to create and sustain in good reading and to foster communion between the reading materials of a library and its readers are as follows:

1. Through library publicity direct appeal can be made to each reader who can realise the existence of a library in his locality and also can feel the necessity of its use. This publicity work is done by:-
   (a) printed booklists, folders, booklets, catalogues, etc.
   (b) talks to local audiences,
   (c) inclusion of stories in the local newspapers and
   (d) local radio and television programmes.
2. Arranging book exhibitions within the library premises or at some other places in connection with the local functions such as village or regional fairs, music and drama festivals, agricultural and horticultural shows, annual days of youth clubs, conferences, seminars etc. The attention of a good number people can be attracted to utilise the library services. The advice and cooperation of the local volunteer and social workers in such types of extension work can enrich and popularise the activities.
3. Arrangement of public lectures in the library hall on eventful occasion from an important branch of extension services. The librarian can contact the speakers and obtain from them in advance the synopsis or points of their talks or lists of basic source materials and books for further reading. He can distribute the printed or cyclostyled copies of the same prior to the talks and display of those copies on the notice boards. Also for promoting better contact with the local children the libraries can arrange story hours and other attractive forms of extension services.
4. An important method of extension services is to arrange week-ends or book weeks with either youth or children or any social institutions. The residential book weekend gives a good chance for real instruction in the use of books; thus their knowledge is spread to a wider circle of friends and

acquaintances. This book week may be allied programme of book exhibitions or public lectures. In many developing and developed countries, a National Book Week is observed every year which is normally followed by a series of public lectures, seminars and book exhibitions, etc.

5. Now-a-days plays reading, films displays, musical and dramatic activities, adult education classes and group discussion are enlisted in the extension services of libraries inorder to lay more emphasis on extending services to groups instead of individuals. Thus the use of the library among the apathetic reading public is encouraged.

6. In developed countries, the provision of non-book materials such as recordings, radio transcriptions, motion pictures, film stripes, lantern slides, television etc. are made for such people of the rural community who never consider the printed books as the best means for communicating ideas.

7. Through book-mobiles of vans carrying books and other reading materials, the reading facilities can be extended to the areas where it may not be possible to establish permanent library centre. Also the public libraries acts of different states have made provisions of mobile library services at district and block levels. This type of travelling library plays an important role in library extension service. The Delhi Public Library has an Extension Services Department which extends mobile library service to different areas all over the Union Territory. Also it has established book deposit stations at different places for extending library services to local people.

8. The library services are also extended to the blinds, children at school, adolescents, inmates of prisons, hospitals and old persons who are unable to leave their homes to visit the library.

9. The modest form of extension service is the celebration of local festivals and special days of the year dedicated to persons on ideas like our Children's Day, Teachers' Day, Lawyers' Day, Labourer's Day etc.

The purpose of all these above extension activities of a library is the encouragement of reading, nourishing interest in useful pastimes and creating communion between the books and the ignorant readers. The success of an effective extension service depends on certain important factors such as:

(a) A well stocked library housed in an attractive building on a convenient site.

(b) Good condition of the reading community to enjoy leisure hours.

(c) A good number of readers with local initiative and adequate interest to utilise the services.

(d) A well trained and experienced staff with sound knowledge, flexibility of mind and the right psychological approach to guide readers in establishing contacts.

The most universal term in contemporary psychology probably is 'motivation'. Motivation explains :how behaviour gets started, is energised, is sustained, is directed, is stopped, and what kind of subjective reaction is present in the organism while all this is going on". That is, motivation helps to explain the "whys" of behaviour; it is the "hypothetical cause of behaviour". In a nutshell, when we discuss motivation, we are primarily concerned with three dimensions which have a direct bearing on the direction, vigour and persistence of an individual's behaviour, and determine in part his thoughts and actions. They are: what energies, activities, or moves human behaviour what directs or channels such behaviour and how his behaviour is maintained or sustained. These three dimensions of motivation from the corner-stones of our study.

Building upon this framework, we can now pose a problem: Why do people behave the way they do? Why does one university librarian closely watch the wrist watch prior to the close of each working day and leave the job promptly at the quitting time while his professional colleague in the next university library puts in two or three additional hours of work every evening after every one has gone home and burns midnight oil in compiling bibliographies so as to be an active participant in the dissemination of knowledge and active research? Why does one Deputy Librarian strongly prefer working for his personal matters during duty hours and cannot tolerate being chained to a desk all day long and enjoy only work which calls for him/her to make a large number of daily contacts with other people while his colleague in the next door section is straining his every nerve to help the librarian to devise ways and means to put his library on modern lines?

Why does on Assistant Librarian feel it below his dignity to help a university teacher to find out an issue of a periodical till his attendant returns from his lunch break while another colleague of his status does not hesitate even to dust and shelve the books? Why are some individuals "Yes men" and afraid of expressing even their sincere and honest disagreement with their superiors while others are not at all reluctant to offer constructive criticism of their superiors for neglecting the library services and for their autocratic behaviour? How can university librarian or other bigwigs in the library organisation understand, predict, and even control what activity or activities a library person may engage in at any particular point of time?

There is no universally accepted theory that can help to explain the motive which arouse and maintain as well as determine and stimulate the individual's behaviour at any given moment of time. Psychologists, however, agree that—with a few exceptions which will be noted subsequently—behaviour is motivated; that people have reasons for doing the things that they do and do them in the way they do; and that behaviour is oriented toward meeting certain goals and objectives. Such goal directed behaviour resolves round the desire for need satisfaction. Every human being—whether an engineer, or a manager, or a librarian—has certain physical, emotional, socially conditioned, or psychic needs which require satisfaction as a pre-conditions to get the best possible performance from him.

Our needs are accentuated by hunger, pain, love and achievement. Our process of thinking, learning, performance, perception and dream including forgetfulness fluctuate in various patterns at different times and influence our behaviour thoughts and actions. A person's needs, therefore, working in conjugation with his emotions and other psychological factors, act as the motives that dictate his actions and motivate his behaviour toward their satisfaction.

Motives, therefore, are an expression of internal need which require satisfaction in motivate individual to give his best in the performance of his job and keep him at work in organisations. When we say that librarians should motivate their sub-ordinates, we mean to say that they ought to give those incentives which they hope will satisfy their needs and induce them to act in a desired course of action. Needs are, thus, "the initiating and sustaining forces of behaviour". It is in this light that motivation is seen as the "complex of forces starting and keeping a person at work in an organisation".

DYNAMIC MODELS OF MOTIVATION

It would seem significant, therefore, for librarians to have a knowledge of needs that are universally important to motivate people. Yet even the psychologists differ in identifying needs.

Freud, for instance, emphasise to basic classes of needs—the life or love instinct, and the death or destruction instinct. Adler focusses primary attention on the drive for power or mastery; and Horney considers "the need for security and safety in a potentiality dangerous world" as a primary motive.

The needs that are usually taken as the starting point for motivation theory are the so-called physiological drives. Undoubtedly these physiological needs are the most prepotent of all needs. What is means specifically is, that the employee is a biological or physiological organism. To sustain such an organism, man every where, at any time, in any place, vitally requires food, clothing, shelter, rest, water, oxygen, exercise, sex, sensory experience, exploration, and the like. Man does live by bread alone, when there is no bread.

All the faculties of an individual in a state of virtual starvation may be directed toward hunger satisfaction; his conscious and unconscious actions become directed by hunger motivation; for him, Utopia is a place where food is plentiful. The receptors and effectors, the intelligence satisfying tools. Capacities that are not useful for this purpose lie dormant or are pushed into the background. A generalisation is now possible, a satisfied need does not motivate; conversely, an unsatisfied need does motivate the behaviour. But what happens to man's needs when there is plenty of bread and when his stomach is full? Maslow's answer is that once other needs emerge, and these rather than the physiological hunger, dominate the organism. And when these in turn are satisfied, again new needs emerge and the process continues "from belly to brain" through the satisfaction of needs at each level. This is what we mean by saying that the basic human needs are organised into a hierarchy of relative prepotency.

Sustaining the physiological level also requires that protection be provided against deprivation, danger, and threat to the job. Having taken care of today, man wants a guarantee for tomorrow. Both economic security and physiological security are involved. Economic security consists of the need for clothing, shelter, and having an environment of a predictable pattern such as job security, pension, and insurance. Physiological security relates to those needs which call for status maintenance and personal adjustment with varying job situation in future.

Arbitrary or unpredictable management actions, behaviour which arouses uncertainty with respect to continued employment, unwise policy statement, inept policy administration, favoritism, inequitable decisions, discrimination and the like stimulate he security and safety needs in the dependent employment relationship, and therefore, are powerful motivators of behaviour at all organisational levels. Such behaviour may or may not help in accomplishing organisational objectives. Supervisors can create the sense of security in their organisations by setting up and enforcing clear standards of behaviour.

No less potent as motivators are the stimuli which rise out of social contacts as man is a social animal. Being gregarious by nature, man has an inherent tendency to communicate, to gain acceptance from his fellows, to give and receive admiration, friendship and affection; in the biblical sense, we all desire to love and be loved. Social needs also include such things as "status and pride". In order to achieve social status and gain the respect and admiration of others, people will work, complete and deny themselves many of the more obvious incentives. Deprived of these incentives man will want them as intensity as a hungry man wants food. When an individual's social needs are thwarted by managers, his organisational behaviour may become anatagonistic and unco-operative as a consequence of the deprivation.

The competitive desire to excel—to surpass the performance of one's fellows—is almost a universal human trait.

This major esteem need, if properly utilised, can produce extremely high organisational performance. A manager's stimulation of these needs and their subsequent satisfaction by the employees lead to the recognition of self-worth, capability, self-confidence, strength and adequacy being useful and necessary in the organisation. But thwarting of these needs produces feelings of inferiority, of weakness and of helplessness. Unlike the lower needs, the ego needs are apparently insatiable.

Even if all these needs are satisfied, we may still often expect that a new discontent and restlessness will soon develop, unless the individual is doing what he is fitted for. A musician must make music, an artist must paint, a poet must write, if he is to be ultimately at peace with himself. What a man can be, he must be. This need Maslow designates "self-actualisation." In the cluster of needs for self actualisation we find the individual's needs for realising his own potentialities—self fulfillment, continued self-development, self-expression and self-assertion. Self-assertion class for freedom of action and independence of thought in work performance. The emergence of the needs for self-actualisation, writes Maslow, rests upon prior satisfaction of the physiological, safety, love and esteem needs. The Maslow, people who are satisfied in the needs for self-actualisation are basically satisfied people, and it is from these needs that we may expect the fullest "creativeness," "independence," "autonomy" "discretion," and "personality expression."

In short, according to Maslow, individual behaviour is motivated by an attempt to satisfy the five basic needs, arranged in a "hierarchy of prepotency". It means that the most prepotent goal monopolises consciousness and the less prepotent needs are minimised, even forgotten or denied. When a particular needs if fairly well-satisfied, the next pre-potent need emerges to dominate the conscious life and to serve as the centre of organisation of behaviour. Since gratified needs are not active motivators, it is the unsatisfied need that dominates one's thinking and acts as a powerful, though often unconscious, motivator of behaviour. Thus, Maslow's theory "predicts a dynamic, step by step, causal process of human motivation," explaining how behaviour is governed by a continuously changing set of "important" needs. Maslow's theory is undoubtedly correct in its broad outlines. Its frame work is not intended to be a static, rigid portrayal of the individual; rather Maslow views human behaviour in dynamic and holistic terms. Its central flaw, however, lies in all men have the same hierarchy of needs.

The asserts that higher level needs normally do not emerge until lower level needs have been relatively satisfied. The five-way classification of needs is somewhat artificial because in a real situation all needs are interacting together within the whole man. The renowned Dobzhausky has rightly pointed out that biological and cultural evolution go together, interacting and usually mutually reinforcing each other. There is feedback between genetics and culture. Social needs are not separate and disparate as Maslow thought, but cultural urges which originate from and interact continuously with the genetic drives. This understanding is important for the librarians, for it makes clear that the drive to secure food, and the urge to acquire money and to be loved, are continuously interactive. To give each sequential priority in terms of an arbitrary hierarchy as Maslow has done does not seem to accord with the facts we know today.

Psychologists agree that deep and perpetual satisfaction can be achieved only the extent that high level needs are net. The higher lever of the need, the greater its power to give lasting satisfaction. It follows that only two top needs of Maslow's hierarchy—the need of self-esteem and self-actualisation, can provide the enduring motivation for they are the only needs that do not blunt a person's satiety, as the economic law of Diminishing Marginal Utility has its limitations in its application here. The greatest motivation, however, is provided by a chance to work towards the fulfillment of the fifth and highest need. People who display the greatest enthusiasm for their work are usually those who have an opportunity for creativity and for continual development of their skills and powers.

One gets support from the experiments carried by Frederick Herzberg, who maintains that positive motivation is provided only by a chance for self-actualisation—for achievement and "the accumulation of achievement may lead to a feeling of personal growth....accompanied by a sense of increasing responsibility". Maslow also writes that for self-actualisation needs, increased satisfaction leads to increased strength. When we examine people who are predominantly growth motivated, "gratification breeds increased rather than decreased motivation, heightened rather than lessened excitement". The ubiquity of the need for self-actualisation is evident, not only in the towering intellectual products of a Spinoza or an Einstein, but also in the first faltering efforts of a toddler to walk unaided or of a pre-school child to print his own name. To most humans, philosopher or carpenter, child or adult, the attainment of desired achievement goals, and the attendant approval occurring to such attainments, are important sources of personal satisfaction and security.

Nonetheless, Maslow's theory of motivation based on the hierarchy of needs is not all moonshine. Due largely to the popularisation of the model by Douglas McGregor Maslow's theory came to be widely discussed and used by both organisational theorists and practising managers. Study by Boris Miai, Jr., supports the model by showing that managers and professionals in the United States highly value self-realisation, whole service and manual workers value job security most highly. Maslow's model also applies to under-developed countries like India, where workers live under below-subsistence conditions. As would be expected, they emphasise basic physiological needs—physiological and security—remain unfulfilled, this can have a serious effect on motivation. Even in developed countries, the managers should constantly bear in mind that most people have needs that spared over the entire spectrum of Maslow's hierarchy of needs.

Herzbergian Model of Motivation

One of the most stimulating, influential and controversial theories of motivation has been presented by Herzberg and his associates variously termed as the "two-factor theory," the "dual-factor theory," and the "motivation-hygiene" theory of motivation. From their supporting data collected on the basis of research Herzberg and his associates purported to find a two factor explanation of motivation. According to them, man has two different categories of needs which are essentially independent of each other and effect his behaviour in different ways. First, is the man's need as an animal aimed at avoiding pain emerging from the environment; and second is his need as a human being to grow psychologically. Herzberg and his associates designate the first category of "hygiene-factors," or "Extrinsic" factors, or "Maintenance" factors because they describe man's environment. In this group of needs are included such things as monetary gains, status, interpersonal relations, supervision, organisational policies and administration, working conditions, job security, and personal life. These hygienic factors, maintains Herzberg, do not serve to promote job satisfaction or motive a man; rather their absence of deficiency can create dissatisfaction. Such a dissatisfaction may be reduced by hygienic measures such as fringe benefits, 'human relations', training for supervisors, or better administrative policies; but such measures won't make workers satisfied. For true satisfaction to be obtained, Herzberg and his associates put forth a second group of factors or job content factors—the 'intrinsic factors,' also referred to as "need motivators"; since they seemed to be effective in motivating people to superior performance.

The "need motivators" include work itself, recognition, achievement, advancement, possibility of growth and development, responsibility, and challenging work. All of these are concerned with work itself, rather than its surrounding—physical, administrative, or social environment. If the worker to be truly motivated, the job itself is to be the major source of that motivation.

All other hygiene factors can only serve to "clean up" the environment and prevent dissatisfaction. Their presence will not motivate people in an organisation; yet they must be present, or dissatisfaction will arise. The presence of "dissatisfaction" may lead to low morale, but its elimination will not enhance motivation. Only the factors contained in the second group, or the job-content factors, are found to be the real motivators, because they have the potential of yielding a sense of satisfaction. Clearly, if this theory of motivation is sound, it does mean that management should seek to enrich the job so as to make it seem more interesting and important. Herzberg, thus, clearly indicates that the factors involved in producing job satisfaction are separate and distinct from factors that lead to job satisfaction but not to job dissatisfaction are classified as "satisfiers," while those that are important for, and lead to, job dissatisfaction are classified as "dissatisfiers".

The major hypothesis of the dual factor theory of motivation is that the satisfiers are effective in motivating the individual to superior performance and effort, but the dissatisfiers are not.

Maslow deals with the general trend of growth in motives among human beings: this has led him to develop theory of motivation based on the hierarchy of needs. Herzberg focusses his gaze on persons in terms of how job conditions help them in satisfying the motives enunciated by Maslow. Maslow is helpful in identifying needs or motives, while Herzberg provides us with insights into goals and incentives that tend to satisfy these needs.

Thus in a motivating situation, if you know what are the high strength needs (Maslow) of the individuals you want to influence, then you should be able to determine what goals you could provide in the environment to motivate these individuals. At the same time, if your know what gals these people want to satisfy, you can predict what their high strength needs are.

The expectancy/valence model is a cognitive theory of motivation. Whereas Maslow contracted upon the broad general objectives of man's behaviour as being need satisfaction; Vroom presented his expectancy theory of motivation to explain why motivation may vary from person and form situation to situation. Drawing heavily on the earlier works of Lewin, Tolman, Vroom's theory projects that human behaviour is to a considerable extent a function of the interactive processes between the characteristics of an individual and his or her perceived environment. In fact, it is the assumed existence of these anticipations, based on the individual-environment interaction, that differentiates expectancy/valence theory most strikingly from other theories of motivation.

In essence, Vroom's model is based on four points that research on human motivation suggests are valid:

1. People have preferences among the various outcomes that are potentially available to them.

2. People have expectancies that certain outcomes will follow their behaviour.
4. If any situation, the action a person chooses to take are determined by the expectancies and the preferences that person has at the time.

In short, Vroom's theory may be put as under:

Force = Valence x Expectance.

In this equation, force is the strength of a person's motivation. Valence is the strength of an individual's preference from an outcome, and expectancy is the probability that a particular action will lead to a desired goal. In view of such a situation, the investigator thought it advisable to control any influence exerted by "personality" as a variable. Emotional stability and instability are believed to the most important factors of personality. Perception and the evaluation on situation are significantly determined by the emotional state of the individual. Thus the emotional stability and instability were considered to have some influence on the perception and evaluation of a working situation.

5

Public Relations in Libraries

Many specialised Public Relations Department to advise both elected members and officers. Such departments normally include a press office which issues press releases and generally deals with press matters. In some authorities it is insisted that all press enquiries are handled by the press office and not by the individual departments. This is part of the corporate dimension of modern local government public relations. Like much of corporate management this has advantages and disadvantages for the public librarian.

On the one hand, it means that PR is handled by one or more public relations professionals. On the other, the fact that library publicity has to be channelled through an intermediary can put a further barrier between the library and the audience for which it is intended. The relationships between the library department and the authority's Public Relations (PR) Department are in themselves quite crucial. It is the librarian's responsibility to give the PRO advance warning of events publications, and other matters that he or she wants publicised. Where, as in Lambeth, the Public Relations Department produces a newspaper of its own, this can provide the library service with an extra channel of communi-cation. A number of librarians, however, have expressed the view that the library's message can sometimes be swamped by the other duties of a local authority's Public Relations Department. Much of British local government PR is concerned with matters such as anti-litter campaigns, or promotions to stop dogs fouling footpaths, or producing posters to persuade people to pay their rates on time.

These are of course important subjects, but one wonders if library publicity might not suffer through being associated with them in the mind of the public. In one local authority, such was the feeling against the library being swallowed up in the corporate identify, that the library staff designed, promoted, and used their own departmental logo in preference to that of the parent authority. There is the further point as to whether public relations staff, more used to designing campaigns of the 'stop dogs fouling footpath' variety, are the best-equipped people to promote the rather different library message.

Library PR Departments

In the United States, many libraries have their own Public relations Departments, some employing specialist journalists, artists, photographers and broadcasters. In a paper prepared for the 1978 ALA pre-conference on library public relations, Kathleen Rummel suggested that a library with 50 to 100 full-time equivalent (FTE) staff should have 2 FTE persons assigned to PR, while in a library with 100 FTE staff and above there should be 'a base of 2 FTE persons assigned to PR with one additional staff person for every 100 staff.' In the British public library context, separate Public Relations Departments simply do not exist. Some authorities, such as Leicestershire, have posts designated for a PR librarian, while other employ publications officers (e.g. Sheffield) and graphic designers (e.g., Shropshire County). With the exception of the graphic designers, most of these posts have been filled by professional librarians rather than by people professionally qualified in public relations. There are some advantages in employing professional PR personnel. In general, the press and broadcasting organisations prefer dealing with fellow journalists.

The media organisations also tend to feel that a professional public relations person will prepare and present materials in the right form for them to use. It is also true that a PR professional is, initially at least, likely to have more contracts than a librarian entering the work for the first time. Both professional librarians and professional public relations people should have communication skills, and there is no doubt that the right kind of librarian can do a very effective PR job. In additions, library public relations does require a person who can understand the library and its functions. Whoever undertakes library PR must be the type who can take the initiative. He or she must also possess sound judgment and really believe in the importance of the library client. Good public relations is not just a matter of informing people about the library and its services, it is also very much about listening to people, to their ideas, enquiries, and complaints.

Volunteers

Some public relations activities lend themselves to the employment of volunteer labour. For example, some libraries use trained volunteers as tour guides. Quite reasonably, trade union members object to volunteers doing a job that should be carried out by paid members of staff. For the sake of good staff' management relationships, consultations with appropriate union representatives should always take place before unpaid help is employed.

Training

It is the task of management to ensure that all staff are aware of the importance of public relations. There may be resistance on the part of some librarians who think that public relations is merely a series of circus acts below their professional dignity. The function of positive public relations should be explained to them; in particular it is necessary to emphasise the importance of human relations.

The earlier this is done the better. Every induction programme for new staff should include a section on dealing with people. A course designed for a new assistant might include all or some of the following:

1. An explanation of the library's policy on everyday matters, such as smoking, wheelchairs, rowdyism, dogs, etc.
2. A session on how to deal with complaints and when to refer them to more senior members of staff.
3. The use of the telephone.
4. Local bylaws.
5. Interpretation of rules and regulations.

Above all, such a course should stress the importance of high standards of service and behavior. In addition to induction course, some libraries include public relations in their general training programmes. Training can play a part in changing staff attitudes to PR. However, this is a long-term process and it would be foolish to suggest that entrenched attitudes can be changed by just one course. As convenor of the Sheffield Libraries Coordinating Committee's Working Party on the Training and Education, the writer was involved in the presentation of a course on library public relations. The course itself was very successful, but a number of participants made the point that the people who would have most benefited from it did not attend. This is perhaps an example of selective exposure mechanisms at work within our own field! In recent years Buckinghamshire and Shropshire Country Libraries have both devoted their annual training courses to public relations, making use of their own staff and outside speakers. In general, however, public relations has not featured in enough internal or external training courses. The staff manual should also include a section on public relations. Indeed, the philosophy of PR should permeate all sections of the manual, especially those dealing with rules and regulations; management should decide just how many rules and regulations are really necessary. Restrictive regulations should be kept to a minimum and where rules do exist, staff should be encouraged to interpret them liberally. Very often junior staff can appear unnecessarily bureaucratic to the client, not because it is in their nature but because they do not have the confidence to bend the rules. It is up to senior management to encourage staff to give people priority over petty procedures. Too many public services in Britain seem to be organised to catch the 1 per cent who abuse them, rather than to help the 99 per cent who want to use them.

Libraries need not, and should not, be organised in this ay. It is up to senior staff to set the right style. One is both encouraged and discouraged by the views of chief librarians on this subject. The diversity of approach is well illustrated by the discussion that took place at a recent meeting of chief librarians. At one extreme there were those who were advocating a new and complicated procedure for registering out-of-authority readers, while on the other there were those who, quite rightly, wanted to make joining any library service as simple as possible, It is worth emphasising that this was a meeting at which the librarians were free from direct political constraints and could express their own views, In so doing, they demonstrated their own attitudes towards the public they serve-attitudes which they are also, no doubt, communicating directly and indirectly to their staff. No doubt, those who advocated stricter control of membership did so on the basis that they would be saving public money. This in itself is arguable, but what is more significant is the costs of such a policy, to individual library systems and to librarianship as a whole, in terms of public relations. For those members of the public faced with such a petty restriction, the library becomes just another bureaucratic organisation placing barriers between the client and the service he or she requires.

The person who is already suspicious or frightened of local authorities may not try to join again. This is not to say that costs are not important: on one would argue that in today's economic climate. Library management needs to be aware of the costs of public relations, but equally it needs to be aware of the costs of not allocating resources to public relations-costs such as lack of public interest or decreased public an political support for the library service.

Public relations rarely appears as a separate budget item in a British public library's estimates. In fact, such a heading is relatively rare in the United States where there is a tendency to call it something else. Also in the US many libraries include programming (talks, film, shows, concerts, etc.) under the same heading a public relations. This makes and assessment of the size of the 'pure' PR budget difficult. Rummel suggests that 'a rule of thumb is that 10-15% of your budget should be applied to public relations, community relations, and programming. When calculating the costs of public relations, it is important to include all the costs involved. For example, the costs of issuing a press release will includes some or all of the following:

1 The cost of posting X number of copies.

2 A percentage of the cost of the office equipment used to prepare and reproduce the release.

3 The cost of stationery used.

4 The costs of any photographs included with the release.

5. Staff costs (time spent creating and writing the release, time spent typing the release, time spent duplicating, etc.).

With PR as with any aspect of management, it is vital to know how and why money has been spent.

Planning

Expenditure on public relations has to be carefully planned. Indeed, planning and preparation can make or break a library's public relations activities. PR should be planned to achieve clearly defined objectives. The planning process needs to include a consideration of the human and other resources available to help attain these objectives, an estimate of the financial resources required, and an indication of target dates for achieving objectives. Priorities will, of course, have to be established within any given timetable. Once overall objectives and priorities have been ascertained and consideration given to the resources needed, the library public relations person is in a position to consider specific matters of detail. As part of this process it is necessary to look at the library service through the eyes of the library's various publics. Clients, staff, non-users, legislators, and suppliers will all have different perceptions of the library and its services. For each of these groups the library will have, in balance-sheet terms, PR assets and PR liabilities. Senior library management should seek to identify these assets and liabilities as an integral part of their public relations planning. In a typical public library, assets light include helpful assistants an accessible location, a reliable reference service, and so on.

Liabilities could include belligerent staff, erratic overdue procedure, negative notices, and the like. One of the functions of library PR is to reduce such liabilities to a minimum. By paying close attention to all aspects of the service, it is possible to draw up a public relations balance sheet listing those things which help and those which hinder the library's image. On the basis of such preparation, one can begin to produce a practical programme of activities tailored to the library's needs and resources. It will be necessary to plan some things well in advance, but a PR programme also needs to be flexible, so that the library service can quickly respond to new events and demands.

As a vital part of a library's internal public relations it is essential to involve staff in the public relations planning process. As stated earlier, there may be staff who are suspicious of the value of the whole idea and it is especially necessary to secure their cooperation and support. There is no easy way of doing this but certainly it will be much difficult if plans are announced to them without any warning.

It is difficult but not impossible. The real problem is that the cost of such measurement may be greater than the cost of the public relations effort itself. To measure the results of a campaign, which attempted to change public attitudes and opinions towards the library service, would require quite sophisticated and expensive research. It would be even more difficult and costly to try and measure the long-term cumulative effects of public relations. Public relations is an act of faith. One of the functions of PR is to act as an insurance against the future. Thus, a library service wants to keep its public informed, not just for immediate short-term benefits, but also for a future time when it may need their help and support. During my tour of the United States we asked every public relations librarian. 'How do you evaluate your results?' The most common replay to my question can be summed up in the response, 'We hope it does some good'.

Faith and hope, then, play a large part in the PR person's philosophy. There is, however, little room for charity. Library public relations does have to justify itself. Certainly, a library committee, spending rate-payers' money on library publicity and promotion, will want some indication of the possible benefits of PR to the library and the community it serves. Of course, before any kind of evaluation can be attempted, it is necessary to know what any particular public relations activity was intended to achieve. No public relations activity should be embarked upon without a clear understanding of what the library hopes to gain from it.

The precise nature of the 'measure' of their effectiveness will obviously vary with the kind of activity undertaken. In the following paragraphs some possible methods of evaluation are discussed. Some of these have been used by American library organisations and others have been tried by commercial public relations concerns on both sides of the Atlantic. In my view, none of the methods described is rigorous enough to give anything more than a general indication of the success or failure of any particular public relations activity. Such a lack of precision is not just a problem in library public relations but in public relations in general.

As two leading PR consultants write: 'The public relations profession is striving for practical, universally applicable methods of evaluation, but it must be freely admitted that for the time being the practitioner and the management area obliged to put their faith in personal observation and empirical evidence of the many public relations programs which have been followed by good results.' A number of American libraries have used various forms of media exposure analysis to measure the success of failure of their press and broadcasting relations. Press cuttings are one yardstick by which a librarian can evaluate his or her public relations activities. If press releases consistently fail to be published, it may be that there is something wrong with the nature of the release or that they are being sent to inappropriate newspapers and magazines.

A very simple measure is simply to count the single-column centimeters of coverage received by the library in the press. Though this will tell you little more than that the library received so many centimeters of coverage, such an analysis can usefully be taken further by examining the type of publication in which the library service does, or does not, obtain coverage. When evaluating radio and television coverage, some libraries in the United States keep a detailed record of all those stations that carry library material, noting the amount of air time devoted to the library service. The report of the one library's Public Relations Department contains an itemised listing of radio and television announcements'.

Another library gathers information from local radio and television stations on their usage of library publicity material. Records can also be kept of the number of people who attend a library promotional event, such as the showing of a library film, though there is some evidence to suggest that the people who attend such events tend already to be well informed about the service or topic being promoted. In general, it is very important to remember that media exposure analysis only shows the extent to which a public relations item has been used by the media. The fact that a library's message has been disseminated does not by any means guarantee that it has any effect. The success or otherwise of a public relations activity does not just depend on the campaign itself, but also on the audience for it. Even when a library has been successful in 'reaching' the public with a message, people still have to interpret that message for themselves. Individual psychological, sociological, and geographical factors will cause some people to discount, distrust, or simply ignore the message. An individual's selective exposure mechanisms can determine just what information he or she pays attention to, It is not unknown for people to avoid actively some forms of information (if you are a smoker how do you react to anti-smoking campaigns?), while others may be simply apathetic. A number of public information campaigns designed to promote some most worthy causes have floundered because of such audience factors.

In exceptional cases, a library service may wish to commission a survey of clients' attitudes before and after a campaign or promotion. Opinion research, is however, likely to be expensive but it is a false economy to attempt to do such work 'on the cheap'. The result obtained from a badly designed questionnaire or poor interviewing are likely to be worse than useless in that they may well be misleading. Personal feedback from clients, councillors, and community leaders may provide information which may be more useful in assessing the library's public standing. The increase in the use of a library's services following a publicity campaign may be a measure of the effect of a campaign, but not necessarily so. It will require quite sophisticated research techniques to isolate the effects of a campaign from all the other internal and external factors that may, or may not, have led to an increase in the use of service.

When attempting to measure the effects of public relations, one must beware of confusing correlation with causation. With some public relations activities it is possible to encourage audience response directly. For example, a coupon can be include with a publication inviting readers to mail a comment or request to the library. New York Public Library has used this technique to measure the effectiveness of its direct mail publications. This particular method can lead to very biased responses and results need to be interpreted with great caution. Similar techniques can be used to measure the method is to include a write-in competition as part of the show. Fund-raiding campaigns may be more directly evaluated by reference to the size of the dollar contributions, though, no doubt, an individual or group donation may also depend on external economic factors.

Research is needed at both the micro and the macro level. There is a need to answer operational questions about such things as the successes or otherwise of a library exhibit, or the extent of press coverage, but also we need to study public attitudes to libraries and to examine the nature of the criticism of library services. We have no way of really knowing if criticisms of library services. We have no way of really knowing if criticisms of library services derive from the services themselves, populist views about public expenditure, or simply- or rather complicatedly-lack of knowledge. It may be that attitudes to a service change with time. Trend studies of attitudes to libraries might help us find out. Research in this area is not going to provide quick or easy answers but that should not prevent its being carried out. Most of the research that has been done on the effectiveness of library public relations activities has been at the micro. Rather than the macro level.

The British Library Research and Development Department has funded some studies of PR techniques. One based in Newcastle attempted to evaluate the effects of promotional techniques on library use, in particular that is small service points. Investigated direct mail advertising as a method of 'selling' the library. Although both were interesting and well-documented experiments, their results were somewhat inconclusive. In Sweden, as Greta Renborg has reported, a few attempts have been made to evaluate public relations activities, particularly those aimed at the non-user. In the United States, Sue Fontaine's study was intended 'to examine the state of the art of public relations in selected 'to examine the state of the art of public relations in selected public libraries. "He report does look at evaluation but reflects the lack of rigorous measurement techniques that we have noted else-where. The commentary to the tape-slide presentation developed from the study states: 'How do you measure public relations successes or failures? ... It's public opinion that counts. Increased use of the library... and increased support in terms of dollars tell how well we are doing our job. Also from the United States comes a report of a pilot project to 'illustrate the effectiveness of a tailor-made public relations campaign'. This was centered on Adel Public Library, serving a population of 2,500, and was primary concerned with the effectiveness of library community relations.

The public relations officer for the State Library Commission of lows has no doubts about the success of Adel's community relations programme. She reports: 'Hundreds of new users... circulation has increased dramatically.... more funding from he city... organisations are contributing money for a new film projector and screen.. a slide projector has been donated... volunteers renovated the basement.... and a Friends group has been formally organised'. These are very positive results and it is to be hoped that the effect of the campaign is continuing and that such good results can be duplicated elsewhere. Few librarians have felt able to be so sure about the effects of their public relations efforts because, as we have noted elsewhere, the evaluation of PR is a difficult and expensive task. However, it is also a necessary one. It is essential to evaluate library public relations in order to establish just how far a library such evaluation should be an integral part of the planning processes for future public relations activities. The evaluation of library services has long been a concern of the Public Libraries Research Group. As part of its current work on public library performance measures, the group has produced a statement on library public relations.

6

Training and Leadership

Personnel management is a 'root and branch' consideration, not to be left to a few interested 'management types' at the top of the tree. Everyone, from first line supervisors to the chief librarian, must play a part in ensuring that there is efficient use of their subordinates, and one of the corner-stones of this efficient use is training. Looking back over the last few years public libraries have been affected by many changes, some from within the profession, some from outside. These changes have inevitably had a bearing on the services of the public libraries and indeed, at times, their ability to offer a 'comprehensive and efficient service' as required by the 1964 Public Libraries and Museums Act. In addition many of these changes have affected staffing resources, and some of these are mentioned below. Since the reorganisation of local government in 1974 Public Library Authorities are much larger organisations, which have tried, in many cases, to offer a broader base of service than hitherto.

One of the consequences has been the development of more specialised functions and roles for library staff at all levels, and there has been a shift in emphasis in what libraries traditionally provide. For instance, the growth of Team Librarianship had meant a complete reappraisal of functions and skills and such massive changes create both opportunities and problems in the management and training of staff. There are many examples of training programmes formulated by public library authorities which are designed to cover a whole spectrum of activities. One can find specimens of programmes designed to cover everything an inner-city service, and some of these will be considered later. One of the depressing influences affecting public libraries (and in fact many service industries) over the last few years has been the economic climate pertaining in the United Kingdom.

After a relatively expansionist period during the late 1960s and early 1970s public libraries, generally, have been made to tighten their belts since the mid-seventies and the cold realities of the eighties have meant that phrases such as 'rate capping', 'procurement cuts' are common parlance in library circles. In the need to economise one of the major targets has been staffing, often with a view to protecting the book fund, but this has come doubly hard at a time when there has been increasing demand on services and a push from within the profession to diversify and widen the scope of provision to the users. It has become, therefore, increasingly important to maximise the potential of existing staff and in this instance training has a substantial role to play.

A more positive factor influencing training has been the realisation by many authorities that it should be tackled on a systematic basis, and one way of ensuring this has been to appoint specialist officers to organise and generate activity in this field. In some cases this has been a full-time training officer, in other cases a personnel function is involved. Less preferably, and more commonly, officers who already carry other responsibilities are nominated to act as the training specialist, apparently in their spare time! Larger authorities such as Manchester, Birmingham and some countries have had specialist personnel sections, including training officers, within the Libraries Department for many years but the last decade has seen a growth in the employment of library training officers both in countries and Metropolitan District either based entirely in the department or operating from a central personnel unit. The factors mentioned above have had a very mixed influence on staff resources in public libraries. In recent years many unpalatable decisions regarding library personnel have had to be taken, but the need to train is nevertheless paramount. Without training we are perhaps jeopardising our relationship with and services to the public who still regard libraries as one of the more acceptable faces of local government.

The librarian must employ all the abilities he or she has as manager in order to maintain existing services as well as introduce new ones, and one of the most effective strategies he or she can use is a well organised and effective training programme. Public libraries have a wealth of resources on which they can draw, both external and internal, to achieve good training practices. These include their own staff, with specialist knowledge and skills, who can be used on internal programmes and courses and local authorities' personnel departments, which can help with general principles and guidance as well as participating in training. Polytechnics, colleges and library schools may be willing to offer their services either in direct nearby library authorities could possibly share the cost of training as well as help organise programmes on a co-operative basis.

The Library Association and other similar bodies regularly organise courses and organisations allied to local government, such as the local Government Training Board, will assist in the setting up of programmes in addition to giving advice on training. Given the necessary commitment there is no reason why good training practices should not be achieved. A half-hearted 'short in the dark' is not to be recommended, though unfortunately this happens all too often. A systematic more positive examples of public library training programmes are described. This is one area of training which is essential and for lack of which there can be no excuse! If systematic training is being organised then this is an obvious starting point. Many textbooks, guidance manuals and accounts of existing practices are readily available to assist the would-be-trainer. One basic text, which given examples, is the Library Association's Sub-Committee on Training Guidelines for Training in Libraries-Systematic Induction, written by P. Robertson. This deals with areas such as the different categories of employees benefiting from induction, the special needs of schools leaves, the training of those responsible for induction, checklists and the use of other resources.

Many public library authorities have well-developed induction programmes, for example Bolton, Cambridgeshire, Hampshire, Sheffield, Tameside an Trafford. Trafford's programme includes an induction package in the form of a folder which is handed to new starters on their first morning at work. The folder contains the appropriate job description, a statement of particulars relating to their conditions of service a number of 'in-house' forms to be completed by the employee and two copies of an induction checklist. There is also an introductory booklet which outlines the work of the library service, describes the major conditions of services, gives a general guide to the locality, including bus and rail routes, and a further reading list which may help the new recruit during the first few weeks of employment. This information pack is backed up by a welcome from a senior member of staff, guided induction training by the appropriate supervisor as well as a four-day induction course which usually occurs within the first six months of employment. Cambridgeshire and Hampshire both have comprehensive induction checklists and detailed instructions relevant to particular posts, whilst Derbyshire provides a checklist for induction of pre-licentiates. Although checklists are now regarded as a traditional form of induction training it is fundamentally important that they are properly understood and used by the supervisor concerned.

Without skilful manipulation the checklist can become so much waste paper to be consigned to someone's personal file, never to re-appear, and, crucially, never to have been of any use in the formative period of someone's employment. The introduction of such a checklist is a beginning but its utilisation by trained supervisors is critical, and to ensure that the qualitative as well as the quantitative aspect of the checklist is secured it is essential that supervisors themselves are fully trained in their use. Some authorities have accompanying evaluation of their induction programme so that at the end of a given time, usually between three and six months, a report on the progress of the new recruit is complied and examined.

Trafford Libraries have such a system, a detailed report on the employee's ability, character and potential being sent to the personnel officer by the supervisor. Any remedial action, including re-training, can then be subsequently taken, as necessary. Other methods and techniques can be used in induction, depending on circumstances. Many country library authorities which are geographically diverse face particular difficulties in ensuring systematic and uniform training and centralised induction, but even some of the most rural have evolved excellent programmes. Cornwall Country Libraries employ a modular approach to their training and this is described in detail in their Staff Training Manual. Different modules are available to suit the particular level of members of staff being inducted, thus ensuring a uniform approach under difficult geographic circumstances. Bolton employs a modular approach to induction courses for library assistants through 1 half- and one-day course.

Other formal aspects of their induction training include a detailed checklist and an interview with a senior member of staff at the end of the first twelve-month period. Derbyshire organises regular headquarters familiarization courses both for new recruits and established members of staff. These course, of three days duration, enable staff to have an opportunity to hear about the work done by the headquarters of a large country library system. Hampshire Country Library holds similar course for both professionals and assistants which are carried out at the library headquarters, whilst Birmingham Libraries have a five day induction course for librarians and assistants held at three separate venues throughout the week.

An important element of this course is public relations training and this is particularly emphasised by the City Librarian in his introduction to the course programme. This area of what one can term attitude training should be uppermost in the trainer's mind during induction. It is relatively straightforward to teach and explain man routines and systems, but not always so easy to inculcate the correct attitudes expected of the staff. However, one can expect problems at a later stage from the new recruit and from their colleagues and supervisors if this aspect is neglected. There is no obvious single method of induction training relevant in every situation, and it is reassuring to see the determined and varied efforts made by public libraries in tackling this important area of training. For those about to embark upon systematic induction programmes we would strongly recommend the Library Associations's publications mentioned previously as a suitable starting point.

Job Training and Instruction

Job training, sometimes known as 'sitting next to Nellie', is practised universally in all organisations either consciously or unconsciously. This common assumption must, as Edwards implies, be challenged by all trainers. Although the instruction of staff takes many forms, for example the simple command or the planned learning programme, it fails to be effective unless the training is given at the optimum time by the most appropriate person. Unfortunately, there is often a tendency on the part of librarians to equate training with short courses carried out away from the work area, but in fact a great deal of the learning process takes place on-site either through direct instruction or through serendipity, the sink or swim approach! It is important that each facet of the job is taught effectively to the trainee, and the key element involved here is the quality of the trainer. Wirral Library Service hold a two-day, in-house course which covers the main areas associated with the organisation and execution of library training.

The emphasis is on a participative approach by course members, and involves role-play, group discussions and case studies designed to simulate live situations in the work place. Traffored Library Service's four-day supervisory course for junior professionals includes one day devoted entirely to training, with the emphasis on job training and instruction. There is a mixture of lectures outlining in a practical way the various elements of systematic training, and this is followed by a participative session where each course member plans and carries out a simple instructional programme using other members as the 'trainee', Sheffield City Libraries have also identified job training and development as an important area. They have held seminars for large numbers of staff on the principles of on-the-job development training, and are planning courses on counselling and coaching skills for librarians and supervisors.

Sheffield has also introduced a self-learning scheme for the Youth Training Scheme trainees within the library service. Instead of the traditional guided tour of the library a Central Library Trail is used in which the trainees, in pairs, explore various departments following guidance notes and instructions provided to them at the outset. There are questions to be answered along the way, and if all else fails they are instructed to ask the staff! In all the five trails covering the departments of the central Library. This is an interesting methods of guided self-discovery which should help in the familiarisation process, and replaces what may be a rather uninteresting piece of conventional instruction form a trainer.

One method more widely employed by public libraries, particularly in the training of library assistants, is that of job rotation. It naturally benefits the trainee to become familiar with all aspects of the library's work in which he or she may have to become involved in the future, and at the same time alleviates the problems of boredom and disinterest. Careful consideration must be given, however, to the regularity of the rotation to ensure that adequate time is allowed for staff to assimilate the necessary skills associated with a new work situation. Clear verbal and written instruction must of course be given at each stage. Staff training manuals can either be a help of a liability in job training, depending largely on their accuracy, up-to-training in mind, using a lucid, step-by-step approach to each facet. They should be used to confirm rather than inform once initial job training is complete. Leicestershire Libraries and Information Service developed their job training programme through the use of packages to cover certain areas of work, including the 'effective use of team time', 'issue and counter routines' and 'basic enquiry work'. This latter package is still used and comprises notes and programmed instructions on the basics of handling requests and dealing with enquiries in the library, along with examples of the necessary stationery.

This type of training can be used for small groups of trainees, or on a one-to-one basis, and enables a uniform and consistent approach to be achieved. It is surprising that this method has not been adopted on a wider scale, particularly where many of the clerical and administrative routines lend themselves to a programmed learning approach. Job training, therefore, requires a well planned and systematic approach from the trainer. The key element is the quality of 'Nellie' and therefore training the trainer must be the first priority.

OFF-THE JOB TRAINING

Off-the-job training is often dealt with in summary fashion by the 'we'll send them on a course' attitude, and it is easy to be led into the subtle trap of using courses, both internal and external as a substitute for properly organised job training. The aim should be a blend of the two, each being used at the appropriate time in a person's training and development Handled skillfully, of course, off-the-job training constitutes a much needed ingredient of staff development both for present post held as well as preparation for a future role the trainee may have in the organisation. As the term implies, off-the-job training takes place away from the work site, and can take many diverse forms- short term secondments to other departments or sections of the service, for example, or educational/training courses such as the City and Guilds Library Assistants' Certificate or the BEC/ COTEC Certificates which include modules on library studies. Internal and external courses, formal and informal group discussions and seminars are also an integral part of off-the-job training.

Trainers often have an ambivalent attitude to the relative merits of external and internal courses. Internal course, if well prepared and carried out can be a much more cost effective methods of training because they can maximise the use of existing resources within the organisation. It is often possible to hide any necessary expenditure and the training itself may be more valid because it can be tailored directly to the needs of the participants.

External courses have to be the paid for in hard cash which necessarily limits the number of staff able to attend, particularly if there are high add-on costs such as subsistence of external courses is often difficult for the Training Officer and the exact level and content of the course sometimes impossible to ascertain. On the other hand external courses often fulfil a specific training need for a small number or even individual members of staff which could not effectively be dealt with internally. Similarly courses organised in-house may have the disadvantage of seeming amateurish, of being too close to home, resulting in interruptions, hit-and-miss attendance through staffing difficulties, or poor presentations by speakers who themselves have not been properly briefed. The Library Association's Working Party on Training gives a basic guide to assessing internal and external courses.

Turning now to externally-based training, and the use made of it by public libraries, there has undoubtedly been a strong tradition amongst organisations in the field of librarianship to offer short duration courses, both nationally and regionally. The Library Association and its groups, notably the Association of Assistant librarians and the Youth Libraries Group, organise many courses across a wide curriculum, a list of which is published in the Record. Other bodies such as ASLIB individual colleges of librarianship and even individual library authorities offer short duration courses on a national and regional basis.

Some of these organisations also offer courses covering a particular aspect of study. This has been examples in recent years by courses provided by the College of Librarianship

Wales and the North West Division of the Association of Assistant Librarians. In the case of CLW the expertise is drawn directly from the college's own resources, thus providing a relatively inexpensive method of training a number of staff.

The AAL courses can be taken to a particular authority and be geared specifically to the needs and requirements of their particular staff. General subjects such as supervisory and personnel management are areas that perhaps best lend themselves to this type of arrangement. There may not be a pool of expertise within the individual authority or there may be other domestic difficulties preventing the organisation of internal courses, and, therefore, this type of training can alleviate these problems. Individual library authorities have, within the last few years offered courses in particular subjects to other public libraries.

Two notable examples of this are the London Borough of Sutton, which has arranged one-day courses on Merchandising within the Library, and Northamptonshire Country Library's course on Local History Publications. Again this is an excellent method of using a skill by a particular authority, sharing their expertise with other libraries which may not have the necessary resources to set up an internal course. It has been said earlier that job training activities form a basic equipment within an organisation, but any public library with a commitment to training will appreciate that there are certain types of training which require staff to be away from the distractions and hurly-burly of their jobs.

Public libraries such as Cornwall, Sheffield and Renfrew all have well developed in-house programmes. Cornwall's Staff Training Manual lists training and development courses for all levels of staff from Assistant Country Librarian to Library Assistant and this encompasses a whole range of modules for each category of staff. Sheffield City Libraries organise internal programmes in a variety of topics. Their one-day customer relations courses use exercises, questionnaires and role-plays as well as extensive audio-visual material.

This type of course can be invaluable not only for new recruits but for the more experienced member of staff. Reference was made under Induction' to the need for attitude training, not only for the new starter but also for others who have worked in the organisation for some time who may not always have picked up the right habits when it comes to dealing with people. Emphasis can easily be placed on the nuts and bolts of clerical and administrative training whilst attitude and interpersonal skills take a back seat, either because they are thought too difficult to teach or merely because of an assumption that everyone knows how to deal with the public anyway. One current area of debate is the development aspect of training and in view of some of the obstacles previously mentioned (financial constraints, etc.) this is becoming a matter of concern. Brief mention has already been made of some of the lengthier training/educational courses available for library staff and this is obviously a very fruitful methods of ensuring their development, both as individuals and as members of the workforce. Whilst it can be argued that some courses are primarily educational, one cannot discount their effectiveness in enhancing knowledge, skills and attitudes.

Some public libraries regard the BBC/SCOTEC and City and Guilds Certificate as a prerequisite for promotion and offer secondment to one or more staff annually. Larger systems, such as Lancashire Country Libraries, are very generous in enabling a number of assistants to attend. The courses are usually organised by Further Education and Technical Colleges, and support by public libraries has been quite encouraging. The City and Guilds Certificate, the shorter of the courses, is of one year's duration and is essentially a practical introduction to libraries and library skills. Students usually attend for half day per week with an examination at the end of the course. It is a fairly gentle introduction to the work of the library for staff wishing to know more about the background to their job. The course covers areas such as the organisation of libraries, arrangements of stocks and use of the catalogue, loan and circulation procedures and office practice in libraries.

The BEC/SCOTEC courses, leading to the National Diploma, are much broader based and more intensive courses. Students are expected to attend for a full day per week for two years. Subjects other than library studies are an integral part of the course and these include accountancy, economic, statistics and the role of the organisation in the environment. The library studies module forms approximately one quarter of the course. Although one might be tempted to argue that this constitutes too small a percentage of the whole, the benefits accruing to the individual may outweigh the disadvantages.

The broader base of subjects covered helps to widen horizons and give better understanding on other facets of local government. Some authorities have found that staff seconded who more aware of their role within the organisation but are capable of assuming greater responsibilities. It is, in addition, a potential stepping stone to higher academic achievement either at university, college or library school. A relatively new innovation in Scotland has been the introduction of a correspondence course leading to the Scottish Certificate in library and information science.

The course lasts for two years and is organised by the Telford college of Further Education in Edinburgh. Students are sent forty-four student units, one every two weeks, and there is a residential week each session at the college. Each student has a personal tutor at the college who keeps in touch and assessment is by regular assignments and college examinations in the residential weeks. He college is also adapting the study units to a produce a one year's course leading to the city and Guilds Certificate for library assistants, will have to spend their own time studying for such a qualification although one hopes that there will be some financial acknowledgment and reward by the employer both during and at the end of the course. For professional staff there are courses, usually leading to a qualification, such as the BA conversion, and the part-time post graduate courses in librarianship, as well as various management based programmes such as the Diploma in Management Studies and MA Librarianship, the latter being offered by a number of library schools. Recently, all these courses have become popular and public libraries have supported their staff on them.

It is, however, the responsibility of the training officer and/or the supervisor to assess and monitor the progress of the member of staff attending such a course. Regular counselling and discussion sessions should be organised to ensure that the person concerned is able to cope with the work and the commitment involved. These sessions also enable a check to be kept on the organisation and content of the course to see whether or not the objectives are being achieved. Sending staff on these lengthy courses is expensive and the trainer must make sure it is not being wasted. Developmental training within the organisation is also an areas which public libraries have recognised as being essential. There is, of course, no clearly defined line between this type of training and that relating and that relating to a person's specific job, as one tends to evolve from the other.

Many of the external professional courses mentioned earlier may form an integral part of a person's development and it may often be the only method that some public libraries use to help staff in this way. Some authorities, however, have taken a more positive approach, realising that there is a need to develop their staff in a more planned and structured way. Certainly few library systems can claim similar training programmes established by examples within the private sector where their managers are pushed through development 'hoops' for most of their working lives, but there are examples where determined efforts have been made.

Liverpool City Libraries in conjunction with the department of Management at the Liverpool Polytechnic have organised development courses for their senior staff, lasting five days. A variety of topics include resource allocation, identification of problems in managing public libraries and an appreciation of performance counselling using a problem-centered approach. The first of these was reported as being highly successful and the course will be repeated as often as necessary. Derbyshire Country Libraries development training is carried out either in-house through courses specifically for library staff or through the Manpower Services Division of the Country Council who offer an annual programme of courses, including management development activities.

Some of the topics covered within this area are management of human behaviour, a middle management programme and post professional training. There is a similar arrangement in Tame-side where the central Personnel department offer a variety of general courses aimed at officers within the whole organisation. Wirral Library Service has also recognised a need for developmental training both through internal and external programmes. In responses to new initiative within the service, such as the introduction of new technology, courses are organised for both professional staff and assistants. Trafford Library Service has recently been looking at this area following discussions by the Authority with the Local Government Training Board. A working party has been established to examine in more detail what can be achieved given the limited resources and other problems such as in-built resistance by some staff to participate in any formally organised scheme! Their considerations have been, up to now, related to management rather than professional development, which may result in a widening of roles for managers and even inter-departmental secondments in the future. Development training, therefore, is of immense importance in public libraries, particularly at a time when a variety of skills and expertise is expected of staff at all levels, combined with an increasingly demanding public and scarcity of resources. As with other training, however, it must be carefully managed. It is a failure by the organisation and manager if this type of training is not given due recognition for there are everyday examples where staff can and need to be prepared for more difficult and demanding tasks, maybe within the scope of their present job as well for roles they may assume in the future, demanding higher degrees of knowledge and skills.

Professional staff in particular are expected to carry our jobs which they may never have considered within the scope of a librarian when they first entered the profession and whilst it can be argued that times change and staff must be adaptable, the onus is one the organisation to ensure they are encouraged and helped through well planned developmental training, either on or off the job. A relatively recent introduction in training has been co-operative ventures between public libraries as well as university and college libraries. There are obvious advantages and benefits in that there is a sharing of expertise, costs, accommodation as well as interaction between staff with varying experience and attitudes. Two examples of such co-operation are in the North East of England and in South Yorkshire where local Training Officer groups have been established to discuss training matters within libraries, and in addition, take a positive approach by organising programmes for staff of the various libraries within the area. The North East group was established in 1980 and, with the support and encouragement of the Local Government Training Board, has provided courses on interpersonal and communication skills and on coaching and counselling staff. An account of their activities in the first two years has been written by Ralph Major who describes the tangible results of the co-operative venture. As well as the two courses mentioned above, these include a compilation of training resources, and co-operation between libraries in enabling staff to attend each other's internal courses.

One course arranged by the group on computerisation was a very co-operative affair involving not only public libraries but also the Department of Librarianship at Newcastle Polytechnic and members of the book trade. The LGTB, too, have assisted on their coaching and counselling skills course. In Sheffield there is a Libraries Co-ordinating Committee involving the city library, university and colleges and within this group is a working party on the education and training of library staff which, as with the North East co-operative venture, organises courses for staff of the various libraries.

The local training officer group (LTOG) in South Yorkshire libraries, organises courses and exchange of experience seminars as well as an annual debate on a current topic of interest within the profession to which all library staff in the area are invited. These schemes are excellent examples of how training can be organised on a co-operative basis. Where one or more libraries may not have the time, financial resources or expertise to arrange off-the -job training a co-operative venture could certainly help, although it would be wise to seek advice before attempting to set one up. It has to be a truly co-operative exercise with everyone playing a part rather than a couple of willing workhorse doing all the arranging and keeping the group together. Inevitably in these circumstances co-operative will not last long! The fourth of the Library Association's Guidelines on training, written by Alan MacDougall, deals with this very subject and gives sound practical advice on setting one up. Off-the-job training provides a splendid opportunity to use a variety of techniques to help and stimulate the trainee which often cannot be used, or would simply be inappropriate within a job-training programme.

Many of the courses mentioned above use case studies, role plays, simulation and in-tray exercises to help in learning. Provided that these techniques are used appropriately within the programme they can often make telling points which the trainee will remember. However, there is often an understandable reluctance on the part of staff to participate in an exercise in which they may be made to look foolish in front of their peer group and it is, therefore, the responsibility of the trainer to make certain that all instructions are clearly understood and that staff are not unnecessarily embarrassed by any such device. There is also, an excellent range of films, video and tape/slide presentations which can contribute much to a particular training situation and these can either be made in-house, by Video Arts. Certain areas of training lend themselves particularly to the use of A/V materials, for example interpersonal skills and supervisory work. Perhaps Health & Safety at Work is the obvious example where films etc., can form the focal point of the training. A clear and concise tape/ slide presentation made by Cheshire Libraries and Museums Service some years ago is a good example of libraries using this material. It is highly relevant in that it describes problems specifically associate with health and safety in the library and can be used either with small or large groups or even as part of the induction of a new member of staff.

The other benefit is that it is portable and can be shown any where, thus saving time on having to organise a programme at one central point. Wirral Library Service in-operation with the college of Librarianship Wales has recently produced a tape/slide package on working with the public, which forms the basis of on-going training in branch libraries. This is the first in a series to be produced by CLW, aimed at library assistants, and may be purchases by other library authorities or individuals. Salford and Bolton Libraries have each produced in-house videos. Bolton's film entitled All in a day's work deals with public relations, and Salford's on story telling to children. Both authorities use them in the context of training programmes for professional staff and assistants. Looking generally at the activity of training in public libraries there have been major efforts made in certain areas during the last few years. Induction training has been recognised as a crucial aspect of the librarian's and supervisor's work and by now the majority of systems at least appear to make use of the checklist. Other training seems to be a more hit-and-miss affair with some authorities having a co-ordinated systematic approach whilst other claim that time and money is not available, and therefore, formalised training must suffer.

Role of the Training Officer

Obviously one of the key figures concerned with public library training is the designated training officer. Large public library systems such as Birmingham and Manchester have employed specialist training staff for some years, and whilst many authorities still do not have such a full-time post within the libraries department there has been a growing recognition of the need for an officer at an executive level to control training and there are examples, even in the smaller metropolitan districts, of such officers. Admittedly, there are many examples where their time is not exclusively given over to training, and there are examples, even in the smaller metropolitan districts, of such officers. There are many examples where their time is not exclusively given over to training, and their posts may encompass other managerial and operational duties. There have been numerous reports in recent years which recommend the appointment of a designated training officer. Foremost of these is the Library Association Education Committee Working Party on post-qualification training, published in 1974.

Research undertaken by LAMSAC for the Department of Education and Science, which subsequently formed the report 'Staffing of Public Libraries', also supports this by recommending one training officer for every 200 non-manual staff, but admits that so much depends upon the training policies of the overall authority. The duties of the training officer are to establish a training policy for the library service in conjunction with his/her fellow management officers, and then to implement the policy-by co-ordinating and generating appropriate training activities. He or she generally 'oils the wheels' of training rather than engaging in its direct policy on a day-to-day basis.

The role is to establish priorities, assess needs in co-operation with line managers and supervisors, organise the most appropriate form of training, liaise with other personnel inside and outside the organisation and carry out the administrative duties of training officer will also attempt to measure the effectiveness of training using evaluation and validation techniques, although to be candid, this is a difficult area which appears not to have been developed to any depth in the public library field. An equally important role for this officer is to ensure that line managers and supervisors are themselves trained in the techniques of training, and some public libraries have recognised this as a significant prerequisite to sound training practice by organising programmes for appropriate officers.

One particular category of staff which should be highlighted in relation to public library training is the licentiate and pre-licentiate. Libraries have always recognised the problem of the newly qualified member of staff, fresh from library schools with little or no practical experience, but expected to assume responsibilities and carry out duties with which they are not always familiar, and more importantly, in which they have received no training. Unfortunately, not everyone has come to grips with the problem and this was recognised by the Working Party on the Future of Professional Qualifications which endea-voured in its report and recommendation to tighten up the Library Association's requirements for a much fuller and wider ranging training programmes for post-qualification staff. This was endorsed by the Library Association Council and has been in operation sine 1982. Public libraries, by and large, have responded to this requirement in a positive way. For each pre-licentiate recruited a programme must be submitted to the Library Association for formal vetting and approval.

This system is intended to ensure that the newly qualified member of staff will receive a sound practical training programme in their duties as well as background information on the work of the library and any other area necessary to equip them for a professional job in the future. This also applies, incidentally, to people appointed to temporary posts, such as schemes funded by the Manpower Services commission, and libraries must recognise their responsibility to offer appropriate training in the same way as with full-time, permanent appointments, whether or not the member of staff concerned is likely to finish the pre-licentiate year with that particular scheme. Newcastle City Libraries have an excellent programme which has been completed by five pre-licentiates to date, and which has, naturally, been further developed in the light of experience since its inception. The aims and objectives of pre-licentiateship are outlined in the written programme, including the responsibilities of the supervising librarian and the requirements of the Library Association in acceptance of the candidate for licentiateship.

The important element of induction is included, along with the general framework and core areas recommended by the Library Association. The component parts of these areas are professional practices (e.g. book selection, stock maintenance, readers' advisory and enquiry work), technical skills (e.g. book acquisition, use of specialised bibliographical tools and equipment) and interpersonal skills, including basic supervisory, management and training responsibilities The programme itself is arranged on a modular basis in order to give a certain degree of flexibility, each module varying in length according to the function and scope of the section or department involved.

The co-ordination of the overall programme is done by the City Librarian, and in terms of the Library Association's requirements he is the supervising librarian. The pre-licentiates meet the City Librarian on a monthly basis for discussion and progress reviews, and arrangements are also made for their visits, projects and logbook of training and experience. Trafford Library Service has a full programme for pre-licentiates. This comprises various elements including on-the-job training, an important aspect because the pre-licentiate is appointed to a specific post and is, therefore, not extra to the establishment. Off-the-job training constitutes secondments and attachments to various sections and libraries lasting from three days to two weeks, and visits to other library systems. The pre-licentiate also completes a detailed logbook which is examined prior to the monthly meeting with one of the Assistant Borough Librarians and carries out a project which is of a practical nature and, where possible, contributes to the work of the

Department. A final lengthy interview with the Borough Librarian and other appropriate senior staff to discuss the training year in general, and the project in particular, rounds off the programme. The licentiate-to-be is given opportunities to continue his/her professional development through attendance at course, meetings and working parties, and is encouraged to join in professional activities of the Association. A further area of training in which public libraries have been strongly involved is that of library schools field work.

Many authorities have recognised that it is important for librarians to assist in the training of the newest 'recruits' to the profession and whilst, as in other training areas, there are good and had examples of fieldwork training, in general public libraries expend a lot of time and effort in ensuring the student is given a sound programme during the limited time they are seconded to libraries. It is easy for experienced staff to criticize the quality of post library schools applicants for jobs, but unfortunately, not so easy to give a commitment to their training in the formative' period within the profession, bearing in mind particularly the nature of library education vis-a-vis practical experience.

Many public libraries organise well balanced fieldwork placements which cover a mixture of practical experience through working in one or more sections or departments of the library with opportunities to see and hear about the majority of the library's service through visits and discussions with appropriate departmental staff.

Community Librarianship

One particular area of training to which public libraries have given recognition during the last few years has been in response to a change in emphasis of the nature of library services and a growing awareness of the need to become more attuned to the requirements of their communities.

Community librarianship, the commonly used term for this change, can involve the preparation of community profiles, the establishment of a community information service as well as the traditional advice and research involved in reference librarianship. There are obvious implications here for the education, training and recruitment of staff. This type of librarianship requires an approach and image which many be far removed from the traditional one, and training is one of the key factors in this brave new world. Community librarianship, particularly inner city provision can be an extremely sensitive area of work, and attitude and familiarisation training is an essential requirement. It can be argued that training in any sphere is a matter of applying certain principles and techniques, and whilst this is true, merely 'putting on one day course' on community librarianship for field work staff is not good enough. It should be rather a much more planned approach, identifying specific needs and then using a combination of methods, making use of both internal and external courses and seminars, job training, coaching and counselling and ensuring that staff at all levels are conversant with the necessary skills and knowledge for their new and possibly difficult tasks and duties. There are some notable examples of training carried out in the field of inner city working and one of the noticeable themes running through this training is the diversity of methods employed.

Manchester Cultural Services have in the last few years adopted a system of team librarianship with emphasis on developing the role of the library in the community. The Manchester area has culturally mixed communities with large Afro-Caribbean and Asian populations in areas of the City. They have appreciated the need for staff to be aware of the pitfalls in serving ethnic minority communities and the City Council has inaugurated a policy of cultural awareness, accompanied by relevant training programmes. Library staff have already attended race awareness courses organised by the Education Department as well as organising their own more professionally based course. This included outside speakers and dealt with areas such as racial bias and the library and racism in books.

Along with other similar library systems Manchester has appreciated the need to ensure that staff at all levels require basic attitude training rather than leaving the whole question of provision to minorities as being the singular responsibility of an ethnic minorities officer, and thereby refusing to acknowledge multi-racial provision as an important area of concern for all members of staff. Similarly, Derbyshire country Library has accepted the importance of race awareness training, and to this end it has organised courses for both professional staff and assistants, and Tameside Libraries and Arts plans to hold comparable courses, dealing with basic problems such as names, language and communication, and information needs of ethnic minorities. Birmingham Public Libraries report that there is on-going training in this area, including seminars for both professional staff and assistants on such topics as understanding different cultures and problems associated with communications in ethnic minority work, the latter using the BBC film Cross Talk. They did, some years ago, organise a week's residential course entitled 'Ethnic groups in Birmingham- a background study'.

Over thirty members of staff attended from a wide range of departments and levels within the City Library and it was, naturally, a full programme on the study of different ethnic cultures in Birmingham. Speakers were used from outside the library, including representatives from the Community Relations Councils, Community Relations Office, the City Education Department and local groups and associations. Whole sessions were devoted to the various ethnic groups and there were practical exercise as well as films and visits to a mosque, a Sikh temple and a Hindu temple. Leicestershire Libraries and Information Service, which has a high percentage of ethnic groups, particularly in the City of Leicester, uses both internal and external courses for training its staff in this area. There has been a series of half-day seminars on services to black communities and participation in the Education Department's series, entitled 'Know your neighbour', which comprises visits to various community venues such as temples. The annual intermediate training course for over thirty library assistants also includes work in the ethnic minority communities.

Community Information

Another area of service which has developed over the last few years, as mentioned earlier, has been community information. There has been a growing number of nationally and regionally organised courses as well as individual public libraries which have conducted their own internal training. Manchester Cultural Services has arranged seminars for professional staff which stressed the need for co-operation with other related organisations and bodies concerned with disseminating this type of information and speakers included representatives from the Citizens Advice Bureaux, Welfare Rights office and the DHSS. Birmingham Public Libraries, as with Services to Ethnic Minorities, have arranged a full residential course on community information. Speakers included members of the library staff as well as ones from outside, such as Bradford Libraries, Leeds School of Librarianship, the University of Nottingham, and from specific agencies, groups and bodies within Birmingham (e.g. Citizens Advice Bureaux, the Urban Renewal Department, Voluntary Service Council). It is interesting to note that along with other sessions on this subject there was one on the implication of training in community information. Since this course there has been a City Libraries Management Team Policy Statement on community information which includes notes and overall guidance to staff. An even more useful tool is their community information training package. Packaged training, can form an important adjunct both to job and off-the-job training or even a basis for actually instructing and guiding staff. Birmingham's is an excellent example of packaged training, including functions such as the acquisition and organisation of resources, enquiry work and referral, publicity and promotion of services and a sample training sheet used in the Small Health Library. As is emphasised in the package it is a basis for training, not a substitute for it! There are guides to books and other information which will be of use in enquiry and advice work as well as notes on the use of the index to information and advice service in Birmingham.

The sample staff training notes for Small Heath Library are a fairly informal but detailed aid to staff who need to know about the basic areas of the community information service.

Training Needs and Staff Appraisal

In the two chapters so far there has been an emphasise what one could term the 'middle part' of training, or actual execution. Training does not just happen, and that has to be starting and finishing points. Whilst one should never assume that training has been complete it is important that each programme should follow some sort of process. One simple way of examining such a process is through which is known as the Training Cycle. The assessment or identification of training needs, therefore, must be talked first and foremost, and one should not be lured into the trap of just 'doing some training' on the spur of the moment without first considering who needs training, what it is they need, who will best carry out the instruction and by what methods.

There are, of course, organisational as well as individual requirements, for instance the introduction of new routines, procedures or services all have training implications, and it is the job of the library supervisor and training officer to recognise these needs initially and to consider how they can be fulfilled most effectively. It is all too easy to say that someone will 'pick up the threads as they go along' or 'if they read the Staff Manual it will tell them.' Staff do not respond well to this attitude and in turn this will be reflected in their approach and commitment to their job. One system which may, if so designed, help in the identification and analysis of needs is that of staff appraisal. This is not particularly widely used in public libraries although there are a few exceptions.

Appraisal tends to be regarded with extreme suspicion by staff and trades unions as a means of disciplinary action, either official or unofficial, as well as being a 'big brother' technique of managerial control. The industrial widely, and an important element of this can be to give both supervisor and supervised active encouragement in the planning of training by using appraisal interviews and records to identify needs. It is of course a technique which requires careful handling and needs a great deal of thought and planning as well as commitment and time once the system is operational. It also requires training of all staff concerned; the appraiser and appraisee must ensure unopen and co-operative environment from which both problems and training needs can be identified and handled correctly. Unfortunately this is not easy to achieve. Some local authorities have adopted appraisal techniques both formal and informal.

The Co-ordinating Librarian in Renfrew District Libraries interviews each member of staff once a year to discuss their future needs and requirements. Whiles the system used is not too formal it appears to be a good way of forward planning from which one can extract a great deal of training information. It is also a continuous process, an important point to bear in mind, rather than a stop-part method which will only serve to confuse and dis-illusion staff. Hampshire Country Library has a staff counselling and career development scheme in operation which takes the form of annual interviews with supervisors. There is an interview summary form completed for each person which is subsequently examined by the Personnel and Training Officer and this provides a good indication of an individual's perception of training needs.

One disadvantage reported in this case, however, is the delay in places being obtained on courses run by the central Manpower Service Department when this method of training may have been identified as satisfying a particular need. This can often be a problem in training, particularly when training resources are out of the control of the client department. However, Hampshire at least has made an attempt to get down to analysing needs on a systematic basis, which, unfortunately a great many public library authorities appear not to do. In a slightly different way Tameside Libraries and Arts participate in an authority-side assessment of needs analysis as part of the annual training plan and budget. Each member of staff receives a Training Needs Assessment form which enables individuals to assist in planning their own training programme.

These forms are divided into sections containing further education, in-service/short external courses and practical/other training, When completed, the forms are checked by the appropriate supervisor and ultimately by a senior member of staff. When staff training requirements have been agreed and approved the form is returned to individuals indicating which type of training will be most appropriate. If completed well, this type of assessment may indicate many areas which will not necessarily be picked up by the usual methods, and could also indicate organisational as well as individual needs. Other public libraries report a much less formal approach to appraisal and identification of needs, preferring to have supervisors identifying those needs on a day-to-day basis. Provided that these supervisors have themselves been instructed and guided, this methods will probably form the bulk of training needs assessment for new library assistants whereby a report is sent by the supervisor to the training officer which assesses their capabilities and identifies weaknesses and further training requirements.

Other public libraries have adopted a similar approach for new staff, but in many cases formal training needs assessment appears to stop once he probationary period has been completed. Overall formal appraisal linked to training does not appear to be a particular or well used technique in public libraries. The examples given above are fairly isolated cases, maybe because of lack of time, but more likely through in built resistance by groups and individuals. However, it might be said in its favour that appraisal need not be ultra-formal, using elaborate systems and complicated forms.

Renfrew's system, whilst probably time consuming, will in all probability identify the vast majority of individual's needs over a particular period, in additional to allowing a senior member of staff to have regular chats with staff, thus possibly creating a climate within the system where everyone excepts to be involved in some training on a regular basis. Coaching and counselling techniques may also be used as a means of identifying gaps in training. These techniques, can assist staff in solving or working through problems by advice rather than taking either a more dictatorial stance on the hand or a 'letting them get on with it' attitude on the other. As mentioned previously, it is a technique being developed by certain public libraries such as Sheffield.

Evaluation

A notoriously difficult area of training is evaluation. It is, to say the least, an inexact science. A great deal of time and effort must be expended in order to ensure that the money and time has been effectively spent. Effectiveness of training can be measured in many ways depending upon the type of instruction used (e.g. course, job-training, programmed learning, etc.) although there appears, even amongst training personnel in public libraries, a natural reluctance to spend a substantial amount of time on it. It is understandable in that many areas of library services are extremely difficult to measures, and staffs' work and training may often be geared to non-measurable standards.

For instance, how is one to measure attitude training in a scientific way without spending an inordinate amount of valuable time? It is more likely that certain responses are sought from trainees at the end, or even during, a programme rather than employing a professional firm of training consultants at unacceptable costs! The trainer will hope, in all probability, that the outcome of such training will be a change for the better in attitude as monitored by their supervisor in a working situation. The popular method of evaluation is the post-course questionnaire, where at least there is an attempt to evaluate the course its (i.e., was it well planned and organised?, were the teaching/learning methods appropriate?, did the course set out to achieve what it purported to achieve?), and with more difficulty, what the trainee learnt and how it may be applied in his/her job in the future.

East Sussex Country Council has developed this a little further by a training evaluation and validation questionnaire which is in two parts. Trafford Library Service adopted a similar method in their series of supervisory courses using a pre-course questionnaire which attempted to stimulate the trainees' thoughts about the forthcoming training. A fairly full post-course questionnaire, giving plenty of room for comments, and linked to the pre-course questionnaire by using related questions in order to ascertain any change in attitude, was sent one month after the completion of the course. This time lag was carefully predetermined in order that more objective opinions and comments on the training would be forth-coming.

Newcastle City Libraries' assessment of their training programme on the Lending Enquiry Desk was a combination of end of course evaluation seminars and post-course assessment forms. A report on the trainees' comments was complied and sent to their Training Working Group for further consideration. Another popular methods of evaluation is the post-course report written by the trainee. This is popular not least because it requires little or no thought and effort on the part of the trainer. Whilst it can be useful for stimulating discussion on the contents of the course as an evaluation tool it is of extremely dubious quality, particularly where no guidance has been given to the trainee. In general there appears to be little activity in evaluation of training by public libraries. It is, as mentioned earlier, a difficult area, often including terminology which is in itself confusing.

The Library Association's Guidelines on Training have included Evaluation as one of the sections, written by Alan Gurr, and this, thankfully, is a clear and concise introduction to the subject. Over the last few years it appears that training in public libraries throughout the country has been patchy. Undoubtedly some library systems do recognise the need to take the matter seriously and have made great strides in the training field. Unfortunately training was a subject much discussed during the 1970s with many courses and meetings organised up and down the country but depressingly at the present time there appear to be other concerns which militate against its development in many systems.

Many libraries today are engaging in strategic planning, scenario building, and other future-oriented exercises. They are trying to understand the future, so that they can prepare themselves with the right combination of skills and resources to meet its challenges. Leadership is one such resource, and the need to focus on its role within the library profession is critical.

Leadership

The question continues on where and how we find leaders. There is a body of literature on the study of leadership which explore whether leaders are born or made, whether leadership is a collection of traits that a person has or whether leadership is a collection of traits that a person has or whether leaders emerge from a unique situation or circumstance. The methodology used by two sets of researchers includes interviews with and observation of acknowledged leaders, as well as discussions with their peers, associates, subordinates and bosses. They examined what characteristics these individuals displayed that lead others to reorganise them as leaders and how these characteristics manifested themselves. Although described in different words, both studies identify five strategies employed by these individuals: vision, communication, trust, risk, and empowerment.

The ability to see or to imagine a future that goes beyond what others believe possible was primary characteristic of the individuals identified by these two groups of researchers. The direction their enterprise should take and the view of what the best possible future should look like was crystal clear. The compelling nature of their vision provided a hook on which other could hang their commitment, their loyalty, and their own sense of purpose. The capacity to envision a unique image of an ideal future is crucial to leadership but meaningless without the ability to communicate that vision. So much of what is truly innovative and has the potential to reshape our views is lost through an inability to be articulate, to fire the imagination of others. The leaders in this study were those who were able to get the people around them to commit to and support their vision.

A high level of trust is needed to take individuals and an enterprise through an ambiguous period of transition into an uncertain future. One way that leaders are able to inspire others to do new thing or act in unaccustomed ways for a greater good is by modeling a particular set of behaviours themselves. Individuals reported that part of their willingness to follow their leader in new directions was derived from his or her demonstrated personal commitment to a goal through consistent, personal efforts. Leaders are also identified by others as those who challenge the status quo, experiment, and take risks. This does not seem to come as much from a desire for excitement as from a desire to learn. Learning is seen as a requirement for growth and change.

The leaders in these two studies showed a bias towards action and viewed the mistakes they made and those made by others as part of the learning process. Partly a strategy in itself and partly the logical result of the other four strategies, individuals around these described leaders felt strengthened by his or her actions and through his or her presence. When leaders create a vision that is a true reflection of the values, needs, and desires of those they intend to lead, their followers feel supported on a very deep level. They are more able to commit to and work toward the goals that have been articulated. They feel challenged and derive a greater sense of meaning from their work. In combination, these five strategies provide us with a model for understanding leadership. One of its strengths is that it makes sense.

Some of us watch leadership from afar as it operates in society at large. Others have been lucky enough to work with a true leader and have been able to observe these actions close at hand. For most of us, this conceptual framework matches with our personal experience. The question still remains as to whether individuals armed with these strategies can provide libraries with the kind of leadership that will be needed to take them into the twenty-first century. To answer this, a better understanding of our anticipated future is required.

THE FUTURE

We look around and we can all see changes and trends that will have an impact on the way we operate both personally and professionally in the future. Gareth Morgan and Joseph Johnston Jr. have identified a number of these trends from which we have chosen those that we believe have the greatest relevance for libraries. Other eras have experienced enormous changes brought on by social, economic and technological developments. The difference today is that, along with the complex and large-scale character of the changes facing us, the rapid rate and ongoing nature of these change processes leave us with a sense of constantly being in a state of flux or transition. Libraries will have to be prepared to add and eliminate services and technologies as need and demand shift. Library organisations were designed to produce a consistent, quality product-retrievable materials. Our structures will have to be revamped to permit us to be more responsive to these shifts. Libraries have always been in the business of collecting organising and facilitating access to knowledge.

The information explosion has already had an enormous impact on the ability of libraries to maintain these traditional functions. We must prepare ourselves as society refocuses its attention and energy into an area that has traditionally been our private domain. We have always seen information as an inexhaustible resource. More and more, we are hearing it described and used as a commodity. We except and our clients except that libraries will continue to offer the same, high quality services that have been offered in the past. The quandary arises when opportunities for new or improved service present themselves. With little or no more money being added to base budgets, it is difficult to see how new programs can be created and the same standards of quality maintained. A larger number of groups of individuals are being recognised as having a stake in the success or failure of an enterprise's endeavors. They can include the staff, the clients, and the suppliers.

Organisations are beginning to learn to exploit their commitment by giving them a larger role in functioning of the organisation. In libraries, we find staff want to be more involved in decisions that will affect the quality of their work life. Libraries are looking to publishers to recognise the partnership in which we're engaged in order to be more influential in the choice of paper used in book publishing of the price of serials. The changing nature of work and the decentralisation of power has lead to organisations that are less hierarchical.

The increased interde-pendence of the various units requires a greater emphasis on collaboration and a need for more and better communication structures. The use of groups in the management processes of libraries has grown phenomenally over the past fifteen years. Traditionally, the role of the middle manager was to pass information up and down through the organisation. With increased access to information at all levels through local computer systems, organisational structures are likely to continue to flatten. The problems that face libraries now and that will confront them in the future will continue to grow more complex. They will require a variety of perspectives to understand and solve them, involving more people in the process. As the choices grow more difficult to make, a greater willingness to take risks will be necessary to avoid paralysis and to develop the kinds of innovative solutions that will be needed. Most library reward systems do not currently support these needs. By focusing only on successful completion of tasks, they discourage attempts to try new approaches which traditionally have greater potential for failure.

By developing our ability to understand and anticipate the future through the analysis of current trends, we also enhance our ability to influence the future. Organisations can no longer afford to merely manage what happens to them. They have a responsibility to increase their effectiveness by trying to shape and influence the elements within their environment. From these projections, we can begin to develop a picture of the kinds of knowledge or skills our leaders will need in order to meet these challenges. First and foremost is the ability to deal with ambiguity, to function effectively in situations where the rules and boundaries are not clear. Because there will be so few anchors, the ability to make choices and focus energy, (one's own and that of others), will also be important.

Most efforts will be collaborative, rather than individual. An understanding of group dynamics and strong interpersonal skills will be essential to effective functioning. These group activities and the multiple constituencies we anticipate will make the ability to communicate clearly critical to personal and organisational success. The leaders the library profession will need in the future must be able to employ the same strategies identified by the leadership studies already mentioned. Because of the ambiguous, uncertain nature of the future that we face, we will need leaders who are willing to take some risks and try new things.

One of those risks will be making a commitment to a particular course of action and focusing the energy on an entire enterprise on the accomplishment of that goal. In order to do that, out leaders will have to share their vision; they will need to communicate effectively their sense of purpose to others. They must possess both a good knowledge of individuals and groups and an understanding of what motivates them to make strengths of others and how to build on those strengths. They need to make people feel uplifted, not diminished, by their commitment to an enterprise, a course of action, and a vision of the future.

Learning to be leaders

There are three issues to be considered in leadership training: what needs to be learned, where it should be learned, and how it should be learned. It the second part of this chapter, we will focus on specific competencies of leadership and how they might be nurtured within library organisation. If we examine current research on how individuals become effective managers, we can find clues that will help up to develop models for effective leadership training libraries. By examining life histories, researchers at CCL were able to identify four arenas that play a major role in the development of successful, high-level executives. They were challenging assignments, other people, hardships and significant events. Challenging assignments included starting something from scratch, cleaning up a messy situation, taking on a project or being a part of a task fore team, increasing responsibility, and switching from a line to a staff position.

There were two ways in which other people had an impact on the development of these individuals: both negative and positive role models were identified; and memorable events of short duration, both positive and negative, demonstrating the impact of interpersonal interactions were described. The kinds of hardships identified by the CCL study were errors in judgment or mistakes that led to failure, problem staff, having to starting over in a new job or career, and personal traumas. They also included career crises, such as demotions, being passed over for promotion, and lousy jobs- specifically, a job that was different from what was anticipated or desired. Other significant events included courses and formal training programs, early work experiences, (especially first supervisory experiences), and an array of personal experiences that took place outside of the work environment. The CCL study sought to discover how these executives learned to be effective or discovered an ability to be effective through these experiences. Participants in the study identified the lessons they believed they earned from these events. The lessons were clustered then correlated with the appropriate event to see which experience seemed to have the greatest impact on the learning of a particular lesson. We have already identified the strategies connected with leadership behaviour. Let us now explore the relationship between what these executives felt they learned from their experience and what we want out leaders to know or know how to do.

Part of the utility of CCL's study is that it helps us to analyse how the competencies that lie behind the leadership strategies could be consciously developed. If we can identify at least some of the components that support and individual's ability to behave in a desired way, then we can develop activities that will enhance that ability. The ability of focus purpose into a unique, meaningful vision that can be acted upon is the characteristic most often identified with leaders. In many ways this is very similar to what the CCL study called setting and implementing agendas.

Four of the lessons related to this quality would be useful in developing visionary potential: knowledge of technical/ professional content, understanding how the business works, strategies thinking, and innovative problem-solving methods. Moving from a line to a staff position was the experience that had the biggest impact on learning in these four areas. It helped the individual to develop a greater appreciation for other areas within their organisation. Staff were also able to develop skills, such as planning, financial analysis, and human resources development that encourage and support a border perspective. Outside coursework was also useful in supporting the development of technical or professional knowledge.

If we wish to construct developmental activities such as these in libraries, there are some key elements to build in and some to avoid. An effective staff assignment should be relatively short, about a year, and involve some form of organisational analysis to encourage abstract thinking. Strategic planning is ideal, but projects that focus on financial analysis or program development could serve the same purpose.

During this process, the individual should report to someone higher up on the organisation. This special reporting relationship makes the experience more meaningful by providing access to feedback that is broader in nature and gives the individual a greater sense of contribution. Routine jobs in personnel and administration do not provide the same kind of the developmental growth. Two other experiences that support growth in this arena are opportunities to start something from scratch and to fix something that's gone awry. As technology changes what is done in libraries and how it is done, we have more opportunities to provide start-up projects for those identified as having leadership potential.

Developing new services for the public and new internal processes and procedures fit into this category. The critical elements are that the individual take full responsibility for the success or failure of the operation and that they work through the constraints and the pressures on their own. There are always areas in our libraries that are not working as productivity of efficiently as possible, and sometimes there are areas that need or efficiently as possible, and sometimes there are areas that need a complete overhaul. Rather than allowing these units to languish, the situation can provide an excellent opportunity to develop diagnostic skills and abilities. Individuals engaged in these kind of undertakings learn the importance of careful analysis before action. It seems that most of our approaches to problem-solving are developed during our earliest work experiences. Libraries that wish to encourage innovative thinking can assist staff by offering training in creative problem-solving techniques. These techniques can be institutionalised through effective meeting planning and their use encouraged throughout the organisation. Kouzes and Posner report that, based on their study of leadership, "inspiration" is the most difficult competency to learn. If we approach it from a pragmatic point of view, this issue relates most closely to communication and influencing skills. In the CCL study, the sections which dealt with handling relationships contain some data on influencing, but communication is not directly addressed. Getting others to implement your solutions was most often learned from the earliest supervisory experience.

The lesson was that in working with people, the people themselves are the key to success.There are many projects in libraries that require "but-in" by, multiple constituencies, such as reorganisations, bringing up an online catalog, introduction of fees for services, and changes in performance evaluation systems. These kinds of assignments provide opportunities for potential leaders to make the connection between their ability to communicate the importance and benefits of an endeavor and its successful outcome. The most critical step in the process of enlisting the support of others is understanding the group or groups with which one is working. In order to be convincing, one must know what ideas and ideals are held in common. In order to tap into these commonalities, we must know their values, what they believe in. The need for an analytical approach must be continually understood.

We have all seen situations where a project was undermined because the appropriate level of the energy and commitment had not been elicited from those who had to make the operational effort. Potential leaders must learn how hat advance preparations need to be made to ensure a successful change operation. If we want staff to develop in this area, we must give them feedback on their communication strategies, rather than evaluating them simply on the content. We should provide critical feedback in terms of the mechanics of the communication process.

The message should be repeated a number of times, in different ways, so that as many people as possible can be reached in as many different ways as possible. Examples of what the new approach has to offer should be credible and vivid, positive and hopeful, and passionate. People want to succeed and forms of formal and informal communication should make them feel included in the vision. Formal and informal courses can also aid in the development of effective oral and written communication skills. The trust of other and self-confidence go hand in hand. It is difficult for other to trust us and have confidence in us if we do not have confidence in ourselves. How did the participants in the CCL study think that they developed confidence?

Surprisingly, the mechanism most often mentioned was coursework, with participation in projects and task force a close second. Through courses, individuals are exposed to information and experiences not available in the workplace, The knowledge should be both conceptual and technical in nature. Classes also provide opportunities for self-assessment: sorting out personal strengths and weaknesses, as well as objective comparison with others. Supporting coursework through release time and direct financial aid is a way for organisations to show their support for individual development.

Projects and task force assignments provide the same kind of proving ground that formal coursework offers and can be designed to deliver a high level of development impact. A tight time frame forces staff to get up speed quickly. The small group size ties the success and failure more closely to the individuals working on the project, If the project requires dealing with a variety of groups, the team members learn not only to coordinate their work with each other, but to negotiate relationships with those outside the group, as well. Bennis and Nanus also identify visible, tangible personal commitment to an idea or project as one of he elements that leads people to trust a leader. In CCL's study, the lesson of singleness of purpose and standing up for one's beliefs were most often derived from adverse conditions or situations. Risk is defined as the exposure to a chance of loss. Our ability to take risks comes in part from our desire to do something different or in a different way, recognising and seizing opportunities, and having the confidence to stand along and act. Learning to final alternatives in solving and framing problems seems to come mostly from early work experiences.

Taking full responsibility was also one of the lessons learned through setting and implementing agendas. Participants felt they learned it from all their experiences but most often it was learned in the process of cleaning up a mess and starting something from scratch. Decision making was the skill they felt they'd acquired, and a bias for action was the attitude that went with it. Being prepared to take advantage of the unexpected was learned from difficult situations that forced the individual to exchange the known for the unknown.

Situations that could foster this lesson are those that encourage an individual to move from an area with which he or she is comfortable and familiar, into an area where they do not have the same level of expertise. We do not take nearly as much advantage of job exchange programs as we could in this regard. A successful outcome will support independent risk taking in the future. No one wants to fail or to see others fail. One of the problem with developing risk taking potential is that, in trying to protect ourselves and others from failure, we often become overly cautious and conservative in our approach. Even with all our precautions, each of us at some point in the past has made a mistake, missed an opportunity, or been the victim of unfortunate circumstances. How the organisation deals with these kinds of situations is the key to what learning is acquired from them. The lesson can be "don't ever try that or anything like that again until you're sure," or it can be "let's find out why that didn't work, so that we can try something else that might."

Rosabeth Kanter has described empowerment as a process that makes power widely accessible within an organisation. Her studies have shown that organisations which support. A leader can only empower other to the degree to which he or she is willing to share these commodities. Some of those who reported about their experiences in the CCL study learned lessons that apply to the development of this competency. These include politics as a part of organisational life, the use and abuse of power, discovering that a single person cannot do it all alone, understanding the perspective of others, and finding out how to develop others. Almost all of these lessons were reported to have come from hardship experiences, from failures, demotions, and personal trauma. To a lesser degree, increased responsibility also contributed to these leanings.

There are few who would argue that we should create situations for people to fail, so that they could derive the appropriate lessons from them. The critical factor in dealing with these experiences is learning how to learn from them. Postmortems are routinely done when someone dies, not to find fault, but to understand why it happened. There are many lessons to be learned when something does not go as expected or hoped. We do not wish to stifle the individual creativity and initiative that leads to vision and risk taking in the process of developing empowerment skills. We do, however, want to find ways to help our potential leaders recognise that other have the same desire to contribute as they do. As can be seen from CCL's study, one of the most poignant ways that individuals learn this lesson is by trying to do things along and failing. The true failure is in not recognising the potential of others.

7

Evaluation of Automation Techniques

Some of the more elaborate systems also provide for such functions as conversion of foreign currencies to dollars; automatic checking for possible duplicate orders; reordering from a second vendor if the first cannot fill the order; computation of such dealer performance measures as average length of time to fill an order, or average discount; and provision of information for cataloguing or circulation functions. Acquisition systems also vary in other respects:

1. By type of material handled (most handle monographs, but many do not handle serials)
2. By type of orders handled (many do not handle standing, blanket or approval orders, or gifts and exchanges)
3. By type of payment possible (some cannot accommodate payments in advance, deposit accounts, or memberships)
4. By type of language representable (most cannot deal with nonalphabetic languages such as Chinese, and many do not provide for diacritics)

One of three major technical catalogues are:

1. Those based exclusively or primarily on unit record equipment
2. Off-line, batch-processing systems using computers
3. On-line systems using various types of remote terminals for communication with a computer

Acquisition systems

The typical punched-card or unit record acquisition system uses a keypunch, a sorter, a collator, and a tabulating machine such as the IBM 402, 403, or 407. Cards are punched with order information, and are then sorted and passed through the tabulator to print orders. The punched cards are then placed, with the help of the collator, in the file of cards used for previous orders, to create an order outstanding file; this file may also be printed out in list form on the tabulator. When the books are received, the price paid for each item is punched into one of the cards, which then serves to update financial records, and in some cases to write vouchers or checks. The public libraries of Decatur, Illinois and Lake Country, Indiana provide early examples of such systems. Decatur began late in 1959 with an inexpensive set of equipment (the IBM Series 50) costing $ 375 per month, and used it to produce not only purchase orders but 14 other products as well, including accounting records, statistics, shelflist cards, and book cards. By 1963/1964, the cost for machine rental, material, and equipment had risen to $798 per month, but payroll, budgeting, and circulation functions had been added, the total staff of the library had been reduced, and the library was operating on less money then it had five years previously.

Among university libraries, the University of Missouri, St. Louis University, and the Joint University Libraries of *Vanderbilt*, Peabody, and Scarritt were early pioneers with punched-card systems. The Missouri system was unique in its use of an IBM machine no longer being manufactured, the "Cardatype," rather than the customary accounting machine. The Cardatype combined a typewriter-like keyboard and printing platen with the ability to read unit record cards, punch them, and perform modest computational chores.

Data entered though the keyboard, read from punched cards, or computed in the arithmetic unit could be utilised in the production of printed orders and other records, and as many as four additional typewriter units could be attached to the central unit, each preparing distinctive documents. The application at Missouri is an excellent example of a unit record system in which the same punched cards are used repeatedly to produce various products. The Cardatype, used at the beginning of the process to prepare purchase orders, also produced temporary cards for the public catalog,

Library of Congress card orders, order records, and report slips. A collator was used periodically to search the file of cards for the books on order, and if items were not received within a specified period of time the same cards were used to produce cancellation notices or claim notices. If the items were reported out of print, the card could also be used to request quotations from out-of-print book dealers, in which case a copy of the request from was again placed in the public catalogue as well as in a *desiderata* file. In the St. Louis University application, the order date was recorded in so-called "Julian" or "shop" date from—that is, the number of the day of the year—and this was used to trigger claim notices.

The files were so arranged tat if the items ordered were not received within ninety days of the time ordered, a claim notice was automatically produced. After operating for several years, the system was abandoned for lack of sufficient volume to justify its cost.

The Joint University Libraries system handled fund accounting, produced orders for Library of Congress catalogue cards as well as for books, printed lists of books on order and in process, and produced temporary cards to be field in the public catalog. A special card punch, the IBM 526 summary punch, was connected to the 402 tabulator so that when purchase orders were printed, cards could be punched with the total amounts of each order for use in encumbering funds. The system was converted to a computer operation in 1966 using IBM 1401 and 7072 computers, and is still in operation at this writing. Numerous special libraries had also begun such systems by the mid-1960s, typically using company equipment for a few hours per week. The one at IBM's Watson Research Laboratory is of particular interests.

As books moved from one step to another, the appropriate cards were manually shifted. Three times a week, an IBM 407 tabular was used to print the file, creating a "Processing Information List," or "PIL," which made information on the processing status of any item readily available. The system was later transferred to an IBM 1401 computer, with "recent additions" in one list and the other five categories combined in a second list, still called "PIL." The status of each item was noted in columns corresponding to the five categories, with "Julian" or "shop" date shown for the day each item moved into each category. By observing which column had the most recent date, one could see at a glance the status of each item.

The computer was programmed to identify items which stayed too long in one category, and produced notices of items that required claiming or exporting. "PIL" lists, increasing in sophistication of typography and production, were to become a common feature of later systems until superseded in the 1970s by terminal displays of the same information.

OFF-LINE COMPUTERISED ACQUISITION SYSTEMS

As general-purpose computers become widely available in the 1960s, off-line, batch-processing computerised systems became (and as for this writing, remain) the most common and popular form of acquisition system. Most such systems still use punched-card input, feeding order information into the system in a way not greatly different from unit record systems, but once data input has taken place information is normally transferred back and forth between magnetic tape or magnetic disk files without the necessity of repeated manual handling of cards.

The typical acquisition system of this type, in addition to printing orders, automatically updates the file of information on orders out standing, encumbers the necessary funds and updates the appropriate financial records, stores the bibliographic information for later use, and gathers statistics. Two public library systems are of interest as examples of the transition from unit record systems to computers. Both used a Univac machine, the 1004 Card Processing System, which had capabilities about halfway between he unit record systems and a small computer as the IBM 1401.

The Suffolk County (New York) Cooperative System began with an IBM 403 tabulating system in 1963, and switched to the Univac 1004 a year later, adding tape drives for storage. A unique feature was the use of mark-sensing pencils to record and input some elements of data, such as the list price and discount in lieu of keypunching the information. The magnetic tape drives allowed the system to store fiscal data and bibliographic information for production of catalogue cards. The Nassau County (New York) Library System began with a similar system in 1964; the system was transferred to a Univac 1005 with magnetic tape drives in 1968 so that order and other reports could be printed faster and the information for them stored more conveniently.

By far the most popular computers for acquisition systems in the mid-1960s, however, were those in IBM's 1004 series, particularly the 1401. The University of Illinois at Chicago Circle began using a 1401 for an off-line acquisition system in 1964, incorporating the "Processing Information List" feature pioneered at the IBM Watson Research Library. The UICC was arranged not strictly alphabetically, but according to a computer-generated code work composed of the first four letters of the author's last name, the author's initials, and the initials of the first two words of the title. Order were printed on three-by-five-inch slips, which were manually sorted by vendor and attached to vendor and attached to cover letters for mailing. Pennsylvania State University implemented a similar system the same year, using a 407 tabulator as well as a 1401 and a 7074 computer.

A unique feature was the use of "change cards," five cards punched with the order number each time an order was prepared, and later used to report changes in the status of a book on order or in process. These cards were placed in cardboard packets and kept in a manually arranged file; if the status of an order changed, one of the card was withdrawn, a code for the change was written on the card, the card was sent to a keypunching section where the code was punched in the card, and the card was then used by the computer to update the master magnetic tape record of orders outstanding. Codes were established for some twenty-five different changes, including "not yet published," "out of print," "book in cataloging," and "processing completed." In addition to a listing of orders in process, with the status of each order shown, the system produced daily lists of books requested by faculty but not yet ordered for each university department or separate fund, about 250 lists in all; when the system was later redesigned, however, this feature was dropped.

Perhaps the example of an off-line batch-processing system of the mid-1960s is the one at the University of Michigan, implemented in 1965 on an IBM 1401, converted a year later to a 1460 and soon after to an IBM 360, and still running strong at this writing. A ten-part order form is generated, which includes slips for the official and public catalogs. The orders outstanding file is automatically updated, but instead of printing it out the university now produces it on a computer-output microfiche (COM) for both economy and ease of handling. Entries for Slavic language works have "Slavic" punched at the beginning of each entry, and orders for music recordings similarly begin with the word "Recording" in order to create separate sections in the list for such works; other entires are alphabetised through the first 83 characters. The Michigan system is one of the few projects for which good cost figures are available. About a year after the initial implementation, an analyst from outside the library evaluated the system in terms of both overall efficiency and costs.

The results indicated that the system did indeed perform efficiently and economically; almost fifty percent more orders were handled by the automated system than by the previous manual system, and the cost per order, when like activities were compared, dropped by seven cents over a two-year span. The librarian principally involved with development of the system has cautioned, however, that "while the information gathered was informative, it can, at best, only be considered as a guide since it is impossible to compare accurately an existing system with something that might have been." In the same year that Michigan's systems was first implemented, Washington University in St. Louis designed a system to control technical processing routines after books left the Acquisitions Department and until they had been fully cataloged and processed. Building on Penn State's "change card" idea, the system was designed to generate "process control cards" that could be inserted in IBM 357 terminals along with a plastic prepunched "badge" indicating the particular change in status to be recorded: for example, that the book has been received, or reported not yet published, or canceled, or forwarded to a particular cataloguing station, or to the card preparation unit, or (finally) that the book was under central of the public catalogue and could be removed from the system. The information would be automatically recorded by a high-speed card-punch (an IBM 1034) in a remote location, and then be transmitted to the computer. Two years earlier, in 1966, Yale University packed up the idea of "process control" and used it in the design of an acquisition system that later served as a model for the automated acquisition system at the Library of Congress.

As implemented at Yale, the technical processing "monitor" checks the status of each order during each day's run, and notifies the library of orders delayed past a predetermined length of time, and of other actions that need to be taken as a result of changes in status. The system represents an improvement in communications for off-line systems, presaging the later development of no-line system; the insertion of prepunched cards in remote terminals eliminates the necessity of manually punching the information in a data processing department and carrying the cards to the computer, and the computer "talks back" by automatically printing action reports regarding particular items when needed. A remarkable thirty-two different outputs were originally produced by the Yale system, including notices to requesters of the status of their orders and large in-process and order number listings, both of which were changed to microfilm form in 1971 because of their size and cost.

First implemented on an IBM 6094-7040 "direct-coupled system," the system was converted in 1972 to run on an IBM 360 Model 67 and a short time later to an IBM 370 Model 155.

IBM 357 data collection devices are still used for recording status and location of items, and IBM 826s are used to prepare order forms while simultaneously punching the same information into cards. Other example of batch-processing off-line systems in university libraries are legion. By 1966, the Joint University Libraries system had converted to a 1401 and the University of Missouri had converted its unit record system to a 1440 computer, in this case not a university computer but one used solely by the library.

In California, the Honnold Library, which serves the six Claremont Colleges, implemented a computerised acquisition system using an IBM Model 40. The fullest bibliographic information available was entered as early in processing as possible, and a book catalogue was produced as the final step in the system. The University of Maryland, which had a unit record system modeled after Missouri's, Converted to an off-line system using several computers in succession, most recently a Univac 9300. Other Ivy League universities were not to be outdone by Yale. Harvard implemented a successful system in 1967, Cornell in 1968, and Columbia between 1968 and 1971.

The Harvard system automatically edits order information for obvious mistakes such as lack of vendor, unusually high price, and invalid fund coding before producing orders. Prices need not be in United States dollars, since the computer has been programmed to convert all foreign currencies into dollars at the current rate of exchange, which can be altered daily if needed. The system checks the outstanding order file periodically, and claims are automatically produced if orders have not been received in the time specified by the selecting librarians; if an item has still not been received after two claims have been produced and a third survey of the files made, the order is automatically cancelled.

The Columbia system is remarkable particularly for the size and power of the equipment used: two IBM 360s, a Model 91 coupled with a Model 7, one of the most powerful complexes in the world at the time it was installed. Input is prepared on IBM magnetic tape Electric typewriter (MTSTs) and converted to machine-readable from on a Digidata System 30 converter. Records for materials in all Roman alphabet languages and in transliterated Cyrillic languages are handled by the system, as are microforms, maps, and speech records, but not serials; and material received through purchase, blanket order, standing order, gift, exchange, deposit, and cooperative acquisition programs are all included. As in the Yale system, the flow of materials in monitored through acquisitions and cataloguing departments and until catalogue cards are field in the public catalog. About 65,000 order are processed annually for a impressed annually for a impressively low 93 cents per order. An acquisition system differing from others in its extensive use of paper tape was implemented in 1968 at the University of British Columbia.

Friden Flexowriters were used to punch the paper tapes as a by-product of such activities as typing orders, processing invoices, and receiving books. The paper tape then served as input to a PDP-11 computer which, in conjunction with a Honeywell 200, did the processing. The usual orders outstanding lists, claims, cancellation notices, and fund reports were produced, as was a list of current accessions, later discontinued for lack of user interest. A system originally developed in 1968 at Florida Atlantic University for use on an IBM 360 was transferred to Arizona State University and implemented there, on a Honeywell 200, in 1971. Of later off-line, batch processing system, one in particular may be noted because of the unusually small size of both the system and the institution involved. This is the acquisition system implemented in 1971 on an IBM 360 Model 30 at Parkland College, a two-year community college in Champaign, Illinois. The system has required the addition of an extra staff member for keypunching, plus $170 per month for a model 129 keypunch, $400 per year for punch cards and magnetic tape, and several hundred dollars more per year for specially printed forms, but the library staff apparently believes these costs are offset to some extent by the fact that it no longer orders items preprocessed at a cost of $2.05 per item. Among special libraries, perhaps the best-known batch-processing system is at the Washington University School of Medicine Library in St. Louis.

The system was begun in 1965 in conjunction with a book catalogue project. The cards were then used to update the magnetic tape record of orders outstanding and orders received, using the university's 1401 computer, Later changes in the status of particular orders were indicated on copies of the order form, them punched into cards, which again were used to update the magnetic tape file. Some seventeen different lists were printed out from the file at periodic intervals. Very few computerised acquisition of this type have been reported in public libraries. Several that developed from unit record systems have already been noted, but only one that was initiated as a computerised system of the

Orange County (California) Public Library: It began as a straight forward book purchasing system in 1966, using an IBM 1460 computer. After converting the system to run ion a 360 Model 30 and then on an RCA Spectra 70 Model 45 computer, the library decided to redesign the system entirely in order to incorporate additional features, including a book catalog. Both library staff and a commercial software firm were used to accomplish the design and programming tasks. The new system, termed BIBLIOS (for Book Inventory Building Library Information Oriented System) was implemented in 1969, also on the RCA Spectra 70 computer owned by the county.

Development costs were just over $100,000 for the acquisitions portion of the system, and the cost of ordering and receiving a title under the system has been calculated at approximately $ 2.23.

On-line interactive systems

In 1967, Connie Dunlap, developer of the University of Michigan system and at that time head of their acquisitions department, spoke to an ALA Preconference on Library Automation regarding the status of acquisition systems. No no-line systems were then in use, she pointed out, and although several were planned, it appeared likely that most institutions would find such systems too expensive. By 1975, however, the costs of on-line storage and the necessary terminal equipment had declined dramatically, and over a dozen such systems were in operation.

Perhaps the earliest to be implemented was at Washington State University in 1968, using three IBM 1050s on-line to an IBM Model 67. Paper-tape readers and punches are attached to the 1050s to provide an alternative means of entry, and as backup to the on-line system. As purchase order information is entered, each field of information is "tagged" (assigned a unique code) by the terminal operator, and the computer edits each field for valid order number, correct budget information, and so forth. When the information has been entered, the operator visually edits the resulting typed version and makes any necessary corrections on the spot. A code indicating that the record has been edited is then entered on the record, without which the record cannot be processed. The entry and editing process requires an average of about three minutes per title.The 1050 terminals are also used to input receiving and involve information, to enter accession numbers, and to indicate that can be cleared from the in-process file. Washington State has adopted the Washington University-Yale University process control technique, and as a by-product of the order entry procedure a book card is created for insertion in IBM 357 card readers to indicate when a book is received and moves through various stages in processing. Because both on-line and off-line input are possible, the library has made comparative studies of the two methods.

The results indicate that operators prefer to work on-line, and make fewer errors as a result. Most errors are identified immediately by the computer, or are recognised by the operator, so they can be corrected at once and the most of erroneous information flowing through the system is drastically reduced. The increased efficiency made possible by improved communication between man and machine is thus concretely demonstrated. The use of the terminal was limited to a seven-day period beginning on the 17th of the month, however, and appears to have been merely a means of avoiding the necessity for correcting the paper tapes and re-inputting them.

No searching was done via the terminal, and although the device could print out information from the computer no real interaction appears to have taken place or been intended. The project was funded through the Computer Center, not the library, and when the funds were cut off in September of 1972 the system was discontinued. Meanwhile, also in 1969 and also in Massachusetts, terminals with visual display screens were being used for the first time in an acquisition system.

The "Book Order and Selection System" (BOSS) of the University of Massachusetts in Amherst uses for such devices on-line to an IBM 370/145 computer. Design of the system began in 1968, and less than twelve months elapsed before the system was operational. Currently BOSS processes about 90,000 orders per year, maintains the on-order file, provides both receiving and invoicing information, and produces claims for items not received. The original order information as well as changes are entered via the terminal; since the visual display shows an outline or "mask" of the information to be entered, no special coding forms are required. If a keying error is caught by the computer, the visual display screen immediately indicates it. After the error is corrected and the computer determines that all required information has been entered, a mask for the next order is displayed.

The order outstanding file can be searched on the 2260 by order number, author, title, or Library of Congress card number. The unit cost for acquisition of an item has been calculated at $2.55, which includes that cost of searching (not normally a function handled by a batch-processing system) and some costs properly assignable to cataloging. Manual file maintenance has been substantially reduced, and the backlog of processing eliminated. A smaller system was implemented at Oregon State University in 1970 using a CDC 3300 computer and a CDC 210 (later 211) terminal with a visual display screen as well as a 3 KSR teletype (keyboard) terminal.

Dubbed LOLITA, the system was developed over a three-year period for around $90,000, a modest figure compared to most other early on-line systems. In part this low cost was possible because an existing time-sharing system at the university's computer center was used, and "programming efforts could be concentrated exclusively on the design of LOLITA and an earlier pilot project... No time was needed to design, debug or redesign the operating system software, as was necessary at Washington State University and the University of Chicago."

One report indicates that "acquisitions personnel have been transferred to other duties, bookkeeping loads on the college bookkeeping operation have been reduced, list of new books are more complete and are produced with less labour, and the system provides input to the cataloguing operation which has resulted in some further saving there. The fund accounting system is sound is now accepted by the state for legal accounting purposes. An interesting feature is as provision for entering orders into the system and "holding" them until funds become available. In a recent fiscal year, the library received enough funds in the last ten days to double monographic purchases fro the year, and despite the shortness of time the library was able to encumber the funds using this capability. Syracuse and Northwestern Universities both implemented on-line acquisition systems during 1971 using keyboard terminals in the IBM 2740 series, and both connected to IBM 370 computers. Despite some similarity in equipment, however, the systems have marked differences. Northwestern's provides input from MARC tapes, converts foreign currency, and writes checks, whereas Syracuse's does not; on the other hand, Syracuse's system automatically issues cancellation notices, checks for duplicate billing and duplicate orders, assigns funds based on the subject matter of the item being ordered, assigns funds based on the subject mater of the item being ordered, produces accession lists and delinquent order lists, and provides a wide variety of other management information, none of which is provide at Northwestern. Unfortunately, no costs for either system have been published.

Perhaps the most sophisticated system presently in operation is Stanford University's BALLOTS. BALLOTS is a combined or "integrated" technical processing system, and includes both acquisition and cataloguing functions. By 1975, over $2.5 million in grants from the Office of Education, the Council on Library Resources, and the National Endowment for the Humanities had been spent on its development. Design began in 1967, but the first production operations did not occur until 1972, when the first part of the acquisition system (the "MARC module") was implemented. The first segment provided the capability of searching machine-readable cataloguing data supplied by the Library of Congress, and using it to order and catalogue books. During the first year only MARC titles could be handled, but by late 1973 other parts of the system had been implemented, and non-MARC titles could also be acquired and cataloged. Serials, standing orders, and approval orders are also now handled by the system, although in contrast to most other acquisition systems fund accounting is not. The equipment used is a large IBM 360 Model 67 computer, a small PDP 11 computer as an intermediary, and a number of Sanders 804 programmable display terminals; cataloguing and acquisition departments share 11 terminals, and others are located at the reference desks in the main and undergraduate libraries, where library staff assist the public in searching the files.

The searching capabilities of the system are in fact its most elegant feature, with many indexes on-line and numerous automatic hints and instructions from the computer as a search progresses. There is also a program for training new users of the system via the terminal itself. A similarly sophisticated system implemented the same year (1972) at Dartmouth College is also of interest. Two cathode-ray tube terminals and two Model 33 teletype machines are used for communication with the computer.

Searching is performed primarily on two files, an in-process file and a vendor file, the latter providing such vendor performance statistics as the average time to fill an order, average number of claims, and average discount Perhaps because the number of orders in process at any one time is relatively low (compared to the large university and public libraries in which such on-line systems are more commonly found) an in-process list is still printed out weekly, even though the same information is available through terminal inquiry. The relatively low volume may also account in part for the fact that the costs of the automated system appear substantially higher than for the previous manual system: about

$8.75 per item processed, versus $6.12 before. One observer has commented the "a tauter, less complex system could provide adequate speed and control at a substantially lower cost," and it is possible that the library is paying a significant premium for the sophistication or the system. A useful contrast, to cite one final example, is the one-line system in operation since 1972 at the Cleveland Public Library. Cleveland had previously used batch-processing systems: an IBM 1401 system from 1968, and an IBM 360 Model 20 system from 1968 to 1972. In 1972 it purchased not one, but two LIBS 100 minicomputer systems from Computer Library Services Inc. (CLSI), complete with all programs necessary to run the systems, for a total price of $57,000 per system. Cleveland's objectives in switching to on-line minicomputer were "to escape from a batch processing system" with separate data processing and acquisitions departments and the many problems arising from split responsibilities, "to get away from the massive generation of reports and listings that were of little value for management purposes, "and" to keep track of the flow of materials and dollars at a reasonable price."

The heart of each of the new systems is a Digital Equipment Corporation PDP-11 with specially designed terminals. Input, receiving, searching, and updating may all be performed on-line. In-process control and a variety of management information are also provided. During the first two years of operation, each system had been out of operation less than 5 percent of the time, and never had both been out of operation at same time. Published cost figures reflect an annual cost of $55,668 per year versus $123,360 per year for the former IBM system; the cost per item processed was an impressive forty-six cents.

It is based on the author's personal knowledge of the state of automation in libraries in Britain and also, to a greater extent, on the published literature describing particular projects in Britain and in other countries. This is not a comprehensive survey: a process of selection has been applied so as to draw attention to the more important individual projects, and it is felt that it will be more valuable because of this. One major problem which arises when reliance is placed on the published literature in this way is the twofold difficulty of distinguishing between projects that are planned for some unspecified future date and those which are actually operational at the time of writing and of learning about automated projects which have ceased to function. It is only natural that projects should be widely publicised at their inception and that their demise should be concealed from the public gaze.

But librarians a body will learn as much from honest reports of failures and the reasons for them as they will from reports about automated systems that are planned newly-implemented. The lack of such a literature about failures is keenly felt, especially in the present context. A second major purpose of this chapter is that it should provide for comment on the systems outlined in previous chapters. These systems are "ideal" and do not necessarily represent any particular real-life operational system. Although they are naturally based on real life, their purpose is to illustrate the principles embodied in real systems.

Accounting Systems

The system design discussed is based closely on one being developed as a co-operative venture by a number of British university libraries. All have access to ICT computers and this has led them to attempt to reduce development costs and to speed the introduction of appropriate automated routines by working together to produce common systems. The fullest statement of the order system specification was given at a conference organised by the group. It is designed to include the majority of outputs that libraries are likely to require from such a system and in order to make it more widely usable it is being programmed in COBOL. The University Library in Newcastle-upon-Tyne has been operating a computer-aided ordering system. The introduction of this system was facilitated in that it makes use of a number of programs already in existence as part of the Newcastle file-handling system. This is a suite of programs written for the English Electric KDF9 computer to facilitate the handling of structured data of the kind found in bibliographical applications. It is interesting to note that Newcastle University library report a small saving in staff time compared with the previous order system which used edge-notched cards. If computer time were charged to the library, however, the automated system would be considerably more expensive.For new books which are included in the Virginia Kirkus Service pre-punched cards are distributed, one for each title, giving the usual bibliographical information. To order one of these books all that a library has to do is to return the appropriate punched card to the data-processing centre indicating the number of copies needed. This is an interesting example of one way in which cooperation between libraries can make for simpler automated systems, save time, and reduce costs.

At the University of Maryland an acquisitions system is in operation utilising punched-card equip-ment only. Orders and auxiliary listings of outstanding orders, receipts, and fund reports are made using an IBM 407 accounting machine. "On order" cards are filed manually in the public card catalogue and pre-cataloguing is carried out whenever complete Library of Congress cataloguing data is available. Shaw has recently described an application of data processing techniques to the accounting side of library acquisitions at the University of Hawaii. He shows that accounting costs are reduced to one thirteenth of their previous level by this very simple system which just uses the computer as a calculating machine. In libraries where funds are limited it is important to remember that modest automation programmers can result in significant savings which can be directed to improving conventional services. A unique computer-aided system for ordering replacement copies of standard books is now operating in Toronto. Public librarians there have selected a standard list of about 2500 titles, all of which are available in paperback editions. Given information on the quality rating of publishers' editions, the computer prepares monthly lists of replacement orders which enable each branch library to have in stock a determined number of copies of all the standard titles, all in good condition.

A number of library systems in the Toronto area are cooperating in this scheme which, because of its size enables substantial discounts to be obtained. A number of other libraries have reported automated acquisitions systems to be in operation. At the library of the University of Michigan a disc memory store is used in the computer processing of order records, while at the Redstone Scientific Information Center a system christened ALPHA (Automatic Literature, Processing, Handling, and Analysis) utilises an IBM 632 electronic typing calculator for key punching the original order records.

Circulation Control

A typical computer-aided circulation control system is now operational at the University of Southampton. It is being implemented in four stages of increasing sophistication the first of which commenced in operation. The first stage, as a by-product of its operation, produces a book card for each book that is circulated, thus building up an "active" collection of books with books cards ready for automatic input of charging data during the second stage of the system. The final two stages provide for on-line interrogation and updating of the loans file. The price which has to be paid for this gradual method of building up an active collection is the heavy work load involved with the first stage. Borrowers fill in slips for each book they borrow and reserve and data-processing staff keypunch one card for each of these transactions and also one card for each book that is returned.

The advantage of a crash programme is that the circulation system can employ automatic collection of charging data right from the very beginning, and that there will be no need to cater for books being circulated without cards. Although cards will be made for many books which will in fact never be circulated again, it will not be necessary to punch cards for books that are returned as at Southampton. Trueswell has shown that for a university technical library where it is the newest books that circulate most, it is more economical to prepare book cards for books on loan during the loan period than to carry out a crash programme for the entire collection. And if all new acquisitions are supplied with book cards at the technical processing stage, possibly as a by-product of an automated order system, then in time only a small percentage of books will be presented for circulation without book cards. However, in a public lending library where a high percentage of the stock is circulated and books have a long "half-life", a crash programme may be appropriate.

Ruecking has made a mathematical analysis of future circulation growth at Rice University in order to make a more accurate comparison between different methods of circulation control. As circulation increases and as filed grow, linear relationships do not necessarily hold, so that it is necessary to include the cumulative costs of a system when evaluating it. His calculations show that over a 6-year period the total cumulative cost of a computerised system would be about half the cumulative cost of any other system.

A number of libraries in the United States have now adopted circulation control systems based on either the IBM 357 or 1030 data-collection units, accepting data from eighty-column punched book cards and readers' plastic badge cards. Among these are Southern Illinois University, Florida Atlantic University, Lehigh University, Oak Ridge National Laboratory, and the University of Missouri. An unusual system operates at Johns Hopkins University which represents one solution to the slow charging speeds which are associated with computer-aided circulation control.

The price paid is an extra operation in the circulation procedure. Charge and discharge data is captured on microfilm by photographing the reader's identification card and the spines of up to twelve or fifteen books being borrowed. After developing the film the data is keypunched and processed by the computer in the normal way. In Germany, two university libraries, Bochum and the Technical University of Berlin, have implemented automated circulation control systems using book cards edge-punched with paper-tape codes for automatic collection of charging data. Circulation control systems using punched-card machines have not yet been displaced by computer-based systems.

One has recently been installed in the Atomic Weapons Research Establishment at Aldermaston. It makes use of the card duplicating facility of an IBM 026 printing card punch to create three transaction cards for each loan from punched book and reader cards. One card is filed manually in the issues file and the other two are used by a computer to apply various controls to the system; to test for overdue books, for example. Eighty-column cards are filled in by borrowers and then keypunched for processing. A computer is used only for printing letters recalling overdue books. Judging from the experience of the University of Hawaii it would be foolish to assume that computer-based circulation systems are the only ones worth introducing in this modern age. The best system for each individual library can only be arrived at after rigorous systems work and careful costing.

Many libraries have produced lists of their periodicals holdings by computer punched-card methods and taken advantage of the opportunities thus afforded for distributing the list widely and updating it easily and frequently. A union list of periodicals held in Institute of Education libraries in Britain was also published in 1966. It was produced with the aid of some programs of the Newcastle file handling system. Experiments are in hand to print new editions of this union list by computer typesetting techniques being developed by the University of Newcastle-upon-Tyne computer typesetting project.

The Atomic Energy Research Establishment at Harwell produced a printed list of its periodicals holdings by punched-card techniques in 1960. The main library at Harwell is responsible for purchasing periodicals for its own collections as well as for those of twenty-two divisional libraries. The use of mechanised methods for compiling the list made it a comparatively simple job to supply each library within the system with a frequently updated union list of periodicals. The most important British union list of serials produced by mechanical means is, of course, the new BUCOP. Input is from punched cards and processing is done by IBM 1401 computer. In the case of a widely used list such as this it becomes important that computer typesetting techniques should be introduced quickly, even though the present frequently updated list is an immense improvement on the older ones.

An interesting holdings list in the United States is that of the Francis A. Countway Library of Medicine, formed by the merger of the Boston Medical Library and Harvard Medical

Library. The incentive to mechanise was the immediate need to merge the records of the two libraries. An impressive number of different outputs have been produced including a KWIC index of current titles. Semi-automated serials check-in systems have a number of attractive features and have been adopted by several libraries. They can be regarded as an intermediate stage between systems producing a list of holdings and fully automated systems embracing accounting, checking in, and binding routines for periodicals.

For libraries which cannot afford to develop a fully automated system directly they are a useful stepping-stone whereby the final goal can be approached by degrees. In Britain a computer-produced checking-in list has been developed at the City University. Periodical parts expected to arrive during the coming month are listed on a line printer. As the parts are received in the library they are ticked off on this list, making it a simple matter to inform library users about the arrival or non-arrival of a particular journal issue. This printed checking-in list gives full titles of journals, unlike systems which punch an eighty-column card for each expected part, where title have to be abbreviated. The system is capable of conversion to a fully automated one, which would require only a minimum amount of keypunching to cater for parts which do not behave as expected.

Another semi-automated system has been installed at the Louisville School of Medicine, Louisville, Kentucky. Using only punched-card equipment, check-in cards are prepared for each expected title. These require the manual addition of volume number, part number, and date of receipt to complete the full bibliographical data for each part. A number of libraries in the United States have reported the installation of fully automated computerised systems.

Bibliographies and Catalogues

The very simplest level at which entries for bibliographies and catalogues can be prepared by automated methods is that involving the use of a paper-tape typewriter or the IBM Document Writer. These machines are used widely in libraries nowadays and their routine application is seldom reported in the literature. Two useful articles which explain how they have been used in particular libraries are those by Wilson and Bernstein. Conflicting reports have been published on the relative costs of producing catalogue cards by tape typewriter and by other techniques.

Mackenzie shows the tape typewriter to be about 75 per cent as costly as either a stencil duplicator or a small offset litho machine. Moore, on the other hand, finds the reverse to be true-duplicating methods works out to be approximately 75 per cent as costly as tape typewriters. The cause of these divergent results is to be found in the relative amounts of clerical time stated to be required by the two methods. An interesting variation on these methods has been reported by Fasana et al. Catalogue records are prepared in machine-readable form and in a special machine-interpretable natural format using a tape typewriter.

Working from the tape punched by the tape typewriter, a special digital machine-the Itek Crossfiler-prepares a catalogue entries. Running this second tape through a tape typewriter produces the required card set directly. Briefly, this technique obviates the need to use a program tape when added entries are being typed and makes for greater flexibility in the production of added entries of different kinds. There is a large literature dealing with various aspects of the production of card and book catalogues by means of punched cards and computer methods. In the following paragraphs only the more important contributions to this literature are mentioned.

Dewey gives a brief historical survey of the earliest catalogues produced by punched-card methods and records that the first non experimental catalogue of books was made in 1951 for the branch libraries of King County (Washington) Public Library System. More widely known are the book catalogues of Los Angeles Country Public Library, first introduced in 1953. Before that date only 26 of the system's 114 service outlets had card catalogues, while the introduction of book catalogue enabled each branch to have a union catalogue of the whole library system. A book catalogue produced by punched-card methods was introduced to the science and engineering libraries of the University of Rochester in 1962. This short-title catalogue, now made using an IBM 7094 computer, is designed as a supplement to the libraries' regular card catalogues and each entry is accordingly limited to one line only.

In the latest editions of this catalogue refinements have been made to the sort programs. Abbreviations are filed as if they were spelled out in full and names which have prefixes such as de, le, van, von, etc., separated from the main name, are interfiled with names where the prefixes are not separated. Among the North American libraries that have made book catalogues by computer are Stanford University Library, where the decision to automate was based on a thorough comparative cost analysis, Florida Atlantic University, where the original intention was that the catalogue should also be searchable by machine and Toronto University Library, which prepared a book catalogue of the combined holdings of five new university libraries in the province of Ontario—the ONULP project. At Harvard University Library a project is under way to convert the entire shelf list to machine-readable form. In that a shelf list is a classified sequence of bibliographic records, the whole job can conveniently be split into small units and one main class keypunched at a time. The first Harvard class, the

Crusades, was completed in May 1965. As with the short title catalogue at the University of Rochester, these printed shelf lists, invaluable as they are, can only be regarded as supplements to the main card catalogue where full bibliographic details are available.

De Gennaro has recently developed this classwise conversion technique into a proposal for creating a national union catalogue in machineable form for the United States. Each class of the Library of Congress shelf list would be converted and machine printout compared with the holdings of other large research libraries. They would add to the machineable records their own locational symbols and titles held only by them, and could print their own book catalogues by selective listing of the master tapes. The medical libraries of Yale University and Columbia University are co-operating in a project which will eventually provide them with a common pool of books and journals the catalogue of which will be in machineable form and accessible through remote on-line consoles. Kilgour has described programs to produce printed catalogue cards as the first stage in this ambitious project.

The programs were written in a symbolic-assembly language to take fullest advantage of the potential of a small computer-a two tape 4K IBM 1401. In another paper Kilgour outlines the advantages to be gained from writing programs in such a machine-oriented language as compared with a higher-level language such as COBOL, which is proposed by Culbertson as a standard language to be used for library data processing. An unusual computer-produced catalogue on microfilm has been operational in the Technical Information Center of Lockheed Missiles and Space Company since July 1966. Using a machine to compose directly from the computer onto microfilm is stated to reduce costs considerably. Access to the catalogue must be by means of a microfilm reader, but film kept in cartridge makes for simple handling and a Xerox Copyflo can be used to produce hard copy quickly and cheaply if this is wanted. The Library of Congress project MARC has had a marked influence on libraries' plans for catalogue automation both in North America and Britain.

The MARC pilot project, in which cataloguing copy was distributed on an experimental basis to sixteen libraries, began in October 1966 and is still continuing. At the time of writing, the Library of Congress is developing an improved format for the catalogue records on MARC tapes, designed to facilitate the communication of bibliographic data in machineable form. Coward describes this new format and discusses the United Kingdom MARC service, which is hoped to be made available within the next few years. It will be firmly based on co-operation with the next few years. It will be firmly based on co-operation has already been established in regard to the actual data going into catalogue records as part of the Library of Congress Shared Cataloging Program.

The introduction of standard book numbering to the British book trade has provided a convenient tag for identifying the records on the British MARC tapes and should reduce greatly the problems associated with matching catalogue records by computer. A possible file structure for the weekly magnetic tapes produced by the U.K. MARC service might be as follows: firstly, a main file consisting of a series of catalogue records in standard book number order; and secondly, a title index to the first part of the file. The index might also be produced in printed form along with a listing of the SBN's of records in the first part of the file. The public library systems of the London Boroughs of Barnet, Camden, and Greenwich have had computer-produced book catalogues for nearly 3 years now. Using the services of a computer bureau and accepting severe limitations on the format and layout of entries, these libraries have been able, nevertheless, to improve their public services by supplying all branches with union catalogues, a virtual impossibility with a manual system. Tait and Anderson, of the Department of Librarianship at the University of Strathclyde, Glasgow, have recently described an experiment to test the effectiveness of an ICT package program for library indexing and cataloguing-NIC. They are using citations from Library Science Abstracts as inputs data to the system. It will be interesting to compare the effectiveness of the indexes produced by NIC (Nineteen hundred Indexing and Cataloguing) with the conventional indexes published for Library Science Abstracts. At the Cambridge Philosophical Library project has commenced to produce by computer a union catalogue of books in the many departmental libraries with in the University of Cambridge.

The entire shelf lists of a sample of these libraries are being converted into machineable form and a thorough investigation will be made into the problems of merging the separate catalogues at the University of Rochester. Unless entries referring to identical books really are truly identical the computer will include them both in the updated catalogue. At the University of Newcastle-upon-Tyne, Hunt is working on a computerised catalogue for the two special collections in the University library. Using programs from the New Castle file-handling system, this catalogue will be indexed by author, binder, provenance, etc. Particularly interesting techniques being developed by the computer typesetting project at the University.In Germany, book-form catalogues are being produced by computer at the University of Bochum. This is a new university and in fact has no card catalogue at all. Germany has also made an important contribution to computer-aided cataloguing methods by being the first country to produce its national bibliography by computer. Type-setting is by means of a Linoquick machine, a normal line-casting machine which can be controlled by paper tape. The main advantage of this data-processing system became apparent with the first half-yearly cumulation, the Halbjahres-Verzeichnis. Normally this job takes from 12 to 15 months, but it has now been reduced to 2¼ months.

Future Developments

The pattern of automated library service in the future can only be predicted by educated extrapolation of the developments that are taking place in libraries today, bearing in mind other factors which will have an important bearing on libraries. Included among these will be an expected continuing exponential growth in population and the increasing the importance of libraries in the developing countries. The expansion of knowledge shows no signs of abating, and libraries will also be faced with a continuing proliferation of disciplines, coupled with a trend towards inter-disciplinary study.

The volume of publications will continue to grow but there should be an increasing recognition by central governments of the importance of libraries and their functions of bibliographic control and information dissemination. The consequence of this recognition will be greater financial support for library programmes. The key requirement in such an age is that libraries should be flexible. This will be manifested in all facets of librarianship; library buildings, systems for subject representation, forms of publications and the reader services provided for the library's clientele. Co-operation between libraries at local, national, and international levels will increase in importance, but it must be flexible so as to ensure that individual, importance, but it must be flexible so as to ensure that individual, seemingly more important goals.

Most important of all, perhaps, is the recognition that libraries serve as an intermediary in process of communication between human beings. They are not ends in themselves and the fact that libraries must deal ultimately with people, not merely with inanimate documents and machines, obliges us to design systems which treat both readers and library staff with understanding and respect for their personal feelings and needs. The computer has a central role to play in such future library systems.

As a reliable, competent, accurate, and cheap manipulator or library infor-mation it can bring to fruition many idealistic concepts about flexible library services. In that it has the capacity to free human beings from much of the repetitive labour that is a necessary concomitant to library work, it can also give us the opportunity to provide personal service to real people. The necessary prerequisite to the wise and proper use of computing machinery in libraries in the future is a body of wise and informed library managers now. It is possible to distinguish two general directions in which computer aided services will develop. Printed lists prepared by computer processing of a basic corpus of bibliographic records will increase in number and in diversity, and facilities for on-lie interrogation of files held in machine memories will become more widely available.

At the present moment computer-aided library systems almost invariably produce as their end product some sort of printed list for human consultation or scanning. In the future, then, we can expect to see more such lists prepared in circumstances where they can be justified either by reducing costs or increasing services. At present, too, a number of experimental on-line library projects are either operational or under development. It is reasonable to suppose that these will be successful and will eventually find application in certain circumstances.

It is possible to divide present-day on-line projects into two broad categories; those involving the automation of one or more library housekeeping functions, and those concerned with information retrieval and the processing of natural language text. The major area of library housekeeping which librarians tend to regard as being suitable for on-line methods is circulation control. Although no system is operational yet, work is either in progress or under consideration at the University of California, San Diego and Los Angeles, and at Harwell and Belfast.

A proposal for on-line accessioning of periodicals has come from the University of Lancaster, and a number of libraries are considering systems for on-line manipulation and cataloguing data. Assuming that it remains essential to make non-programmable alterations either to ordering data or catalogue data from a central agency before it can be added to a library's own catalogue file, then an on-line visual display console equipped with a keyboard and light pen would appear to be an attractive piece of hardware for doing this. All of these on-line systems, however, involve only minor modifications to existing patterns of library activity. More far-reaching changes to present-day methods of library use appear to be implied in on-line systems for information retrieval and text processing. Those that come closest to everyday library operations involve the on-line interrogation of a file of bibliographic records. This enables a search to be directed in the first place to the names of authors, editors, etc., titles, class numbers, or coden.

Secondary search of a body of records retrieved by one of the above terms can be by means of a subject term; publisher's name, date of publication, place of publication, language, or location. The details of the system have yet to be worked out, including the bibliographic record format to be used, but the body of records will be indexed in four ways corresponding to the four data categories by which primary access to the file may be obtained. Presumably, search statements can combine more than one term in logical relationship. A project is also under way to create an on-line union-catalogue for the public libraries of metropolitan Toronto. Here, in addition to the design of the machine system, difficulties have to be overcome in respect of the machine system, difficulties have to be overcome in respect of differences of cataloguing practice between co-operating libraries. It is likely that this project will provide for only limited degrees of search complexity, and will handle only abbreviated bibliographic records in order to minimise the size of file required.

Kessler is conducting an interesting experimental project at Massachusetts Institute of Technology which permits on-line searching of bibliographical records by various novel search strategies. Articles from twenty-one specially chosen physics journals are "indexed" for the system, but conventional subject indexing is not employed except in so far as it is made available in Physics Abstracts. Search strategies can be defined on the basis of journal titles, author's names and—words in titles. Citation-orientated searching is also possible, for example, one can search for all papers which cite a chosen article or alternatively, all papers that have a stated number of references in common with the chosen article. Kessler has introduced the concept of bibliographic coupling to describe the linkage formed between papers which have references in common. Two papers are said to be bibliographically coupled with coupling strength of one (two, three etc.) when they have one (two, three etc.) references in common. Kessler has found that groups of papers coupled in this way are quite similar to the groups of papers coupled in this way are quite similar to the groups made by a conventional subject index.

Indexing by means of bibliographic coupling is likely to become more common in future than it has been in the past.

Relying on the authors of papers for the intellectual efforts which is required for a good index, it demands the use of new search strategies on the part of library users. The technique is particularly suitable for machine applications in that no intellectual effort is required to construct the index.

The printed volumes of Science Citation Index are compiled on these principles and make it possible to experiment now with search strategies which will be appropriate with some future on-line information retrieval systems. A detailed description of an imaginary on-line library system has been given by Licklider. Termed a "procognitive system" in that it exists for, or to serve, knowledge and learning, it replaces the codex and the card index of present-day libraries by direct-access computer memories containing the same information. Computer processors in the procognitive system are able, in an unspecified way, to organise and mull over the data in store, and also to search it.

An experimental approach to such a system has been described by Bobrow *et al.* A program named SYMBIONT enables a number of basic operations to be performed on textual matter. Once a document has been input to the system, 150-word "pages" of it can be displayed on the face of a console. Pages can be turned forwards and backwards, and selected passages of text can be named and stored for future reference. Searches can then be made using these names. Project INTREX is another experiment in the same general direction. Begun in late 1965 it is a research programme whose main aim is to provide, a solution to the problems of large libraries by means of on-line computing techniques similar to those of SYMBIONT and the procognitive system.

There is, of course, a dual problem here. Not only must some very sophisticated computer programs be developed, but they must be related to an understanding of language and of the way human beings interact with the body of knowledge which these systems plan to hold in computer memory.

The fact is that we are woe— ignorant of the ways in which scholars approach the literature of their subject, or the reason why readers come into a library. To design on-line computer systems which perform limited file-searching functions may be to miss the real needs of most library users. The automation of library operations can very readily be regarded as a way of escape from the pressing problems of everyday life in a library; ordering and cataloguing books, answering awkward reference questions, tracing lost books. Automation will certainly simplify many of these tasks, but it must be built upon a sure foundation of good library practice which, as far as possible, prevents problems from arising. Librarians best know what the problems are in cataloguing, acquisitions work, reader service, and circulation control, and it is important that their knowledge be brought fully to hear on the job of designing automated systems in the first place.

8

Problems and Prospects

Availability of computer processing time has been a problem for numerous library projects; the lack of priority given by the computer center to the development of library systems has been another complaint; and a third is the lack of control by the library over decisions regarding continuation of a project. The experiences of the M.I.T. library with its acquisition systems and the Florida Atlantic University library with its book catalog project were as examples of all three of these related problems. A fourth problem involving computer centers and their personnel is what Veaner has called "system instability".

In a survey of twenty-four institutions conducted in 1972, he fond that "this was more the rule than the exception, especially in software, operating systems, hardware configuration, and pricing. Wherever an academic computer facility was used for library development, the same broken record always seemed to be playing: the facility was always being taken apart and put together again."

Rice University's experience with its circulation system affords another example. It was begun on unit record equipment,

transferred to an IBM 7040, then to a Burroughs B5500, an finally to an IBM 370 Model 155. At times during the period when the system was being switched from one computer to another, the "daily" print-out of the circulation file was literally months out of data, and since the transaction records were on tape instead of punched cards there was no way of telling where the books were. Attitudes of computer center personnel may also be a source of trouble. Ignorance of libraries and their operations has frequently led to a assumption that the problems to be solved are simple or trivial, or at best, to the glib conclusion by systems analysts and programmers that they understand both the problems and the solutions, Elitism—"the notion that the masters of the computer are inherently superior to and have better judgment than computer customers"—is also common.

A relate problem is the fact that most of the good programmers and systems analysts are naturally interested in facing new challenges and are apt to become disinterest in library projects once they become "production" systems. And ear also may play a part; to many computer centers, it has sometimes appeared that the library, in addition to its usually well-established role on campus or in the community, could become the largest of the computer center's users, and "in some facilities this recognition may have in-duced a fear of being taken over or overwhelmed by the user, who would then be in a position to dominate and dictate the direction of further development an operations." A host of other attitudes and emotions may affect library system projects.

One system expert with long years of experience says. "We have seen computer center staff force users out of compatibility with other installations in matters that are completely standard for reasons that seem to range from downright incompetence, to an arrogant desire to exert control over other people's work, to regarding the computer as a toy for their personal amusement and a vehicle for practical jokes that verge on the malicious."

Suppliers

At least five type of problems can be identified on this category. The first is the failure of suppliers to deliver the necessary equipment. The Orange Country Public Library designed and programmed a circulation system but never implement it, simply because the company which was supposed to supply the hardware never delivered. A more common (indeed, almost universal) problem is the failure of suppliers to deliver the required software (i.e., the programs and related documentation), either on time or at all. A third familiar problem is inadequate service r, which plagued most of the projects using paper-tape machines and still troubles most libraries using automation projects are simply poor machines, either poorly engineered or poorly built, a case in point being the IBM 1050 which most libraries have discontinued using because of constant breakdowns.

Library staff

Perhaps the most serious problem originating with the library staff itself is the failure to distinguish legitimate research and experimentation from operational improvements, or to provide separate funds for research. Some of the development in library automation have been funded by grants (usually given to initiate expected operational improvements, not for research) but most have been funded from the operating budgets of individual libraries. Only a few libraries have deliberately set aside a portion of their budgets for research ad experimentation.Because most experimental techniques were attempted under the guise of operational improvements, those that did not work were considered failures by the librarians. Money that have been used for more books or more staff had been wasted, it appeared, and mismanagement or (more charitably) misjudgment was often suggested. Yet see properly as needed research and

experimentation—the only way a profession advances—many of these "failures" were in fact successes. To the extent that they demonstrate methods which did not work, they made a valuable contribution to this part of librarianship. The real failure of many librarians involved in these projects is the lack of reporting to the profession on the problems encountered.

A few projects have been reported frankly and in full, but most have die silently, almost secretly. Perhaps because they were intended to be immediate operating improvements, their cessation was viewed with embarrassment and even shame, and those in charge refused to discuss them. In such cases, the failure goes beyond the mere missing of an opportunity to contribute to the advancement of the profession; a real harm results, because other libraries are apt to repeat the process with the same results, needlessly wasting money, manpower, and time. Unfortunately there are far too many examples of this problem. Florida Atlantic's projects were begun with great publicity, but after implementation of the projects the profession was kept almost completely in the dark regarding how well the new systems had worked.

Rumors of trouble abounded, feed by reports of staff members accepting positions elsewhere. When the Director of Library and Information Retrieval Services resigned early in 1967, "it became apparent that the experiment which had been launched with such confidence and such fanfare had failed," yet only when a later director of libraries published a summary report did many of the facts become known. "Those involved chose...to blanket the difficulties encountered with silence, ignoring the fact that progress in a technologically oriented society is as dependent upon the analysis of projects which fail to achieve goals as it is on the resounding successes."Networks have had a particularly high mortality rate, especially those designed to do centralized processing, but reports by the librarians involved on the reasons for discontinuance tend to be

elusive. ANYLTS (the Association of New York Libraries for Technical Services) began like Florida Atlantic University with a considerable amount of publicity, and some $2.5 million was reported spent on its development, yet when it died in 1972 there was no general report to the profession.

Apparently development efforts had fallen considerably behind schedule, and the income-producing activities of the project could not sustain it after Federal funds were with drawn. In the absence of a formal report, however, it is impossible to know for certain the reasons for its failure. Despite the "stability of long-established procedures", an-other problem in many library automation projects has been that the library staff really did not understand the existing procedures, at least not with the precision and detail required for designing al-ternative methods of accomplishing the same tasks.

As a result, systems were implemented which could not handle various exceptions to normal procedures. simply because the exceptions were not maintained or understood, and not uncommonly the whole project failed as a result. Library staff have also created problems by failing to agree on the desired characteristics of the final product of a system. As might be imagine, cooperative projects and networks have been particularly vulnerable to this vice. The Colorado Academic Library Book Processing Center (CALBPC) died in part because the participants constantly disagreed on the format of the catalog cards all of them were to receive, some catalogers insisting on treating cards as works of art, others insisting on petty variations to suit "local conditions", and still others insisting on the maximum in economy. The CALBPC effort also exposed other difficulties librarians seem to have in working with each other, such as head librarians feuding or jockeying for status, institutional jealousies, and simple parochialism. Even when library staff members do agree on what they want, difficulties have frequently occurred in communicating these decisions.

Veaner found that "many did not understand how to together a specification document; particularly they did not know how to account exhaustively for all possible cases of alternatives: Librarians were unaccustomed to defining their data processing requirements quantitatively or with precision—both absolutely indispensable to the computer environment... Few library users understood the relationship between the system specifications and functional results, and fewer still understood the significations of performances specifications."

Poor Planning

Some of the problem that have troubled library automation projects are not the sole province of any one of the above group of people, but may originate with any or all of them. The first category of such problem may be thought of generally as poor planning, and at the head of the list of planning problems may be idea to initiate a project in the first place. There are many valid reasons to begin an automated systems, or to provide a new service provided of course that the resources are available to pay for it. But many projects have been started, not for any of these reasons but because of pressure from the institution's administration to "be modern" or "automate the library", to keep up with the Joneses of the library world, to promote a personal reputation, or simply because somebody on the library staff is gadget-happy and needs a new toy. Systems thus initiated, or begun without sufficient analysis of the goals and objectives of the project, are apt to fail early, and even if they proceed past the implementation stage lack of clearly define objectives will awake evaluation of their success difficult if not impossible.

Another problem in planning that is frequently encountered is the lack of market research—that is, the failure to establish in advance that the planned product or service is needed or wanted. The reports of the Washington University

School of Medicine library on its book catalog and serials list project provide good examples of this problem, as well as a related one: the products cost too much for the benefits derived. These twin problems—insufficient demand and inordinate costs—run through the reports of many troubled projects and seem to be the principal reasons for the failure of every example of a particular type of network not yet mentioned: the kind set up to transmit materials between libraries by facsimile transmission instead of by conventional interlibrary loan techniques.

The best-documented and most extensive such project was the Facsimile Transmission System (FACTS) in New York State, which involved fifteen libraries and ran from January 20, 1967 to March 31, 1968. An impressive amount of time and money was spent in constructing this network, but the results in terms of user response were disappointing. Apparently the principal problem was that there was little demand for the fast but expensive service the system was set up to provide. Perhaps the biggest problem at the planning stage is simply wishful thinking. Unrealistic assumption are commonly made regarding the time required to complete and implement a project, the effort involved, and most of all the cost. Assumptions regarding the benefits that will result may also be at fault, a problem experienced by the Colorado Academic Libraries Book Processing Center. It was presumed at the planning stage that larger discounts would result if book orders were pooled, but in fact this never happened. Libraries were not buying the same titles as much as had been though, and even when they did, it was it different times so the orders could not be pooled. With the added costs of processing, bookkeeping, and paperwork at the Center, the cost was higher, in fact, than if each library had ordered its books separately.

In their early enthusiasm and eagerness to get started, library system planners may also forget to do their homework—that is, to search the literature, to learn (through various means, including contact with the professional associations) of similar projects which have been attempted or implemented, and then to take the experiences of these projects into account. For a profession with the communication of information as a goal, the incidence of this failure is disturbing. The numerous information retrieval projects of the previous decade were particularly guilty in this regard, but examples exist for virtually every type of project. Even terminal-oriented circulation systems, of which hundreds now exist, continue to be developed from scratch, without building on the experience of others. In some cases, this failure to profit from the lessons learned and the work done by other systems occurs not because of ignorance but because of what Brong and Pasternak have called the "N-I-H" or "Not-invented-Here" syndrome.

The planners know of other systems which do what they wish to do, but they refuse to adopt such systems (or even to study them) simply because they were developed by other institutions. The excuse may be that the existing systems were designed for public institutions rather than private ones (or vice versa), or that they do not accommodate "local conditions," but the real reasons are often ambition, arrogance, and indifference. One other problem in the planning category should be mentioned. Occasionally the planning for a system is based on the existence of "soft" money—i.e., money from grants or one-time gifts or appropriations—or the assumption that such money will be available to fund the project in the future. This is both appropriate and desirable if the project is developmental or experimental and designed either to terminate when the funds run our or to continue operating (perhaps at a reduced level) with identified, regularly budgeted funds. Incredible as it may seem, however, not a few projects have either assumed that soft money would continue to be available indefinitely, or have simply failed to consider what would happen when such funds ran out.

Poor Design

The actual design of many systems also falls prey to wishful thinking and unwarranted assumptions: for example, that acquisition data can be reused, without major changes, for catalog cards, or that serials are regular and predictable enough that irregular serials will not be a major problem. System designs may also fail to provide for editing and proofing procedures, as in the Florida Atlantic book catalogue project, where it was assumed that "untrained clerical personnel could be relied on to code Library of Congress copy for keypunching without having their work revised."

And some systems have omitted routines for handling exceptional circumstance, which again may be due to wishful thinking. A second problem associated with the design stage is poor choice of hardware. The machinery chosen may be satisfactory for the functions it was originally designed to perform, but unsuitable for use in another context. Equipment designed for intermittent use may fail when used in a high-volume, production environment; and conversely, equipment designed for constant use may fail when used intermittently, as was the case in the Hawaii facsimile system. Occasionally the misuse of hardware or software occurs because the designer has a pet technique, or a pet piece of equipment, and attempts to apply it to every system problem, simply because it is familiar and has worked for him before. A good systems designer starts by analysing the problem, conceptualizing alternative approaches to a solution, rigorously determining the advantages and disadvantages of each approach, and selecting one. If the project is large, specifications will then be drawn up, and only then will equipment selection begin. Unfortunately poor designers sometimes reverse the process and a poor system is almost inevitable. Occasionally, too, a particular designer or approach becomes a favorite not of a particular person but of a large number of libraries; in short, a fad. If the system design is basically a good one, such as the terminal-oriented circulation system, everyone profits; if the system design is basically bad, such as the arrival card serial control system, everyone suffers. The proof against this problem, of course, is conscientious inquiry into the actual results achieved by similar systems.

Poor Implementation

Once systems reach the implementation phase, most of the problems will have already been create or encountered, but some projects still falter at this stage. A common fault is that those charge with the implementation, whether librarians, systems people, or administrative staff, fail to take the human element and human values sufficiently into account. Unless it is made clear to all staff members affected by the new system that the goal is better service or more assistance by the purpose of the system are understood, fears for job security are likely to be rampant even if not expressed, and failure to provide reassurances on this score can have serious re-percussions. Temporary inconveniences or additional workloads caused by the one-time necessity of converting records must be explained, and disruptions must be anticipate and counteracted. Presumably back-up procedures will have been incorporated in the system during the design phase, but manual back-up procedures must also be provided during implementation in the event of total system failure.

The consequences of omitting this step can be disastrous, as a final example from Florida Atlantic illustrates. The systems at FAU had been designed on paper at the University of Illinois at Chicago Circle, but never actually implemented; nevertheless it was apparently assume "that the preliminary work done at Chicago made it possible to bypass manual backup systems during the period when the new computer-based systems were being tested and debugged..... No serious discussions were ever held regarding what would happen in unforeseen difficulties arose with either the software or the hardware," the consequences of which "were serious. When the computer-based systems failed, the students and faculty were let without many of the services which even the least sophisticated library user takes for granted." Throughout design and implementation, documentation of the system and all procedures must also be produced, and some library systems have come to grief on this matter alone.

A system may be implemented and working well, but if knowledge of the system is partly or fully in some key person's head and that person leaves or his services are otherwise lost, the solution of subsequent problems may be difficult if not impossible. All systems change, or a least should change, since any library is growing and the requirements imposed on the system consequently differ. If documentation is faulty, changing the system may be a major problem, even in some instances enough to cause its abandonment.

Any catalogue of woe such as the foregoing is naturally depressing, and inevitably runs the risk of seeming overdrawn. Fortunately there have been many systems that avoid most if not all of the problems cited, and successes probably outnumber the failures. To cite these in the interest of "balance", however, would be contrary to the purpose of this chapter, and at any rate no one expects a paper on pathology to conclude with examples of healthy patients. Library automation is basically healthy, despite the problems mentioned, but it will more so when all of these involved can discuss, openly and candidly, the difficulties and even the failures that all sooner or later experience.

Prospects

The recent history of library automation systems is characterized by several strong trends brought about by changes both in technology and in the economic situation confronting most libraries. Unless radical change in either technology or the economy occur, these trends seem likely to continue dominant, and to determine the course of library automation development for some time to come.

Networks

Chief among these trends and easily the most conspicuous is the heavy emphasis being placed on library networks—that is, systems involving more than one library. The entire programs of the 1973 Clinic on Library Applications of Data Processing was devoted to networks, and the log-awaited draft report of the National Commission on Libraries and Information Science contained as its major recommendation a proposal for a national network, evolving from the existing local and regional ones. As Bierman has noted, "the folly of individual libraries proceeding on their own to develop major automated systems solely for their own use seems well recognized and accepted." Networks come in many styles and flavors. One of the most common is the cooperative center for providing catalog cards (and sometimes relate cataloging products), of which the outstanding and most successful example is OCLC, the Ohio College Center.

As mentioned earlier, many other state and regional network are now tied into OCLC and dependent on it to a greater or lesser extent for the services they offer. These include NELINET (the New England Library Information Network of about 40 libraries); FAUL (the Five Associate University Libraries of Upstate New York, which despite the name includes seven members, one of which is not a university libraries); SUNY (the State University of New York, with seventy-two libraries); the Pittsburgh Regional Library Center; PALINET (the Pennsylvania Area Library Network): SOLINET (the Southeastern Library Network, with almost 100 members); the Cooperative College Library Center in Atlanta, Georgia; and AMIGOS (which stands for nothing in particular, but includes several dozen libraries in Texas and the Southwest organized into a network by the Interuniversity Council).

A second type of network is also concerned primarily with technical processing, but attempts to provide a means of cooperative acquisitions as well as cataloging. Successful ones (at least if success is measured by continued operation) include the BCL (Books for College Libraries) program in Massachusetts and the College Bibliocentre program in Ontario, Canada. The mortality rate for this kind of network is high, however, as the deaths of CALBPC (the Colorado Academic Library Book Processing Center) and ANYLTS (the Association of New York Libraries for Technical Services) make clear.

A third type of grouping sometimes called a network is merely a loose consortium of libraries with special procedures for expediting interlibrary loans, often using teletypes. Most of these are not automated in any significant way, and so lie outside the sphere of this book, but some have been working for years to implement on-line networks for the same purposes, a prime example being NYSILL, the New York State Interlibrary Loan Network.

At this writing, the largest category of networks would have to be labeled “in planning” or “in process of implementation”, which some efforts dating back several years. CAPTAIN (Computer Aided Processing & Terminal Access Information Network) is intended to handle acquisitions and processing for New Jersey’s eight state collages, but despite occasional signs of life has experienced constant difficulties in becoming fully operational. MALCAP (the Mary land Academic Library Center for Automated Processing) has had a similar experience. The Washington Library Network, run by the Washington State Library, is "about ready" to go on line after years of development.

Others are mere gleams in various bibliothecal eyes. Indiana is planning a network through INCOLSA, the Indiana Cooperative Library Services Authority. Academic Librarians in the Midwestern state of Michigan, Wisconsin, Minnesota, Ohio, Illinois, Iowa, the Dakotas, Nebraska, and curiously, Indiana have proposed one tentatively labeled MIDLNET or MILINET. Stanford has offered its BALLOTS files for use by other libraries in an attempt to start CLAN (the California Library Automation Network).

The nine universities comprising the Oregon State System of Higher Education have proposed another. And the Rocky Mountain states, not to be left out or outdone by anybody, have proposed SALIENT, the Satellite Library Information Network, for which they have been awarded "designated user" status on the Communication Technology Satellite to be launched by the space program in late 1975. This universal interest in networks has several minifest causes For one thing, declining library budgets and the startling increase in book and serial costs have made the need for cooperation between libraries more urgent. "Resource-sharing" has become a byword, and the resources implied are both bibliographical and financial.

On-line networks enable libraries to know quickly and efficiently which books are in other libraries, and it thus among a group of libraries, reducing the number of duplicate copies needed. Bibliographical data can be shared more effectively, too as the OCLC system demonstrates. A final and forceful incentive is that the sources of funds for purely local automation projects have almost dried up; the Federal grants that were plentiful in the 1960s disappeared in the 1970s, foundations have been less willing to fund projects unless they were truly innovative, and most libraries own budgets are being held static or reduced instead of being increased. Money for cooperative projects that can reasonably be expected to reduce operating costs can usually be found, but not money for local experimentation. Several technical developments have also helped to make the network trend possible. The improvement in communication between computer systems and system users has already been noted, but it should be pointed out that this extends to communication between libraries as well.

Telephones and teletype have long made some interlibrary communication possible, but on-line networks allow librarians in many different libraries literally to share the same working files and catalogues in real time, almost as if they were working in one giant library. Technology has also lowered the cost of storing units of data by several orders of magnitude and the cost of on-line terminals has declined almost as dramatically, while labor costs have continued to rise. The combined force of all these factors has made the economic argument for networks compelling.

Work in the development of standards has also facilitated networking. Without MARC as a national standard for machine-readable bibliographic data, most of the successful networks would not have been possible, and credit for this success must go not only to MARC's brilliant developers at the Library off Congress but also to the many librarians and others who worked hard to promote widespread acceptance of the standard though professional organizations such as the American Library Association (especially its Information Science and Automation Division Standards Institute and the International Standards Organization. The recent introduction of International Standard Bibliographic Descriptions for monographs and serials opens the way for standard Serial Number offers promise for eventual control of what sticky body of data. These and other standards activities have done much to stabilize the future of networks.

Minicomputers

The problems many libraries have experienced in using large, general-purpose institutional computers may also help account or the network trend, since a cooperative system used only for library purposes is one way of avoiding the necessity of sharing a computer with non-library users in an institutional environment. Another way around this problem, apart from networking, is the use of minicomputers owned, controlled and used solely by a single library, and this alternative appears to be growing in popularity. Mention has already been made of the library-owned 1440 used by the University of Missouri, and 1401s have also been dedicated to library purposes, notably at Harvard, and 1401s have also been dedicated to library purposes, notably at Harvard. Minicomputers as currently defined are smaller than the 1400 series, however, most of them taking little more space than the average secretarial desk.

A Favorite is Digital Equipment Corporation's PDP-11, often used as a satellite processor to freed data to and from large computers and do some processing itself, but now increasingly used on a stand-alone basis. The PDP-11 used by the University of British Columbia and the University of South Carolina for their circulation systems provide examples of the former, and the PDP-11 used by the University of Houston for its circulation system offers an example of the stand-along type.

The Houston system also illustrates another growing trend, the interest in "turn-key" systems developed and offered by commercial firms. The reasons behind this trend area similar to those for networking: they avoid the cost of local systems development, and they eliminate concerns about priority and availability. Presumably they lower the risk of failure, too, since the company supplying the system will normally have undergone a considerable amount of debugging prior to installation. Commercial systems have had a mixed in library automaton, however.

Several large companies have been active for many years in the field, but have been more successful in supplying hardware to libraries than in designing complete systems. Lack of knowledge of the market—in this case, libraries—seems to be the problem, rather then lack of technological capability; systems have been proposed which were based on the company's experience in running its own special libraries, without any apparent realization that larger libraries and libraries of different types have different problems and operate in different ways. To some extent, the failure of some commercial designs may also be due to the fact that the companies involved are large and have interest in other fields. Similar companies are a different story. Most of them have concentrated on the library market alone, so they tend to know the market and the business better, but they also tend to be know the market and the business better, but they also tend to be undercapitalized and hence are prone to financial instability. Not a few have gone bankrupts as well as to themselves.

Many of the better-run firms seem to have established themselves on a reasonably sound footing, however, and in recent years have made a significant contribution to library automation. Several have offered book catalogs successfully for so many years that the service is now routine, a few have found markets for cataloging and searching services, and "package system" companies have been successful in installing dozens of ready-made acquisitions and circulation systems. The package (or "turn-key") systems appear to offer numerous advantages. Normally they include all necessary equipment programs, instruction manuals and prepaid training for staff members as well as maintenance contracts and guarantees; in short everything necessary to operate a well-defined area of library operation, such as circulation. The cost of a library systems staff is thus avoided as in the cost of program development efforts to reach fruition, so common with earlier projects, are also bypassed, and the problems of relations with a central computer do not arise.

The problem of overinflated claims, both for operation of the system and service, still makes caution necessary, however, just as caution has always been necessary in the purchase of equipment alone. An additional cause for caution is that such systems are a relatively recent development and it is just as easy for their designers to underestimate the difficulty of automating library operations as it was for library systems staffs before them. For some types of projects and in some libraries, moreover, a local, in-house effort may continue to be the only feasible alternative, and without continued experimentation little further progress in the field is likely to result. Commercial firms do have risk capital, however, and most libraries do not, so the availability of well-designed and fully supported commercial systems offers a welcome alternative for library automation to many libraries in the future.

Future Developments

Assuming that the trends mentioned above continue the development of library automation in the near future can be predicted with some degree of confidence. For catalog card production, very few new projects are likely to be choose to join a network tied to OCLC or a similar service, using it for catalog searching and resource sharing as well as for card production. Attempts to use such networks cooperative acquisitions are less likely to succeed, and seem destined to fall into disfavor, Acquisitions work is more likely to be done on commercial package systems Development effort of Columbia, Chicago, and Stanford universities found that acquisition procedures differed so widely that a joint effort at systems development in this field was impractical. This situation is unlikely to change in the near future, and local systems will therefore continue to be built, with an increased use of on-line techniques. Book catalogs will probably remain popular with public libraries where the ease of producing multiple copies makes them particularly attractive, but most of them will come from one of the various commercial book catalog services rather than from new projects initiated by the libraries themselves.

Academic libraries will continue to use book catalogs to a lesser extent, although the increasing need to share resources and the concomitant need to make existing resources more widely known my lead to a greater use of book catalogs than heretofore. Circulation control will be dominated by commercial, stand along systems, which appear likely to increase rapidly; a recent telephone poll revealed literally dozens of libraries planning to order or already installing such systems. Only in serials control is the picture still cloudy.

The CONSER project is energetic and exciting at the moment, and the fact that OCLC, with its proven record of achievement, will host the project offers hope for its success. The experience of most other serials projects however, offers very little encouragement, and CONSER's approach to the problems engendered by the "baffling bibliographic instability" of serials system similar to the one at UCLA's Biomedical Library, the improvement in library operations and service may be enormous. If they fall, it may be years before another attempt is made. Predications based on current trends of course ignore one importance factor. Technological advances are often unpredictable, and frequently the most exciting and the most significant are those which can least be foreseen. The odds are probably excellent that one or more real breakthroughs will occur within the next decade and offer a new approach, perhaps even begin a new era in library diminished support were merely growing pains, we may hope and the reports of most recent projects show an expertise in planning, design and execution that augurs well. When breakthroughs come, therefore it seems reasonable to think that the profession will be ready for them, and eager to put them to effective use.

The use of computers and the creation of a standardized MARC format were significant achievements in the evolution of library automation, but their full impact was best realized within the context of other important development occurring between the aid-1960s and the mid-1970s. The cornerstone of these development was a radical change in mass market computer technology, characterized by faster processing, increase storage capability, and decreasing hardware prices.

Systems such as the IBM 1401, popular in library use during the early and mid-1960s, comprised what came to be known as second-generation computers. Faster and incorporating far greater memory in less physical space than the vacuum table based computers of the 1950s; The rapid and quantum advances were made in solid state computer technology that even by the mid-1960s, newer models of computers were so much more powerful than the IBM 1401 that a third generation was hailed. The magnitude of technological advancement even within the third generation can be shown by comparing two disk transport systems, the IBM 2314 and the IBM 3330, from the late 1961s and early 1970s. The 2314 utilized removable pack; a piece of information could be assessed in an average of 75 milliseconds, and information could be read into memory at a rate in excess of 800,000 characters per second. As processing speeds and storage capabilities were increasing, the size and price of the machinery were decreasing. By the early 1970s, computers appeared on the market that were comparatively so small and inexpensive that they warranted the label of "minicomputer." Slower and less powerful than their contemporary larger counterparts, minicomputers processed capabilities that matched and exceeded the most sophisticated second-generation computer of barely a decade before, and at a mere fraction of the price. In a 1977 issue of Library Technology Reports, William Scholtz put the comparison in perspective:

In 1960, the IBM 1620 computer needed a room that was approximately 20 by 30 feet....In 1974, a similar machine in terms of capability took up a space that was approximately 3 feet by 3 feet. [and] could perform identical tasks to those performed by the IBM 1620 in about one quarter the time. And finally, the cost to buy the 1974 machine was about what it cost to rent the IBM 1620 for one month. The chief implication of these technological advancements in terms of library application was to usher in the era of online automation. Although the minicomputer would play its own role in this development, earlier online library systems in the last 1960s were based on use of the larger third-generation computers. The computers for these systems were shared among a number of users and invariably were located outside the library in a centralised data processing facility.

Another difference between second-and third-generation facilities was the extent of the latter's timesharing capacity. Second-generation systems were generally not capable of timesharing; the computer processed one job before moving to the next job in the queue.

The remarkable advancements in speed, all tasks associated with design, and storage capacity in third-generation systems allowed them to process a number of jobs simultaneously—or so it seemed. In actual fact, the computer still performed one task at a time, but could handle several jobs coincidentally and execute tasks so quickly that it appeared to each user that the computer was interacting exclusively with their programs, files, and commands. Although the technological environment for online library systems has been in place since the late 1960s, their realization by the late 1970s was still in a stage of infancy if viewed within the context of the totality of libraries in the United States.

Despite the decrease in computer hardware prices that characterised the late 1960s, the design, implementation, and maintenance of an online system were still prohibitively expensive for all but a few libraries during the late 1970s, and even most of these required special grant funding. Between the late 1960s and late 1970s, three trends evolved in the development of online library systems. The first consisted of pioneering in-house projects in single institutions.

The second centered around the evolution of what came to be known as "bibliographic utilities." The third trend was the emergence of private enterprises developing prepackaged "turnkey" automated library systems. Much as with unit-record equipment and computerized online batch processing, the earliest online library system focused on circulation.

Illinois State Library System

One of the first online systems was at the Illinois State Library in Springfield, in late 1966, at a time when many other libraries were designing full offline systems. The backbone of the system was an IBM 1620 computer located in the state processing facility. The equipment in the library consisted of IBM 1033 prints and 1031 card readers, which were similar in operation to the 357 Data Collection System, requiring insertion of machine-readable book cards and borrower identification badges. Rather than producing transaction cards or recording transaction data on tape, however, the 1031 at the Illinois State Library transmitted data directly to the computer. By later standard, the online system at the library was primitive. Although transaction information was conveyed directly to the computer as it occurred, it was stored on a separate daily transaction pack and was merged with the main circulation file only on a once-a-day batch processing basis.

The system did not include item-specific online query, so that it was still necessary to use offline batch-produced circulation lists to trace circulation information pertaining to a given item. For these purposes, the system was much like wholly offline batch processing systems. What set it apart from those, however, was its ability to perform two important functions online: checking borrower registration numbers for validity and checking each returned item against an online holds file. Each time a borrower identification card was inserted into the designated slot of the 1031, the borrower number was automatically checked against a computer-stored file of valid borrower numbers. If the borrower's number did not have a counterpart in the file, that fact was generated immediately on the 1033 printer. This was a major improvement over completely offline operations. Where such validation, if done at all, could be performed only by manual lookup in a printed directory of borrower numbers.

The other important online function of the Illinois State Library system was checking holds, and that had equally important implications. When the book card of a returned item was placed in the 1031 for discharge, the call number was checked against an online list of call numbers of items placed on hold. If the cell number of the returned item matched a call number in the holds file, a message was automatically generated on the 1033 printer showing call number, identification number of the patron who had placed the item on hold, and the data when the hold had been placed. In this manner, greater control over holds was realized than was possible in offline batch processing computerized circulation systems.

Midwestern University System

Another early online circulation system was implemented in late 1967 at Midwestern University in Wichita Falls, Texas. The Midwestern system was unique in that it was, at least insofar as its designers know, the first and perhaps only online circulation system to operate on an IBM 1401 computer, a decidedly second-generation machine. Like the Illinois State Library system, Midwestern used IBM 1031 input stations and 1033 printers, validated borrower identification numbers, and checked items against an online holds file. But it went further than the Illinois system in several important respects. Not only did the Midwestern systems check borrower numbers during a charging operation for general validation, but it also determined if a borrower had any outstanding overdue items or unpaid fines. If so, the computer generated an immediate list of the charges on the 1033 printer.

The Midwestern system had an online query capability, albeit restricted to searching on a borrower number. The keying in of a number prompted the computer to respond by printing a list on the 1033 containing all items charged to that borrower. But perhaps the fundamental difference in the Midwestern system was that the main circulation file was online in the strict sense of the term, with the file being updated immediately upon completion of each transaction, rather than in a batch mode.

Eastern Illinois University System

In September 1968, the Booth Library at Eastern Illinois University in Charleston began to operate its own version of a online circulation system using a third-generation IBM 360/

Model 50 computer and the IBM 1031 input stations and 1033 printers. The Booth system had the basic functional characteristic of the Midwestern system, but with an important additional query feature.

The Midwestern system had query capability by patron number; the Booth system supplemented this with item query by call number. By entering a particular two-digit code followed by a call number, a terminal operator could retrieve bibliographic information and current circulation data about a specific item. Queries of this nature were made using an IBM Cathode Ray Tube (CRT) terminal located at the circulation desk. A further extension of this search capability was a scanning command that displayed bibliographic entries in call number sequence.

Since the Booth Library online file was an inventory file containing an abbreviated bibliographic record for nearly even item in the library—not just items currently charged out—the scanning capability allowed shelflist searching of the entire library collection. The structure and search capabilities of this system suggested possible extension as a public-access tool, and in fact plans were announced to locate a public-access CRT terminal near the card catalog in fall 1971. Still, the known item query capability of the Eastern Illinois system allowed more immediate information about the circulation status of an item—ever if the query had to be generated by a circulation attendant—than was possible in an offline system.

Minicomputer-based Hybrids

In the early 1970s, a number of academic libraries began to incorporate minicomputers in their circulation operations. A significant feature of these systems was that at least part of the processing hardware was located in the library itself, although a larger computer, outside the library, still played an integral role. Typically, the minicomputer in the library contained certain files for immediate online access and captured transaction data for later batch transmission to as larger computer located outside the library on which the main circulation file was stored. While some of the operations remained offline, this setup realized the benefits of online processing for certain critical purposes. One of the most common minicomputers in this type of configuration was the IBM System/7 in use in circulation control in at least six libraries by early 1974.

In the system operational at the University of Pennsylvania in Philadelphia, five online files were stored in the minicomputer. Each of these contained critical information against which various types of transactions were checked. There were three item files against which renewal attempts and discharges were checked. A call number file contained the call number of all items placed on hold, the access number file contained a list of all items recalled, and a reserve book file contained all items for which in request had been placed to transfer the item to a reserve book collection upon its return.

Another file, against which all patron identification numbers were checked, was the restricted patron file, containing a lost of borrower identification numbers of all users whose further attempts to charge materials were to be blocked for some reason. The fifth online file was the daily transaction file, which recorded the day's activity. Once a day, this file was transmitted to the main computer, an IBM 370/Model 168, located at the university data processing center, for batch updating of the main circulation file. This transmission, usually involving information for about 3,000 transactions, required about 30 minutes. For the most part, improvements, gained in the Online circulation systems of the late 1960s and early 1070s over what was possible in an offline system were focused on immediate access to information about restricted items, such as holds, and better control of patron privilege. Although improvements regarding access to information about restricted items enhanced public service by allowing more rapid reshelving of returned items and a better system for regulating holds and ensuring identification upon return, these benefits were not always immediately evident to the average library user.

The second common capability, immediate access to Online delinquent patron files, could as likely cause ill feelings as goodwill between the library and its users. The lack of reliable backup measures, inexperience in dealing with online systems, and continued reliance on batch-produced circulation lists combined to make early online circulation systems less than revolutionary in terms of public service. At least one facility, the Simon Fraser University Library, had so many problems and so much user discontent with its online system that it abandoned online and reverted to its earlier offline system."

Ohio State University System

Perhaps the outstanding example during the early 1970s of online circulation system that could, in fact, facilitate user services to a degree not possible in an offline system was demonstrated by Ohio State University's Library Control System. The entire philosophy behind the design and application of the system for the Ohio State University libraries was, as described by Hugh Atkinson, "that the system should be one which would speak to the problems of its users rather than simply the problems of the library." These problems included, among others, a decentralized library structure consisting of a main library and more than 20 branches. Only one catalog—the main library's—contained complete information for all items in all 21 libraries.

Similar to several earlier online circulation systems, Ohio State opted for an "inventory" file approach in which the main machine-readable database contained records for all items in the libraries rather than an "absence" file, which would have contained records only for those items in circulation. This principles as fundamental at Ohio State since the system was to be used as a locator file as well as for circulation operations. A massive conversion effort—perhaps the largest of its kind carried out by any library to that date—was contracted to a vendor, which put into machine-readable form records containing call number, unique item number, author, title, date of publication.

Library of Congress card number, language code, from of publication code, and holding for each of 1 million distinct titles and 2.5 million items. The key to the Ohio State system was its items query capability. Searching was possible by call number, title key, and a combination author/title key. When the desired item was retrieved, it was possible to see which library or libraries on campus owned a copy of the item, and whether each copy was charged out. Search terminals were available in the main library and in most of the branches.

Thus, the entire union catalog of the libraries' holdings could be assessed from any library in the system. Although this in itself was a fundamental improvement over the single union catalog in the main library. An item not already checked out in one library could be charged on terminals located in any a copy was found to be available in a different branch library, the circulation attendant could issue a command that would generate a charge slip in the branch library that had the copy. The item would be retrieved in that library and placed on a shelf to await later pickup by the patron.

The online union catalog, showing location and circulation status of each item throughout the system, combined with the capability of remote charging to remove much of the patron uncertainty that was inherent under prior circumstances. The Ohio State University library system, like all other online system, was not entirely free of problems, but many of them could eventually be alleviated by design changes and the system was such an improvement over earlier conditions that the problems were of comparatively minor consequence. The impact of this system on library service was probably best exemplified by the fact that, during the first 18 months it was in operation, circulation at the Ohio State University libraries increased by more than 40 percent.

The system was an important achievement owing to its scale of implementation, its query capabilities, and its emphasis on public service problem solving. The same system was later taken by Atkinson to the University of Illinois and implemented; today it is the basis of an important networking system in libraries throughout Illinois. Apart from circulation, the late 1960s and early 1970s saw the development of a number of online technical processing systems.

One of the earliest acquisitions systems was designed at the Washington State University Library in Pullman and was implemented in 1968; an online serials control system was up and running at University Level in Quebec the same year. Predating both of these was the beginning of a comprehensive online library system at the Redstone Scientific Information Center in Alabama. Some parts of the system were operational as early as 1966. And by the early 1970s, acquisitions, cataloging, authority control, serials check-in, and circulation were online. Offline computerization had been an important development in acquisitions, providing for machine-assisted production of purchase orders, improved methods of fiscal control, and more timely updating and generation of status lists. Still, a significant amount of from handling and paper file maintenance remained in many of these systems.

The online acquisitions systems developed in the late 1960s and early 1970s represented major improvements by reducing the amount of manual handling and maintenance of paper products, as well as further enhanced those functions that had been performed well in offline computerized system.

Acquisitions

One of the more ambitious projects in the late 1960s was carried out at the Oregon State University Library at Corvallis. Christened LOLITA, this online acquisitions system required nearly seven "staff years" in programming, systems, and clerical labor to develop. It contained three Online files: order/in-process file contained three display screens of information input when an order was placed, and updated as an item passed through the acquisitions and cataloging procedures.

The first screen included basic bibliographic data, the second screen contained accounting data, and the third screen allowed for local cataloging information such as call number and location. The amount of time and file maintenance that this system saved the staff, particularly when compared with a manual system, was considerable. LOLITA generated four paper copies of each order, two going to the vendor, one later used as a cataloging workshop, and one retained as a general hard copy record for the library.

The two copies for library use were a reduction over most offline systems, and some libraries went even further. With the online acquisitions systems in use at the University of Massachusetts Library and the Dartmouth College Library, neither library retained any paper copies of the order form in technical processing at all. One of the greatest contributions made by online systems in general was the expansion of access points, and these early acquisition systems were no exception. It was possible with an offline system to produce lists or maintain paper copies of order forms by more than one point of access, such as by order number, author, and title if desired, but that merely increased the number of lists to be consulted or files to be maintained. As a result, the number of listing parameters was usually minimized in offline systems. In online systems, all files and their indexes could be maintained in the computer, and multiple access points to a single record would not mean an increase in hard copy materials to be consulted or maintained. LOLITA, however, only provided to access points, order number and author, to each record in the system. The early online acquisitions systems retained some of the capabilities that had been included in their offline predecessors, but the newer systems were much improved in quality, speed, and ease of handling. LOLITA, along with several other early systems, provided for handling of partial shipments and authorization of partial invoice payments, capabilities that were handled, if at all, only with some difficult by offline systems.

The fund accounting component of LOLITA was also successful. A year-end encumbrance report could be generated in 20 minutes, and LOLITA was to only much faster, nut also judged more accurate and detailed in a controlled comparison with manual ledgers. Perhaps the most important characteristic of online acquisitions systems was that, in most cases, it was only one part of a broader integrated technical processing system that brought the acquisitions and cataloging functions closer together.

The online order record, upon receipt of an item, became an online cataloging record. This greatly reduced duplication between acquisitions and cataloging and also provided an end product consisting of a machine-readable bibliographic record for each item entering the collection. In LOLITA, the final steps in the online processing after an item had been received were for a cataloger to verify the bibliographic information originally entered by the acquisitions department and the complete the record by adding local cataloging data.

The completed record was removed from the online file, but not before it had been copied onto magnetic tape as a permanent machine-readable record.

An important feature in the development of online technical processing systems was the incorporation of Library of Congress MARC records. Records on MARC tapes were transferred into the local online systems in various ways. A common feature across systems was that each new order was searched against a locally maintained MARC file, and when a match occurred, the appropriate MARC record entered the local system as the source for bibliographic information for ordering and eventual cataloging. One of the most comprehensive uses of MARC records evolved in the University of Chicago Library Data Management System. Orders could be searched against the MARC files, and there was a retrospective searching capability whereby incoming MARC records were searched against the local bibliographic file to identify previously created local records as potential candidates for bibliographic upgrading by the new matching MARC record.

These features in one from or another could be found in other systems, but an interesting feature of the Chicago systems was its use of MARC tapes as a collection development tool. Subject profiles, defined by Library Congress classification numbers and ranges of numbers, could be maintained online, and each incoming MARC tape was matched against them.

The result was an offline list of items falling into each subject profile for use in identifying potential orders for the library. The system also allowed access to these lists online if a bibliographer wished. The system also allowed access to these lists online if a bibliographer wished. Supplementing the LC class number profiles were certain national bibliography online profiles used to identify potential orders from an area studies prospective. In addition to profiles designed to identify items of potential interest for the library, the University of Chicago system also included a capability designed to assist in better control over blanket orders from publishers. The first four digits of an International Standard Book Number (ISBN), MARC field 020, are unique to each publisher. Each record on the MARC tapes was automatically searched on these first four digits at Chicago. The system could then generate lists of items published by each publisher with whom Chicago had a blanket order arrangement, and these lists could be used to assist in monitoring receipt of blanket order items.

BALLOTS

Several of the largest research libraries in the United States were interested in the concept of an online integrated technical processing system as early as the mid-1960s, although actual systems could be implemented at these institutions only after several years of planning, design, and experimentation. These of the more well publicized of these large-scale efforts included the Northwestern Online Total Integrated System (NOTIS), the University of Chicago Library Data Management System mentioned earlier, and Standford University's Bibliographic Automation of Large Library Operations using a Time sharing System (BALLOTS). Without minimizing the importance of achievements elsewhere, BALLOTS was perhaps the most sophisticated online technical processing system developed in the early 1970s. Because of its later adoption as the online bibliographic component of the Research Libraries Group (RLG), its impact on American librarianship during the 1970s and early 1980s has been greater than any other system originally designed for use by a single institution.

An experimental version of BALLOTS was brought online as early as 1969, but it was not until 1972, after further design and modification, that the system was dully implemented. It ran on the Standford University campus computer, an IBM 360/ Model 67, with a Digital Equipment Corporation PDP 11 minicomputer in the library as a front-end communications processor. The terminals initials selected for accessing the system were programmable Sanders PDS 804s. The hardware for BALLOTS was in itself an important achievement. The selection of terminals with a programmable capability was based on the design requirements for the terminal display features desired. Two important functional considerations were to allow for protected fields in an online record that could not be modified by a terminal operator, and at the same time to permit line insertion to allow expansion in length of certain nonprotected fields.

At the time BALLOTS was being designed, either one of these further could be incorporated by using a nonprogrammable terminal, but not a combination of the two. Only a programmable terminal, such as the Sanders model could allow both protected and expandable fields. In addition, it was possible for several programmable terminals to share a single communications line rather than each requiring its own dedicated line. BALLOTS was designed around several modules and contained four online files critical to technical processing. One was a MARC file, which held the most recent 6 to 12 months of MARC records from the Library of Congress.

A second was an In-Process File (IPF), which contained a record for each item anywhere in the processing stage from initiation of an order to final cataloging. Once received and cataloged, the record was transferred into a third file, the Catalog Data File (CDF), which contained an online record for each item fully processed on BALLOTS. Fourth was a Reference File (REF), which included see references, see also references, and explanatory and history references. When a request for an order was submitted, a terminal operator first searched the MARC file to see if as corresponding MARC record was available. If a match was found, the operator requested an online ordering work form, which contained mnemonic fields into which information could be entered. Appropriate bibliographic data were automatically transferred from the MARC record to the work form, requiring the terminal operator to input only the additional information pertaining to the order, such as vendor code and accounting data. An online order record could easily be created for an item where there was no available MARC record, but this naturally required more time since bibliographic information had to be supplied from other sources and typed onto the Online work from.

Offline products, such as purchase orders, a cataloging workslip, and a temporary order slip, were printed each evening for all items entered into the In-Process File during the day. Stanford found the traditional 3" x 5" slip too small for its purposes and, as described by Veaner, "because copies of certain forms no longer had to be filed, the forms themselves could be designed around their data requirements rather than a filing cabinet size." The online order from was updated as its status changed, such as when an item was received. After receipt was indicated, the item was given to the cataloguing department for final processing.

One of the helpful features of BALLOTS was its tracing procedure; the location of an item within the processing unit was kept up-to-date online ever to the name of the specific cataloguer handling the final processing. It was the responsibility of the cataloguing department, with item in hand, to verify and, if necessary, modify the information on the online record created in acquisitions and to add any additional pertinent data. Catalog cards and spine labels were then printed offline, with the day's production of all cataloguing cards sorted into filing order sequence. The online record was transferred into the Catalog Data File as the permanent bibliographic and holdings inventory record.

BALLOTS had a number of built-in features that made input and modification of records easy for a terminal operator and at the same time reduced the likelihood of operator error. Fields that were inappropriate for operator input or modification were automatically protected so the operator could not even place the cursor in those positions on the screen display. After entering information into a nonprotected field, the operator could move the cursor to the next nonprotected field simply by depressing the shift and tab keys. Throughout the procedure were default protocols that assumed the operator's next most logical step but these could be overridden by the operator if an item required atypical treatment. The system also had validation capabilities for certain types of information such as account codes. When an account code was entered by an operator onto the online order work from, the system checked the code validity.

This check did not prevent a valid inaccurate code from being assigned to an item, but it did insure that nonexistent accounts could not be charged. Ordering selected volumes of a multipart set hard always been a problem in acquisitions systems, but BALLOTS handled this in a way that minimized the work of the terminal operator and still allowed flexibility in subsequent processing. If, for example, volumes 1, 2, 3, 8 and 9 were being ordered, the operator merely typed 1-3 and 8-9 in an appropriate field on the order work from, and the system automatically "exploded" the record into five distinct records, one for each volume ordered. These separate records for each volume allows receipt of partial shipments and individualized processing. One of the strongest features of the BALLOTS system was its search retrieval capabilities. Unlike most other technical processing systems. BALLOTS offered a wide complement of sear fields and allowed searching on truncated words, variant forms of entry, and keywords. A terminal operator could search the MARC file by Library of Congress card number, personal name, corporate or conference name, and title. The Catalog Data File allowed for searching by all these elements, but also by Library of Congress subject headings, call number, and BALLOTS ID number. Searching of the In-Process and Reference files was more restricted than searching of the Catalog Data File, but less restrictive than searching the MARC file. As an automated technical processing system, BALLOTS was a landmark project far more sophisticated than earlier offline systems and more successful than its online contemporaries of the early 1970s. As might be expected, it had a tremendous impaction Stanford's operation, such as integrating technical processing functions more closely than before.

The Acquisitions and Cataloging departments, although remaining under separate supervision were physically consolidated. They had previously been located on different floors of the library. In addition, the number of staff was reduced. One-third of the staff positions in the Order Division were eliminated, as were several positions that previously had been responsible solely for typing unit entry cards, duplicating and typing headings on them, and sorting them into filing order: all functions that were computerized under BALLOTS. By the mid-1970s, automated efforts in technical; processing were turning to shared systems.

BALLOTS remained an exemplary illustration of an in-house system, and itself became the basis of a networking system, first among several libraries in California, then in a wider geographic area in the western United States, and still later among a number of major research libraries across the country. Although serials control is an integral part of technical processing, development of automated systems for serials handling has usually been carried out somewhat independently of acquisitions and cataloging. This had been the case with unit-record and offline batch processing systems and was equally typical of online development. Offline systems allowed libraries greater control in some aspects of the serials operation, particularly in claiming, and enabled holdings lists to be updated and printed much more frequently and with far less staff effort than in unit-record systems.

A considerable amount of manual card and paper handling still was required, however, and the offline lists were a problem in that they tended to be generational, with periodic supplements to other periodic supplements to less frequent master cumulations. Online capabilities offered the potential of reducing the amount of handling and making available up-to-date records of holdings in one place. In the early 1970s, and on perhaps a somewhat less dramatic scale, the system developed at the UCLA Biomedical Library was to serials what BALLOTS was to acquisitions and cataloging and what the Ohio State University system was to circulation.

Although not the first online serials control project to be implemented, the UCLA system was generally considered more sophisticated and flexible than its contemporaries. Design objectives included, among others, the elimination of all card handling and the generation of fewer hard copy lists. By 1972, there were records in the serials control database for about 12,000 titles, slightly more than half the library's current subscriptions. The format of the online records was similar to MARC, but with fewer fields. When an issue of a title was received, the operator retrieved the online record and updated it by keying a simple code. Other codes were defined for updating holdings when back or skipped issues were received. In additional to the check-in operation, the system had automatic overdue detection and binding status monitoring. Keyword searching of the database could be performed, an especially crucial capability given the complexity and similarity of serials titles. The search component also allowed retrieval of titles by fixed field. Online systems had many advantages over those based entirely on batch processing. The volume of paperwork and hard copy files was reduced, as well as the amount of staff time required for their maintenance. Although the "up-to-the-second information" characteristic of online was highly touted, many of the earlier systems only partially had this capability, as evidenced by some circulation functions that used minicomputers as front-end communications systems. Nevertheless, even those systems were able to store some of their more critical files in virtually current status. One of the most important characteristics of online systems was search retrieval capability. Again, some of the early ones are very restricted in inquiry capability, but others were considerable sophisticated, such as at Ohio State University, Stanford, and the UCLA Biomedical Library described earlier.

The design, implementation, and continuing operation of the more sophisticated online systems were landmark achievements, but their costs were correspondingly high. In many instances, funding was aided throng grants or heavily subsidized by the host institution's general operating budget; the costs were far out of reach of the vast majority of libraries. It was estimated, for example, that the continuing production and development costs in operating BALLOTS doe a single month in 1974 were $34.225, and this figure pales in comparison to the design and development costs incurred before the system's implementation.

Bibliographic Utilities

Left with an alternative of in-house, single-library development projects, only the largest and most well endowed libraries could have used an online system for any technical support systems during the 1970s. As early as 1967, however, a second alternative was being formulated, and the outgrowth of this and similar efforts was the evolution of four system—OCLC, RLG, WLN, and UTLAS—whose use by the early 1980s, extended into several thousand libraries on the North American continent.

OCLC

Although some libraries continued to develop their own in-house systems for certain library functions, it was apparent by the mid-1970s that automated cataloging in particular was evolving in a different direction. The basis of this transformation was the Ohio College Library Center (OCLC), a system based on the simple premise that, recognizing minor local variations, cataloging data for a given item were essentially similar from library to library. The Library of Congress MARC project had been as major breakthrough in the concept of shared cataloging information in an automated environment, but the general pattern of sharing had been unidirectional and on an institution-by-institution basis. MARC tapes were sent from the Library of Congress to subscribing institutions, each of which then loaded the tapes and manipulated the data on its own computer.

The idea that evolved for OCLC was a central file of cataloging records that could be maintained on a single computer system and accessed through terminals sharing dedicated communications line connected to that computer. Not only would this enable libraries to share a MARC file, but it would centralize development costs of the system and virtually eliminated the need for each participating library to use the host institution's computer system. Because the Library of Congress cataloged only portion of the universe of materials received by libraries, and since the MARC tapes included only the OCLC online system was the capability for allowing original input of records, using the MARC format, by the participating libraries themselves. The impact of this is seen by the fact that even by the end of the decade, less than one-fourth of the master bibliographic records in the OCLC database had been supplied by the Library of Congress. OCLC was chartered in 1967 and Frederick G. Kilgour named as its executive director. System production first began with offline batch processing in 1970; 54 member academic libraries in Ohio submitted punched IBM cards with Library of Congress card numbers of items for which they wanted catalogue cards produced.

The punched cards were searched against a file consisting of the Library of Congress MARC records, and when a match occurred, catalogue cards were generated and sent back to the requesting library within two weeks. In 1971, OCLC went online, installing terminals that allowed each library to search the growing OCLC On-Line Union Catalogue (OLUC), the bibliographic database of the system. The library could order catalog cards merely depressing a couple of command keys on the keyboard attached to the CRT display terminal. During the first several years of OCLC online operation, a number of far-reaching decisions were made that would enhance-and sometimes plague—the cooperative effort.

The display format revolved around the concept of a bibliographic "master record"; in theory there was to be only one record in the database for any given bibliographic entity. When this master record for an item was retrieved by a library, any of the MARC fields could be modified to reflect local practices with respect to subject headings, forms of name entry, local call number, and so on; virtually any element in the record could be modified. All local changes were reflected on the catalog cards printed offline at OCLC and mailed to the library (and eventually on the library's magnetic tapes of its cataloging activity when this service became available). These modifications, however, were not stored permanently online for the library. Therefore, when a library retrieved a record it had previously used for cataloging, the bibliographic master record was displayed online, without the local modifications that the library had previously made. The lack of capability to permanently store local information was probably justifiable in OCLC's initial stages. The amount of storage required to maintain this data for each cataloging use of each record by each library would have been enormous, especially since most members of OCLC at that time had a low incidence of adding copies for titles they had already cataloged once.

Nevertheless, it was not long after the system went online that some members began to express concern over the lack of a permanent online record containing local modifications for previously cataloged materials. A characteristic of OCLC during the 1970s was a perpetual gap between announced plans and actual implementation, and the permanent storage and display of local cataloging data—or at least of a scaled-down version of local holdings from selected fields—perhaps provides the most exemplary illustration. In early 1974, "Definition and Use of the 049 Holding Field," detailing a critical field used to record local data for card production and tape purposes, was published by OCLC partially in anticipation of an impending change, which would allow storage and display of modifications to master records.

The actual change proved far less than imminent. Five years later, in 1979, OCLC's development schedule projected the capability of local holdings display for current cataloging records to be available to members in January 1980, with access to local information for previously cataloged materials available sometime later. But less and less discussion of this capability emanated from corporate headquarters and the capability eventually disappeared from all development schedules. The strategy initially used in creating the online file of bibliographic master records in OCLC revolved around the creation of as large a database as possible in as little time as possible. This may be overgeneralization, but there is little doubt that it was prevalent enough so that a great many of the permanent master records entered into the database by member libraries in the early years suffered in quality and completeness of information.

Master records, particularly for retrospective cataloging entered into the database, were frequently created from a description taken solely from the shelflist card of the first member library to convert the title. Thus quality and completeness depended in great part on any given library's past shelflisting practices, on the library's policy for input of new records into the database, and, beyond that, on the accuracy of the terminal operator. The philosophy of rapid creation of a database at the expense of detail and completeness of record could be seen in OCLC's approach in 1975 to providing records for serials titles, for which a specifically designed MARC format had only recently become available. To greatly increase the number of serials records in a short time, tapes of the Minnesota Union List of Serials (MULS) were loaded into the OCLC database. Although MULS contained accurate information as far as it went, it was primarily a locational tool and provided very abbreviated bibliographic data for cataloguing purposes.

Perhaps the greatest quality control complication in the long run was the extreme difficulty of upgrading master records when a mistake was detected or information found to be incomplete. Written forms had to be completed by a member library and mailed to OCLC; when received, the master record was examined by OCLC staff and modified according to the reported additions or changes. This process was time-consuming and cumbersome for member libraries, and not exactly a foremost staffing priority at OCLC.

The result was that a library could easily retrieve a master record containing an obvious typographical error that presumably had been modified locally by any number of other libraries for their own card production, but that remained in the master record due to backlogs at OCLC in record upgrading. Owing to the prominent role of the OCLC database in the Conversion of Serials (CONSER) project, a limited number of libraries were given the capability of making permanent online modifications to OCLC serials master records from their own terminals, thus bypassing the manual error reporting procedure. This proved a tremendous success.

The possibility of enabling a small number of libraries a similar online capability for records in other formats was a topic of discussion for several years, and was finally initiated in mid-1984. The approach used in creating its database and the difficulty in correcting errors in master records earned OCLC a reputation in some quarters as a "dirty database." To be certain, many early records in the database did suffer from lack of quality control. An often overlooked factor by critics, however, was that OCLC was an experiment without direct precedent and included among its membership a segment of the library community that had virtually no previous experience with any type of library automation. OCLC was not the first online system used for collective representation of cataloging data fro a number of independent libraries, but immediate predecessors were based on centralized input and thus centralized control.

This was quite different from the structure of OCLC, in which any member library could input an original bibliographic master record for an item. Given this degree of autonomy and decentralization, combined with the lack of previous experience with library automation on the part of most of its members, and a lack of precedence to gauge the implications of shared databases, the early 1970s were an individual and cooperative learning experience for OCLC members which served to demonstrate both the strong points and the problem areas of cooperative ventures in library automation.

During its first year of online operation. OCLC remained a cooperative venture of Ohio academic libraries. During 1972, membership was extended to Ohio nonacademic libraries, and in 1973 to libraries outside the state. Although the major computer facilities were to remain centralized at OCLC headquarters, a decentralized approach to the provision of general support services emerged by the mid-1970s. OCLC and various independent state and regional agencies entered into contracts for the brokering of OCLC services and for provision of training and ongoing assistance.

Some of these networks had predated OCLC; others were formed in direct response to the need for an agency to provide OCLC services in a particular area. Two exceptions to the general pattern of independent brokering were the formation of OCLC Western (referred to as PACNET-the OCLC Pacific Network), consisting of several branch offices on the Pacific Coast, and OCLC Europe, both being service agencies under the direct administration of OCLC. The independent affiliate networks, which have usually numbered about 20, have remained administratively separate from OCLC a relationship that has at times worked to the benefit of OCLC and at other times served as a source of conflict. Within four years after OCLC's decision in 1973 to expand its base of participation beyond Ohio, the number of libraries using the system had increased to more than 800.

Increasing numbers of public and special libraries were joining, but the majority of new members continued to be academic libraries. These included many members of the Association of Research Libraries as well as medium-sized university libraries, but an influx of new participants continued from among the ranks of four-year colleges, a pattern that underscored OCLCs role in introducing automation into smaller institutions. A major factor in the opportunity for these smaller academic libraries to join OCLC during these years was the availability of implementation grants from the Kellogg Foundation. By 1977, it had become apparent that OCLC governing structure had not kept pace with the growth of the system. General "membership" and positions on the board of trustees were still restricted to libraries in the state of Ohio, with libraries in other state defined as "participants" and having no elective say in the governing body.

The Arthur D. Little firm in Cambridge, Massachusetts, was commissioned to study OCLC's governing structure and to suggest alternatives. With recommendations based on a report submitted in June 1977, the Ohio OCLC membership later that year voted to adopt a new governing structure to reflect its national character. During the same year, OCLC changed its official name to the acronyrn by which it had become known, and in 1981 it adopted the name of OCLC Online Computer Library Center.

RLIN

The concept of resource sharing was the basis for the formation of a number of formal cooperative ventures during the 1970s. One such, begun in 1974, was the Research Libraries Group (RLG), comprised of Harvard, Yale, Columbia, and the New York Public Library. Its board goals focused on the sharing of resources, collection development, and preservation and conservation of library materials. RLG felt that a common automated bibliographic system would enhance cooperative efforts among member libraries. By early 1978, the four systems under final consideration for adoption included OCLC, Standford's BALLOTS, the University of Chicago Library Data Management System, and the New York Public Library bibliographic control system.

In spring 1978, RLG announced agreement with Stanford for the use of BALLOTS as the group's automated bibliographic component. Although RLG may merely have chosen what it considered to be the best available system, the choice drew strong reactions from within and outside the group. In June of the year, Harvard announced withdrawal from RLG, although Director of Libraries Douglas Bryant indicated that the choice of BALLOTS was not the motivating factor.

A wide spectrum of emotions was expressed throughout the library community concerning RLG's decision not to go with OCLC, which many saw as the emerging national bibliographic network. In comparing the online features of BALLOTS and OCLC, there is no question that BALLOTS was the far more sophisticated and flexible technical processing system. Unlike OCLC, it also provided for online storage and display of an individual library's cataloging data in a network environment, as well as other features such as searching by title keyword and subject, not available on OCLC.

Although on a smaller scale than OCLC, BALLETS had also proved capable of serving as a shared system as early as 1975 when seven public libraries in California entered into a networking arrangement with Stanford, and the number of libraries using it has increased since then. The greatest source of resentment among OCLC libraries about RLG's selection of BALLOTS was probably not so much the choice itself as it was the accompanying implicit, and sometimes explicit, attitude that OCLC and its "dirty database" were unacceptable, and that the needs of RLG members were somehow quite apart from those of the rest of the library community—including those of many prestigious research libraries that remained ardent supporters of OCLC. Equally crucial in the reaction, OCLC had come to be recognized by then as much more than a shared cataloging database. Because of library identifier symbols attached to each bibliographic record, OCLC had grown into a tremendous tool for facilitating interlibrary lending and, to many, was the most current and reliable source of occasional information available in the United States.

The selection of another system by RLG virtually cut off those libraries and their collections from this source of information and ejected a major obstacle to their participation in resource sharing on a broader scale. To many OCLC libraries and even to those using neither system, this detachment seemed a conscious and motivated effort to minimize the role of RLG members in the broader context of American library cooperation. The reaction to RLG did little at that time or later to discourage the image of elitism.

Full membership in RLG, in essence, required a library to be a member of the Association of Research Libraries (ARL), and this restricted potential membership in RLG to a pool of early 100 libraries. RLG permitted other libraries to apply for participant status, meaning a library could use and contribute cataloging data, but the feeling was that this did little to soften the image of elitism. BALLOTS, which in the RLG environment became the Research Libraries Information Network (RLIN), may have been functionally superior to OCLC as a technical processing system, but not all of its distinctions were carried over into the new network. At Stanford, the system had been, and remained, a full technical processing system, which traced an item and built on its online record from the initial point of ordering to its final point of cataloging. Crucial in this progression was the In-process File (IPF), described earlier in this chapter.

Although any RLIN member library had searching access to Stanford's IPF, there was no capability for other members to build a similar file for their own institutions. Thus, one of the strongest features of the original BALLOTS, which provided the continuity for its realization a more complete technical processing system, did not exist under RLIN in its earliest manifestation for any library other than Stanford.

WLN

During the 1970s, work was also being conducted at the Washington State Library on the design of an online bibliographic system. Supported by a $1.2 million start-up grant from the state legislature, the system went online in 1978, the Washington Library Network (WLN) was being used in 12 public and 9 academic libraries in the state, along with 2 libraries in Alaska. Later that year, 3 libraries in Idaho and 1 in Oregon joined WLN. From the start, it was apparent that WLN was a well-designed and highly sophisticated system. It included retrieval of local information, subject access, and, not long thereafter, authority control. WLN took a cautious approach to building its bibliographic database.

As in RLIN and OCLC, Library of Congress MARC tapes were loaded, but unlike the other two utilities, WLN established a standing policy to centrally review all records input by member libraries. In January 1979, the library press reported that the National Library of Australia had signed for membership in WLN had sold its system software to the National Library. The distinction was significant. All three of the major utilities—OCLC, RLIN, and WLN—were based on a centralized computer system linked through telecommunications lines to terminals in member libraries; none of the utilities up until that time had attempted to transfer any part of its system for use in another computer. In 1978, it was not entirely clear to American library community what role WLN would assume in national bibliographic networking. Although WLN was focusing on regional cooperation in the Pacific Northwest, OCLC had also been a geographically limited system at one time, and BALLOTS had been implemented in a single library. It seemed possible that a third nationally competing system may have been emerging in the form of WLN. In 1979, however, the network reaffirmed its regional emphasis, adopting a policy that expansion outside the Pacific Northwest would-be restricted to sale of the WLN software in a manner similar to what had taken place with the National Library of Australia.

In the years immediately following, a number of such transactions occurred, including sales to the South-eastern Library Network (SOLINET), the University of Illinois, and the University of Missouri. Membership in the WLN network in the Pacific Northwest had increased to 60 members by 1980 and, as OCLC had done slightly more than two years before, WLN modified its government structure to reflect the expansion of its membership base beyond a single state.

UTLAS

Although its impact in the United State has been limited, the University of Toronto library Automated System (UTLAS) was a fourth major online bibliographic networking system to have emerged on the North American continent during the 1970s. Implemented in an online networking mode during the mid-1070s, UTLAS had increased its membership to more than 200 libraries by the end of the decade. UTLAS membership was limited primarily to Canadian libraries, with some important exceptions. In 1980, the network signed its first member in the United States, the Rochester, New York, Institute of Technology. The following year, UTLAS signed a million-dollar agreement with a Japanese firm to broker UTLAS in Japan.

The system did not make concerted efforts to expand into the United States, but it is noteworthy that in 1981, in a comprehensive comparison of the four major utilities, the

University of California at Berkeley ranked UTLAS first in overall technical capability. The University did not, however, opt for UTLAS. In 1984, UTLAS opened a U.S. branch office in New York, and it will be interesting to see what impact this will have on its position in the nation. Over the years, each of the four bibliographic utilities has strived to become more than simply a shared cataloguing database.

Development efforts by one or more have gone into acquisitions subsystems, serials check-in capabilities, circulation systems, interlibrary loan communications, online union lists, provision of Computer Output Microform (COM) catalogs, and terminal compatibility for searching other databases. WLN, OCLC, and RLIN made a tremendous impact on librarianship in the United States during the 1970s in terms of providing online cataloging capabilities, but their impact in circulation control, acquisitions, and serials check-in was negligible. Some libraries continued to develop their own in-house systems to handle these functions. However, another alternative emerged, particularly in the area of online circulation, in the form of commercial vendors of automated library systems.

Commercial Online Systems

Commercial enterprise played a pivotal role in library automation long before the advent of online systems. Automation via unit-record equipment had been almost the exclusive domain of IBM. Remington Rand offered unit-record equipment comparable to IBMs, but its impact on the library market was negligible. IBM continued its domination into the early 1960s, when offline computer processing came into use in some libraries. As the decade progressed, however, computers manufactured by other firms began to appear in universities, corporations, and municipal facilities. By the end of the decade, IBM was still the predominant name in computers for library applications, but it no linger maintained the exclusively it had once enjoyed. During its years of dominance, IBM had been responsible in devoting time and effort to assist in applying its equipment to the library environment. Libraries certainly did not receive an undue share of attention, but IBM representative were often assigned to help libraries with implementing applications, and the corporation published descriptions of and guides for use of its equipment in library applications. The company also sponsored seminars, the most notable being a symposium held in Endicott, New York, in 1964. Although IBM and its new competitors expressed at least nominal interest in library applications during the 1960s, it was evident that this was an infinitesimal share of the total computer market.

According to estimates in the early 1970s, less than one-tenth of one percent of the computers in the United States were being using by libraries in the way. To make these facilities still less conductive as a market, even those with computers were inevitably using equipment purchased by host institutions for a variety of applications, the foremost usually not being those of the library. Libraries had little control in either the selection of equipment or in the decision to replace one manufacturer or model with another. As long as large-scale, multipurpose mainframes were the only available computers, libraries were essentially at the mercy of their host institutions. Although some libraries established excellent relations with their computer centers and did play a role in automation decisions, procurement was an unpredictable and uncontrollable environment for many. The advent of minicomputers radically altered the computer field for libraries, enabling at least the large ones to perhaps purchase their own equipment and create a more predictable environment.

A number of libraries did purchase their own equipment and designed applications software in-house in the 1970s, but another alternative began to emerge in that decade—the library-specific commercial vendor of automated library systems. In terms of the total computer market as viewed by larger corporations, libraries were too few to attract a great deal of attention, but the potential volume demonstrated a suitable market for smaller and specifically library-oriented commercial ventures.

CLSI and Circulation

One early commercial venture came from Computer Library Systems, Inc., later shortened to CL Systems. Inc., and later again simply to CLSI. The company's first automation efforts involved acquisitions systems, and one of its first installations, in 1972, was at the Cleveland Public Library, which had been using a batch processing system on IBM equipment for eight years. In a description of the CLSI system at Cleveland Public, Richard Palmer observed that, over a five-year period, the cost of the new online system was expected to be less than one-half the cost of the IBM batch processing system, had it been continued. In addition, the new system offered broader and more library-specific features. CLSI soon turned its attention toward circulation control. Its LIBS 100 system and other vendor-supplied systems introduced subsequently come to be known as "turnkey," a reference to the premise that, upon delivery and installation, virtually all that was required to make the system work was to plug it in and turn it on.

Although in practice this has not always exactly proved to be the case, the idea was essentially sound and formed the basis on which these systems would become cost-effective alternatives to in-house development. As so many libraries had learned in implementing their own online or even batch processing systems, the cost of design and development were considerable. With a mass-marketed system, such up-front development costs could be distributed among many customers and hence would be far less for each library then independent design and development. With a turnkey system, programming expertise was not required of the library staff or even at the host institution. Perhaps most importantly, the library's minicomputer could be operated and maintained within the library itself, and the software was marketed by vendors whose entire business was specifically library applications. Other vendors joined CLSI in the online circulation control market during the early and mid-1970s, nut for several years the field was fairly unstable.

Various companies entered and left the market, were purchased by other companies, and radically redesigned their systems. By 1975, five commercial vendors were offering turnkey automated circulation systems with varying degrees of online and offline capacity. Two years later, three of them had cased marketing efforts in the United States and another had been sold and its system totally redesigned. CLSI provided the only continuity in this short span of time. The year 1977 was pivotal, however, in that several new vendors of circulation control systems entered the market and would prove more stable than most of their predecessors. Among these were Data Phase, Geac, and Universal Library Systems.

Entering the 1980s, CLSI was still the leading force in the commercial market, with 177 installations and more than 300 other libraries remotely accessing computers located at one of the installation sites. The fastest growing computer was Data Phase with 50 installations, followed by Geac with 22. Gaylord, active since 1978, had 11 installations by 1981. Although not actively marketing in the United State since about 1977, the Plessey online circulation system popular in Great Britain had 9 users in the United States and Canada.

Acquisitions, Serials Control, and Cataloguing

With the exception of early CLSI efforts, commercial activity in online acquisitions and serials control has lagged behind circulation control and did not really begin to make an impact until the late 1970s and early 1980s. The primary source of commercial developments also differed between the two areas. For the most part, vendor-supplied online circulation control systems have resulted from new commercial ventures into the library marketplace. In acquisitions and serials control, in contrast, many of the earliest efforts came from long-established library vendors; book jobbers for acquisitions and subscription agents in serials control. Baker and Taylor's offline BATAB system was available to libraries since the 1960s, and by the late 1970s the system had been redesigned, enhanced, and offered online as LIBRIS.

Around the same time, Brodart also announced availability of an online acquisitions system. By the early 1980s, book jobbers had been joined by other vendors, such as Ringgold and Innovative Interfaces, in offering online acquisitions, as well as by each of the four bibliographic utilities. In addition, several vendors of circulation systems were in the process of testing acquisitions modules, promising even more competition. Commercially available online serials control systems have appeared comparatively recently.

Two major subscription agencies, Ebsco and Faxon, each announced plans for an online system in 1981, capable not simply of ordering, but encompassing functions such as check-in and claiming, and not limited to titles ordered through the respective agency. Ebsco eventually abandoned development of its own online check-in component, while Faxon did incorporate one into its online system. Also in 1981, the MetaMicro Corporation of San Antonio, Texas, announced a serials control software package for minicomputer application, although active marketing of this system eventually ceased.

Activity in the not-for-profit sector also showed signs of life in the early 1980s, exemplified by marketing of the CHECKMATE serials control system by the California Library

Authority for Systems and Services (CLASS) and by OCLC planning efforts to make its rather dormant serials check-in subsystem more attractive. Changes in the OCLC sub-system were made in 1983, but had a negligible impact in attracting new users. An interesting activity occurred with CHECKMATE, as Ebsco began to market that system when it abandoned development of its own online check-in module. Although the bibliographic utilities emerges during the 1970s as the clearly predominant supplier of automated cataloguing systems, there were a few commercial attempts to penetrate the cataloging market.

One of these was the BIBNET system, announced by Information Dynamics Corporation in 1974. BIBNET was to operate similarly to OCLC in a number of ways: it was principally intended to be a shared cataloging database; it was to contain member input master records as well as LC MARC records; the master database was to be stored on centralized computers; and library identifier symbols were to be affixed to each bibliographic record as an aid to interlibrary loan. Several features of BIBNET were planned conspicuously different from OCLC and attempted to answer some of OCLCs more pressing problem areas.

Keyword-in-title search capability was to be available, along with plans for the eventual introduction of subject searching of the database. BIBNET users would be encouraged to access the system though a minicomputer housed in the library to facilitate local production of offline products and to reduce telecommunications cost. By using a minicomputer, libraries could retrieve records from the master database, copy them onto a cassette tape, and then break the telecommunications link. Master records copied onto the cassette would then be displayed on a CRT terminal connected to the minicomputer, modifications made to the records, and the revised records copied into a second cassette. Catalog cards and other offline products could be printed locally, based on the modified records on the second cassette. Although access to BIBNET could be gained through means other than a minicomputer, the front-end interface was strongly promoted as the most useful for allowing flexibility. Information Dynamics had ambitious intentions for BIBNET. Not only was it to contain post-1968 LC MARC records, but there was a plan to centrally input access points into the online system for more than 3.5 million Library of Congress manual cataloging records created between 1953 and 1968. When a library retrieved such an index entry, it could notify Information Dynamics through the system that it would like a full record in the database for that title. Information Dynamics would then create a record in MARC format for the title requested and load it into BIBNET within four days.

BIBNET'S entry into the marketplace coincided with the rapid and successful expansion of OCLC. The system simply never established a firm position. A more successful venture was launched several years later by Informatics, Inc., with the introduction of MINIMARC. It was minicomputer-based, but with no pretense as a networking system. The entire LC MARC database was supplied on floppy diskettes.

The library retrieved these records locally on its minicomputer and modified them according to need. For titles not found on the LC MARC database, the library could create and input records into its own working file. Catalog cards and other offline products could be locally produced. Since a premise of MINIMARC was local processing, the system did not incur the telecommunications charges as did use of a bibliographic utility, and the overall cost were not as per-unit-dependent. On the other hand the initial investment could be as tenfold that of joining a bibliographic utility, and monthly maintenance and other costs were substantial enough to make participation in a utility more economical for smaller libraries. A limiting feature of MINIMARC was that, as a nonnetworking system, its core database was restricted to LC MARC records and was therefore smaller than those of the bibliographic utilities.

Since its emphasis was so much on being a local system, it did not serve in any capacity as an interlibrary loan locational tool. In 1981, however, Informatics, RLG, and the California Library Authority for Systems and Services (CLASS) announced availability of an interface whereby MINIMARC users would be able to search the RLIN database through their MINIMARC system equipment, an arrangement that would enhance MINIMARC as a local system with access to a broader utility. By 1981, more than 30 libraries had installed MINIMARC, and the number had increased steadily since then. Another successful commercial venture into automated cataloging was the Carrollton Press REMARC project. In 1980, Carrollton announced a five-year project in which it would convert more than 5 million Library of Congress cataloging records, not included on MARC, to machine-readable from. Libraries could submit brief data to Carrollton, in either machine-readable or nonmachine-readable form, to match against both the LC MARC database and the REMARC database being created by Carrollton. For items for which a record could be found, Carrollton would supply machine-readable bibliographic records containing relatively complete LC cataloguing data.

In addition to MINIMARC and REMARC as alternatives to the bibliographic utilities, a number of commercial book jobbers and COM vendors were maintaining machine-readable cataloguing databases for their customers. These were really a quite different matter, since initially with these stored databases, a customer did not have direct online access to its own database. This circumstance has been changing, as some of these vendors now provide online access. In the late 1960s, the only choice for libraries implementing an online system was to design and develop it in-house and use a large mainframe computer housed in central facilities at their host institution. During the 1970s, additional alternatives emerged: systems designed and developed be bibliographic utilities and commercial vendors; systems that could be operated on library-owned minicomputers and, more recently, on microcomputers. What was once a very restricted environment has broadened into a increasing range of options. As with unit-record equipment and batch processing computerized systems, the use of Online has been a learning experience for those libraries implementing their own systems, for the bibliographic utilities, and for the commercial vendors.

Index